Lourens de Vries
The Greater Awyu Languages of West Papua

Pacific Linguistics

Managing editor
Alexander Adelaar

Editorial board members
Wayan Arka
Danielle Barth
Don Daniels
Nicholas Evans
Gwendolyn Hyslop
David Nash
Bruno Olsson
Bill Palmer
Andrew Pawley
Malcolm Ross
Dineke Schokkin
Jane Simpson

Volume 657

Lourens de Vries

The Greater Awyu Languages of West Papua

ISBN 978-1-5015-2720-3
e-ISBN (PDF) 978-1-5015-0695-6
e-ISBN (EPUB) 978-1-5015-0691-8
ISSN 1448-8310

Library of Congress Control Number: 2020941880

Bibliographic information published by the Deutsche Nationalbibliothek
The Deutsche Nationalbibliothek lists this publication in the Deutsche Nationalbibliografie;
detailed bibliographic data are available on the Internet at http://dnb.dnb.de.

© 2022 Walter de Gruyter Inc., Boston/Berlin
This volume is text- and page-identical with the hardback published in 2020.
Photo credit: Village of Wanggemalo (2006), Dineke Groen
Typesetting: Integra Software Services Pvt. Ltd.
Printing and binding: CPI books GmbH, Leck

www.degruyter.com

Contents

Abbreviations — IX

Chapter 1
Introduction — 1

Chapter 2
Phonology — 7
2.1 Aghu — 8
2.1.1 Aghu vowel phonemes — 8
2.1.2 Aghu consonant phonemes — 9
2.1.3 Aghu syllables and roots — 9
2.2 Digul Wambon — 10
2.2.1 Digul Wambon consonant phonemes — 10
2.2.2 Digul Wambon vowel phonemes — 10
2.2.3 Digul Wambon syllables, stress and phonological processes at morpheme boundaries — 11
2.3 Kombai — 12
2.3.1 Kombai consonant phonemes — 12
2.3.2 Kombai vowel phonemes — 13
2.3.3 Kombai syllables, words, stress — 14
2.4 Korowai — 14
2.4.1 Korowai consonant phonemes — 15
2.4.2 Korowai vowel phonemes — 15
2.4.3 Korowai syllables, words, stress — 15
2.5 Conclusion — 16

Chapter 3
Morphology — 18
3.1 Introduction — 18
3.2 Nouns — 20
3.2.1 Possessive pronominal prefixes — 21
3.2.2 Plural suffixes with kinship nouns — 23
3.2.3 Derivation of (verbal) nouns — 26
3.2.4 Noun compounds — 28
3.3 Adjectives — 30
3.4 Personal pronouns — 31
3.4.1 Basic forms — 31

3.4.2	Emphatic forms of personal pronouns —— 33	
3.4.3	Reflexive and reciprocal pronouns —— 34	
3.5	Deictics and demonstratives —— 36	
3.5.1	Introduction —— 36	
3.5.2	Demonstratives, definiteness and topicality —— 37	
3.5.3	Demonstratives and verbs of coming and going —— 40	
3.6	Verbs —— 41	
3.6.1	Overview of Greater Awyu verb systems —— 41	
3.6.2	Verbs in Yonggom Wambon —— 53	
3.6.3	Verbs in Korowai —— 62	
3.7	Question words —— 70	
3.8	Quantifiers —— 71	
3.9	Numerals —— 71	
3.10	Adverbs —— 76	
3.11	Postpositions, conjunctions and connectives —— 77	

Chapter 4
Syntax —— 78

4.1	Introduction —— 78	
4.2	Noun phrases —— 78	
4.2.1	General overview of noun phrase structure —— 78	
4.2.2	Possessor nouns as modifiers —— 80	
4.2.3	Noun phrases and compound nouns —— 81	
4.2.4	Adjectives —— 83	
4.2.5	Relative Clauses —— 85	
4.2.6	Demonstrative modifiers —— 90	
4.2.7	Coordinate noun phrases —— 90	
4.3	Clauses —— 93	
4.3.1	General overview of clause structure —— 93	
4.3.2	Experiential clauses —— 95	
4.3.3	Clauses with posture verbs —— 95	
4.3.4	Copula clauses —— 98	
4.3.5	Grammaticalization path of nde/te —— 99	
4.3.6	Clauses with invariant existential-locative predicates —— 101	
4.4	Postpositions —— 102	
4.4.1	Syntactic clitics —— 102	
4.4.2	Postpositions expressing semantic roles —— 103	
4.4.3	Topic and focus postpositions —— 107	
4.5	Clause combinations —— 109	

4.5.1	Introduction —— 109	
4.5.2	Clause chaining —— 110	
4.5.3	Subordination —— 115	

Chapter 5
Discourse —— 120

5.1	Introduction —— 120	
5.2	Recapitulative linkage —— 120	
5.2.1	Tail-head linkage —— 120	
5.2.2	Generic verb linkage —— 123	
5.3	Quotative framing —— 125	
5.4	Representation of emotion in discourse —— 128	
5.5	Argument distribution —— 129	
5.6	Thematization —— 132	
5.7	Tracking of topical participants —— 134	
5.8	Verbal semantics: actions and their components —— 137	
5.9	Concluding remarks —— 139	

Chapter 6
Language in Greater Awyu society —— 143

6.1	Introduction —— 143	
6.2	Clans —— 146	
6.2.1	Korowai clan names —— 147	
6.2.2	Marriage and bilateral clan links —— 148	
6.3	Language and identity —— 148	
6.4	Language names —— 150	
6.5	Linguistic ideologies —— 152	
6.6	Lexical substitution —— 153	
6.7	Linguistic and cultural practices of personhood and person reference —— 155	
6.7.1	Social personhood: humans, witches and demons —— 156	
6.7.2	Clan and kinship in person reference —— 158	
6.7.3	Korowai joking avoidance —— 164	
6.8	Language in *kampung* and clan lands —— 165	
6.9	Language of humans and demons —— 168	
6.10	Cultural geography and spatial orientation —— 169	
6.11	Conclusion —— 173	

Chapter 7
Greater Awyu languages in context — 175
7.1 Introduction — 175
7.2 Genetic context — 175
7.2.1 The Awyu-Dumut language family — 175
7.2.2 The Greater Awyu language family — 177
7.2.3 Genetic links between Greater Awyu, Greater Ok and Asmat-Kamoro — 177
7.2.4 Greater Awyu and Trans New Guinea — 179
7.3 Areal context — 181
7.3.1 Headhunting — 184
7.3.2 Linguistic effects of Marindinisation — 186
7.3.3 Patterns of peaceful contacts between Greater Awyu speakers and their neighbors — 189
7.3.4 Mandobo (Greater Awyu) and Muyu (Greater Ok) — 191
7.3.5 Counting, numerals and areal diffusion — 195
7.4 Typological context — 196
7.4.1 Introduction — 196
7.4.2 Phonology — 198
7.4.3 Morphology — 199
7.4.4 Discourse preferences and syntactic continuities — 202
7.5 Where did Greater Awyu speakers come from? — 203
7.6 Summary — 205

References — 207

Appendix — 215

Index — 251

Abbreviations

Kinship terms:
B	brother
C	child
D	daughter
F	father
H	husband
M	mother
P	parent
S	son
W	wife
Z	sister

1	first person
2	second person
3	third person
I	primary stem
II	secondary (suppletive) stem
III	tertiary (suppletive stem)
NON1	second and third person
/	rising intonation, medial/pause
#	falling intonation, utterance final
ADJ	adjective
ADH	adhortative
ADV	adversative
AGT	agentive
ASS	assertive
CA	common argument
CAUS	causative
CIRC	circumstantial
COM	completive
CONN	connective
COP	copula
COORD	coordinator
CS	copula subject
CC	copula complement
C	consonant
CNJ	conjoining connective
DEM	demonstrative
DUR	durative
DS	different subject (switch reference)
DST	distal deictic
EMP	emphasis
EXCL	exclamative
EXIST	existential

FOC	focus
FUT	future
GEN	genitive
HAB	habitual
HOD	hodiernal past
HN	head noun
HIST	historical past
IMP	imperative
IMM	immediate (past or future)
INT	intentional
IRR	irrealis
ITR	iterative
LNK	linking element
LIG	ligature
LOC	locative
MED	medial distance deictic
MOD	modifier
NEAR	near (past or future)
NEG	negative
NP	noun phrase
POSS	possessive
PL	plural
PRED	predicative
PRES	present tense
PROH	prohibitive mood
PRX	proximate deictic
Q	question marker
QUOTE	quote marker
RFL	reflexive
RLS	realis
RPAST	remote past
SBJ	subject
SEQ	sequence
SIM	simultaneity
SG	singular
SS	same subject (switch reference)
SUB	subordinator
TOP	topic
TNG	Trans New Guinea
VN	verbal noun
VOC	vocative
V	vowel

Chapter 1
Introduction

This book presents a description of major patterns found in languages of the Greater Awyu language family (see fig. 1): their phonology (chapter 2), morphology (chapter 3), syntax (chapter 4) and discourse (chapter 5). Chapter 6 discusses major aspects of the anthropological linguistics of Greater Awyu languages. Chapter 7 concludes the book by placing the linguistic patterns of Greater Awyu languages in genetic, typological, areal and historical contexts.

The book is a synthesis of the linguistic research carried out between 2009 and 2014 in the framework of the project The Awyu-Dumut family of Papuan languages in its linguistic and cultural context, financed by the Netherlands Organization of Scientific Research.[1] Lourens de Vries, Wilco van den Heuvel and Ruth Wester formed the Awyu-Dumut research team at the Vrije Universiteit, Amsterdam.[2]

The book builds on linguistic research by Drabbe, Voorhoeve, Healey and others, from the early 1950s until more recent survey work done by linguists of SIL International (Jang 2003; Hughes 2009; Kriens and Lebold 2010). The book also builds on the rich ethnographic and anthropological work done by van Baal, Boelaars, Welsch and especially Stasch. His dissertation on Korowai, his subsequent work in the linguistic anthropology of Korowai and his generosity in sharing his field notes, lexical data and insights were fundamental for understanding and describing Greater Awyu speech practices, linguistic ideologies, lexical domains, patterns of language contact and many other topics dealt with in this book.

---

[1] Netherlands Organization of Scientific Research project number 360-89-020. An additional Distinguished Visiting Scholar grant of the Cairns Institute of James Cook University, an International Collaborative Award of the Australian Research Council and my role as Partner Investigator in the Australian Research Council Discovery Project "Why Languages Differ, and How" (DP 130101361) allowed me to fully concentrate on research and writing while at James Cook University (Cairns campus) during four months in 2010 and 2014. Thanks are due to Prof. Aikhenvald and prof. Dixon for their support and input.
[2] I thank Wilco van den Heuvel and Ruth Wester for their support, critical comments and re-thinking of my work of the 1980s and 1990s. Our disagreements were particularly useful to me. They also read earlier versions of this book, gave detailed critical comments and pointed out very many mistakes in content and presentation. All remaining errors and flaws in this book are entirely mine and may well result from not better listening to them. Antoinette Schapper, Bruno Olsson and an anonymous reviewer deserve my deep gratitude because of the many improvements in linguistic argumentation, style, updating me in the field of Anim studies and stimulating me to compare Greater Awyu patterns with patterns found in other language families of the New Guinea area.

https://doi.org/10.1515/9781501506956-001

Unpublished data in the form of word lists, survey data, transcribed texts and sketch grammars were provided to the Awyu-Dumut project by missionary linguists and SIL linguists who now or in the past lived and worked in the area. I thank Gert van Enk (Korowai), Hong-Tae Jang (Wambon), Jaap Groen and Dineke Groen (Kombai), Sun-Kyu Chi (Kombai), Dick Kroneman (Kopkaka), Melissa Williamson (Nagi) and Peter Baas (Tsaukambo) for sharing their insights, pictures, notes, maps, tables and data with me. This was a tremendous contribution to our understanding of the Greater Awyu family and proved fundamental to establish the northern boundary of the Greater Awyu family, where Greater Awyu languages meet Ok-Oksapmin languages, also called Greater Ok languages (see Map 1).[3]

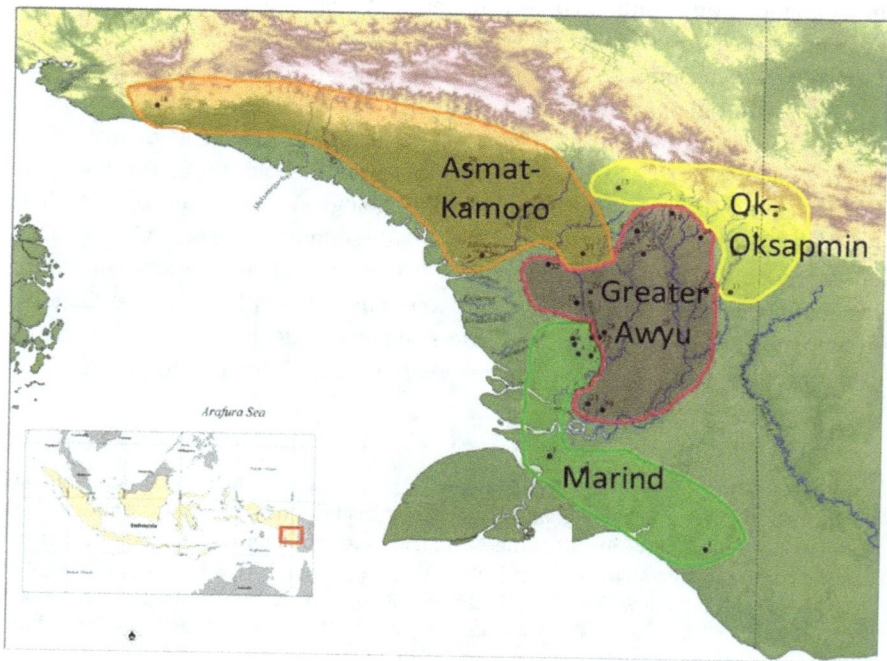

Map 1: The Greater Awyu language family and its neighbors.

---

3 I thank Jaap Fokkema, VU University Amsterdam, for Maps 1 and 2.

De Vries, Wester and van den Heuvel (2012) proposed to integrate the Awyu-Dumut family in a wider grouping, the Greater Awyu language family, with around 45,000–60,000 speakers. The Greater Awyu family has two branches, the Becking-Dawi branch and the Awyu-Dumut branch (de Vries, Wester and van den Heuvel 2012: 290–312) (see Map 2).[4] The Becking-Dawi branch consists of Korowai, North Korowai (spoken along upper stretches of Becking river, Hughes 2009), Tsaukambo (Baas 1981) and Komyandaret (Hughes 2009). Korowai is the only language in this group for which there is a grammar (van Enk and de Vries 1997). For the other languages we only have field notes and word lists. Komyandaret is a dialect of Tsaukambo according to Baas (1981), who noted the mutual intelligibility of the two varieties. The close relation is supported by the 60% lexical similarity between Tsaukambo and Komyandaret described by Hughes (2009: 7).

Map 1 shows the Greater Awyu family and its neighbors, the Asmat, Ok and Marind (sub)families (Marind=Marindic-Jaqajic in Usher and Suter 2015).

The close genetic relation between Korowai and Tsaukambo is strongly suggested by the systematic correspondences in (bound) morphology in pattern and matter, described by de Vries (2012b).

The Awyu-Dumut branch has three subgroups (de Vries, Wester and van den Heuvel 2012):
– Awyu (Pisa, Shiagha, Yenimu, Aghu)
– Dumut (Mandobo, Yonggom Wambon, Kenon Wambon (=Digul Wambon))
– Ndeiram (Kombai, Tayan, Wanggom)
– Sawuy (unclassified)

The Awyu and Dumut subgroups are well-established subgroups, with proto phonologies (Healey 1970, Voorhoeve 2001, Wester 2014) and proto morphologies (Wester 2014). The Ndeiram subgroup needs much more research, both in terms of its internal composition and its position within the Awyu-Dumut branch, since Kombai is the only well-documented language of the Ndeiram subgroup (de Vries 1993a). By comparing the Kombai data with her Awyu-Dumut proto morphology, Wester (2014) confirmed the hypothesis of Voorhoeve (2005) that Kombai is a member of the Awyu-Dumut branch. The few data presented by Voorhoeve (1971) on the Sawuy language indicate that Sawuy is an Awyu-Dumut language but we need more data to determine its position in the Awyu-Dumut group.

The Awyu subgroup has been surveyed by Kriens and Lebold (2010). They draw attention to dialect continua and their consequences for language names

---

4 The following overview of branches and subgroups was taken from de Vries, Wester and van den Heuvel (2012: 270–273).

and language boundaries: "The Awyu people [. . .] speak a number of closely related languages. In addition, there is a great deal of language "chaining" from one village to the next, which makes it difficult to define the boundaries between these languages". (Kriens and Lebold 2010: 5). They also observe that language names used in earlier surveys and decades appear to have vanished.

We use Drabbe (1950) as our source for Pisa, Shiagha (Shiaxa) and Yenimu (Jenimu) and Drabbe (1957) for Aghu. The points on the Awyu dialect continuum where Drabbe and Voorhoeve obtained their data from, are indicated on Map 2. Aghu (Axu, also known as Jair) is the best known language of this subgroup. Drabbe 1957 is a detailed grammar of Aghu containing ten texts. Drabbe's work is all in Dutch and his Awyu-Dumut grammars and text collections, although extremely valuable, are not easy to follow, even for linguists reading Dutch. Van den Heuvel (2016) translated and adapted Drabbe's 1957 *Spraakkunst van het*

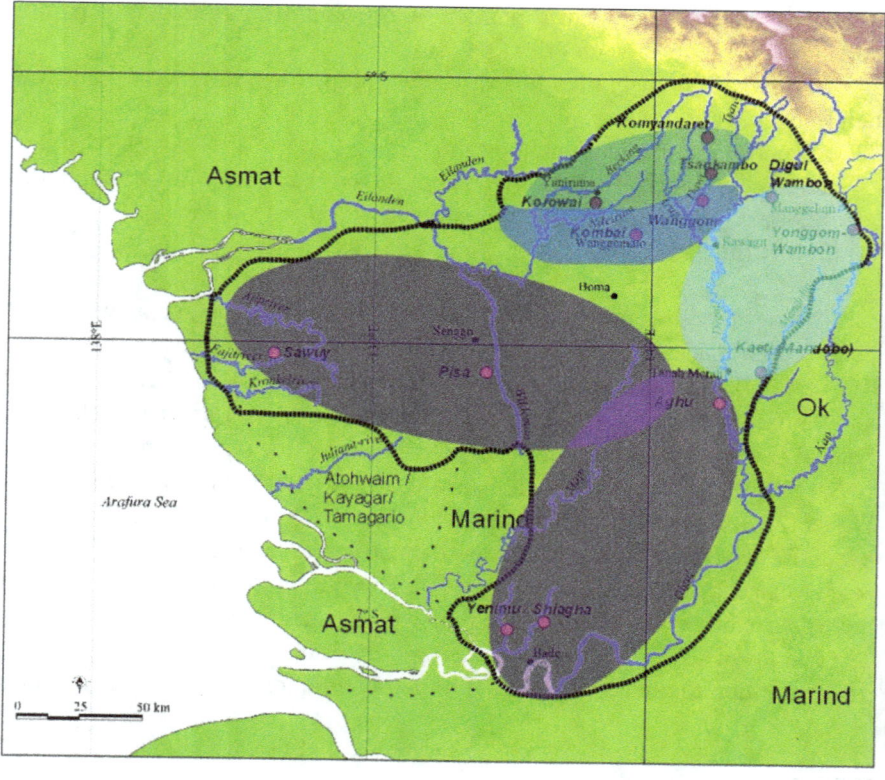

Map 2: Greater Awyu languages discussed in the book.

Aghu-dialect van de Awju-taal. He made the complete Aghu text collection, all lexical material and the grammatical analysis of Drabbe (1957) available in English, carefully distinguishing between Drabbe's analysis and his own.

The Dumut group has been surveyed by Jang (2003). Basing himself on lexical similarity counts, Jang (2003: 20–27) distinguishes two major Dumut groupings, Mandobo and Wambon, each with minor groupings:
- Wambon: Ketum Wambon, Upper Wambon (=Kenon Wambon=Kenondik Wambon=Digul Wambon), Lower Wambon
- Mandobo: Kokenop Mandobo, Upper Mandobo, Central Mandobo, Mariam Mandobo

Map 2 shows the location of Greater Awyu branches and subgroups in relation also to neighbouring families Asmat-Kamoro, Greater Ok and Marindic-Jaqajic (shortened to Asmat, Ok and Marind on Map 2).

Map 2 contains red dots with language names and those represent places where consultants lived who provided data for the languages discussed in this book. The grey area with Pisa, Aghu, Sjiagha and Yenimu is a rough approximation of the location of the Awyu subgroup, light green indicates the area of the Dumut subgroup, with Mandobo(=Kaeti), Digul Wambon and Yonggom Wambon. Blue represent the Ndeiram subgroup with Kombai and Wanggom. Dark green the Becking-Dawi branch, with Korowai, Tsaukambo and Komyandaret.

Dialect chains play a major role also in the Dumut subgroup. But it is not yet clear whether the Mandobo and Wambon speech varieties form a single unbroken Dumut dialect chain. Our sources for Mandobo and Yonggom Wambon were the descriptions by Drabbe (1959) and for Digul Wambon the descriptions by de Vries and de Vries-Wiersma (1992) and Jang (2008). The points on the Wambon and Mandobo dialect chains where the data were obtained are indicated on Map 2.

The Ndeiram group (see fig. 1) consists of Tayan, Kombai and Wanggom (de Vries, Wester and van den Heuvel 2012). According to de Vries (1993a: 1), Kombai speakers said that they could understand both Tayan and Wanggom speakers, although they spoke differently from them. These Ndeiram dialects probably form a dialect chain that extends from the border with Asmat to the Upper Digul river where the Ndeiram chain meets languages of the Dumut subgroup (de Vries, Wester and van den Heuvel 2012). Intelligibility judgments of informants, quoted in a survey by Hughes (2009: 9), also indicate that Wanggom speakers and speakers of Kombai understand each other. Versteeg (1983: 22) gave a lexical similarity percentage of 61% for Wanggom and Kombai. The morphological data on Wanggom are limited to a few paradigms written down in Baas' field notes (Baas 1981). We have no data whatsoever on Tayan. Kombai is the only language of the Ndeiram group that has been described (de Vries 1993a).

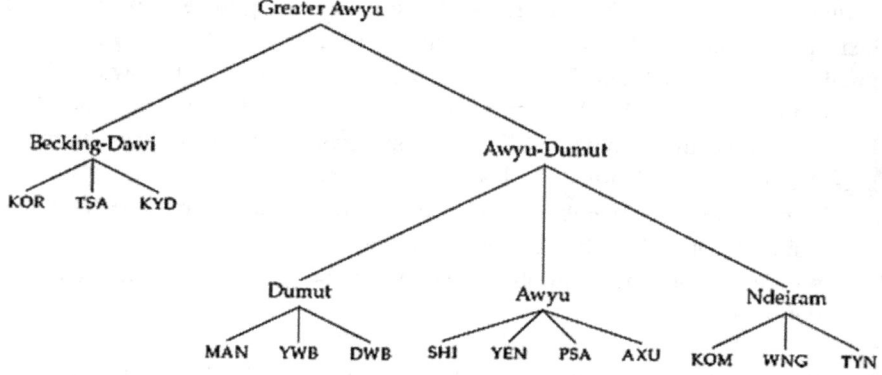

Figure 1: Provisional family tree of the Greater Awyu family (from Wester 2014: 5).

KOR=Korowai
TSA=Tsakwambo
KYD=Komyandaret

MAN=Mandobo
YWB=Yonggom Wambon
DWB=Digul Wambon

SHI=Shiagha
YEN=Yenimu
PSA=Pisa
AXU=Aghu

KOM=Kombai
WNG=Wanggom
TYN=Tayan

We do not claim to be complete in our list of (possible) Greater Awyu speech varieties. Healey (1970: 998) refers to Airo-Sumaghage as a possible Awyu-Dumut language but gives no data. Language names for Greater Awyu speech varieties come and go. We discuss the background of the uncertainty in language names, in areas ascribed to languages and in the number of languages and dialects in chapter 6, as this uncertainty and multiplicity reflects both linguistic processes of dialect chaining as well as conflicting linguistic ideologies and naming practices of Greater Awyu communities and outsiders (missionaries, civil servants, traders).

Greater Awyu text collections can be found in van Enk and de Vries (1997) (Korowai), de Vries (1993a) (Kombai), de Vries and de Vries-Wiersma (1992) (Digul Wambon), van den Heuvel (2016) (Aghu), and Drabbe (1959) (Mandobo and Yonggom Wambon). There is an appendix at the end of this book with texts from Mandobo and Yonggom Wambon, transcribed by Ruth Wester, based on texts in Drabbe (1959).

Chapter 2
Phonology

The morphologies of Greater Awyu languages are better documented than the phonologies, which tend to be sketchy. We will present short summaries of the phonologies of Aghu, Digul Wambon, Kombai and Korowai as representatives of all the subgroups and branches of the Greater Awyu family.

Wester (2014: 33), building on the work of Healey (1970) and Voorhoeve (2001), reconstructed an inventory of proto Awyu-Dumut consonantal phonemes. All consonants, with the exception of the palatal semi-vowel *j, are articulated at three places of articulation (bilabial, alveolar and velar): voiceless plosives *p, *t, *k, voiced and prenasalised plosives * ᵐb, * ⁿd, * ⁿg, two nasals *m, *n, one liquid *r and a semi-vowel *w.

Wester (2014: 34) found 20 regular sound changes in these consonants between proto Awyu-Dumut and daughter languages. These sound changes as a general rule tend to affect the mode of articulation and voicing rather than the place of articulation and therefore we see changes such as *t>s, *t>l, *t>r, all at the alveolar place of articulation, or *p>f, *p>β and *p>w, all bilabials. A striking exception is the regular sound change initial *p>h in Digul Wambon. For the full reconstruction see Wester (2014). Here I will just illustrate these developments with the changes affecting proto Awyu-Dumut *p, all from Wester (2014: 26–27).

Initial *p>/f/ in the Awyu subgroup (and in Kombai): *peta>fete 'to see' (Shiagha), *peta>fera 'to see' (Kombai). Wester (2014: 25) notes that there are some words with initial /p/ in the Awyu subgroup but she agrees with Healey (1970: 1000) that these must be borrowings into proto Awyu because none of these words have cognates with a reflex of /p/ in any of the other languages (see Wester 2014: 26, Table 2.5). Initial *p>ø (zero) or /h/ in Dumut subgroup, e.g. Yonggom Wambon *peta>eto 'to see', Digul Wambon *peta>hetak 'to see'.

Medially *p dropped (Mandobo) or fricativized into a voiced bilabial fricative in the Dumut subgroup: *kip(V)i>kiou (Mandobo) 'wind', *kip(V)i>kiβui (Yonggom Wambon), *kip(V)i>kiβin (Digul Wambon). Medially *p>f in Awyu subgroup: *kip(V)i>kifi 'wind' in Shiaga, Yenimu, Pisa and Aghu.

Finally *p dropped in the Awyu subgroup, e.g. *atop 'vagina'>ato 'vagina' in Shiagha, Yenimu, Pisa and Aghu, final *p was retained in the Dumut subgroup (*atop 'vagina'>atop 'vagina' in Mandobo, Digul Wambon and Yonggom Wambon). In Kombai *p>/f/ between vowels *ap> af-a 'house-PRED' or dropped in word final position *atop> aro 'vagina'. (The Kombai example also illustrates another regular sound change initial and medial *t>r in Kombai, see Wester 2014: 26–27)

2.1 Aghu

Aghu represents the Awyu subgroup of the Awyu-Dumut branch in this phonological overview. The Awyu subgroup owes its status as a subgroup to two major innovations from proto Awyu-Dumut, denasalization of prenasalized plosives and word final consonant deletion (Wester 2014: 35). The Aghu summary is based on the phonological description of van den Heuvel (2016: 9–24).

2.1.1 Aghu vowel phonemes

Aghu has the 6 oral vowel phonemes of Table 1 but they have also 6 nasal and 6 long phonemic counterparts. This makes the Aghu vowel system extraordinary complex in the context of Trans New Guinea vowels inventories that tend to have 5 vowels, symmetrically ordered (Pawley and Hammarström 2018: 84). On top of the nasal and long vowels contrasts in the final syllable Aghu also has a rare asymmetrical 6th vowel /y/, a close tense rounded vowel.

Table 1: Aghu vowel phonemes (van den Heuvel 2016: 9).

i y		u
ɛ		ɔ
	a	

Van den Heuvel (2016: 9) gives the following minimal pairs of vowels: *mi* 'drink'; *mü* 'blunt'; *me* 'upper stream'; *ma* 'Ma clan'; *mo* 'back end'; *kumu* 'with' vs. *kimi* 'hold'; *osu* 'go up' vs. *osü* 'go down'; *jobo* 'fyke' vs. *jobu* 'sharp object'; *ko* 'tree species' vs. *ku* 'youngest shoot of palm tree'.

In word final position, oral vowels of Aghu are in contrast with nasal vowels and van den Heuvel (2016: 11) explains this in terms of the Awyu subgroup innovation of deletion of final stops and nasals. The deleted final nasals were absorbed in the preceding vowel in the form of lengthening and nasalization.

Some Aghu contrasts between nasal and oral vowels: *kiã* 'pointed bamboo' vs. *kia* 'story'; *xã* 'bread tree' vs. *xa* 'bark'; *õ* 'leaf' vs. *o* 'say'; *ẽ* 'eat' vs. *e* 'stand', *mĩ* 'firefly' vs. *mi* 'come down'; *dũ* 'bow' vs. *dü* 'sago' (van den Heuvel 2016: 11).

In addition to nasal vowels, Aghu has contrastive vowel length: *aː* 'women's house' can be contrasted to *a* 'rain', while *iː* 'bird' can be contrasted to *i* 'lie' (van den Heuvel 2016: 13). It is likely that long vowels are the result of compensation in vowel length when final C deletion took place that separated the

Awyu subgroup from the other Awyu-Dumut languages, for example Aghu *i:* 'bird' is a reflex of proto Awyu-Dumut **et* 'bird'. The word final contrasts between oral vs. nasal and short vs. long vowels add another twelve vowel phonemes to the basic six of Table 1.

Vowel harmony occurs in Aghu, as in all Greater Awyu languages. It occurs in different forms, is often optional and speaker-dependent but sometimes obligatory and tied to specific affixes. The direction of vowel harmony is also unpredictable: backward, forward or in both directions. Drabbe (1957: 2) reports obligatory vowel harmony in the case of the Aghu same subject suffix *-de*, for example *fimi-di* 'think-SS', *xo-do* 'go-SS', *musu-du* 'come.up-SS', *ü-dü* 'stick-SS', *ete-de* 'see-SS'. In other cases it is optional, for example the specific article *fe* optionally harmonizes with the final vowel of the word that it specifies: *dü fü* 'an (other) clump of sago' (van den Heuvel 2016: 22–23). Van den Heuvel (2016: 23) mentions forward and backward harmony in the case of the affix *–mV* that sometimes assimilates to the vowel of the preceding root and in other cases to the vowel of the following suffix.

2.1.2 Aghu consonant phonemes

Aghu consonants (see Table 2) occur word medially and word initially but do not occur in word final position, as a result of the final C deletion rule that separated the Awyu subgroup from the other subgroups. The phoneme /d/ is realized as [ɾ] between vowels and /s/is realized as [ʃ] when followed by *iü*, as in *siü* 'banana', *posiü* 'old' or *püsiü* 'very'.

Table 2: Aghu consonant phonemes (van den Heuvel 2016: 13).

	Bilabial		Alveolar		Palatal	Velar	
	unvoiced	voiced	unvoiced	voiced		unvoiced	voiced
Plosive	p	b	t	d		k	g
Nasal		m		n			
Fricative	f		s			x	
Approximant		w			j		

2.1.3 Aghu syllables and roots

Van den Heuvel (2016: 20–21) describes the form of Aghu lexical roots as consisting of one to four (C)V syllables, with the stipulation that only the last (C)V sequence may have a nasalized vowel as nucleus. An example of a minimal Aghu root is *a* 'rain' or *u* 'voice'. Word stress is a weak accent on the last syllable of words. There are not enough reliable data to establish whether Aghu allows VV sequences and how to analyze the glides.

2.2 Digul Wambon

Digul Wambon represents the Dumut subgroup of the Awyu-Dumut branch in this overview. The Dumut subgroup retained the prenasalization of the voiced plosives of proto Awyu-Dumut and also retained final consonants (see Table 3; Wester 2014: 35). This summary is based on Jang (2008) and de Vries and de Vries-Wiersma (1992).

Table 3: Digul Wambon consonant phonemes (de Vries and de Vries-Wiersma 1992).

p	t		k
ᵐb	ⁿd		ᵑg
β	s		ɣ
m	n	ɬ	
w	l	j	

2.2.1 Digul Wambon consonant phonemes

Jang (2008) does not have a velar fricative phoneme. Instead, he has a /h/ phoneme which Wester (2014: 25) regards as a reflex of proto Awyu-Dumut initial *p. Since /ɣ/ has a [h] allophone (de Vries and de Vries-Wiersma 1992) and lenition of velar fricatives to /h/ occurs in the Becking-Dawi branch, the difference might be just a matter of the choice of basic allophone. Jang (2008) interprets [ɣ] (and [β]) as voiced fricative allophones of /k/ and /p/ in intervocalic conditions.

2.2.2 Digul Wambon vowel phonemes

The mid vowels (see Table 4) have tense and lax allophones that vary freely in open syllables (de Vries and de Vries-Wiersma 1992: 11).

Table 4: Digul Wambon vowel phonemes (de Vries and de Vries-Wiersma 1992).

ι		u
ε		o
	α	

2.2.3 Digul Wambon syllables, stress and phonological processes at morpheme boundaries

There is one syllable type (C)V(C). Phonological words may have up to six syllables. Stress is a weak accent on the penultimate syllable.

Wester (2014: 23–24) mentions a number of common phonological processes that operate at morpheme (and word) boundaries in some or all Awyu-Dumut languages. One of these processes, nasal epenthesis, occurs in all Awyu-Dumut languages but also in the Becking-Dawi branch. Other boundary processes occur in subsets of the Greater Awyu family, for example intervocalic change of voiceless stops into voiced approximants or voiced fricatives is found in Dumut languages, in Korowai and in Kombai.

The description of Digul Wambon by Jang (2008) presents phonological boundary processes in some detail as they function in this Wambon dialect: intervocalic voicing, plosive devoicing, geminate consonant elision, intervocalic nasal epenthesis, clustered vowel elision, glided vowel semi-vowelization and vowel epenthesis. In order to derive the correct surface forms these rules are ordered, for example the geminate consonant elision should take place before vowel epenthesis, followed by the plosive devoicing process (Jang 2008: 10). I will briefly discuss intervocalic voicing of plosives and nasal epenthesis.

Voiceless stops of Digul Wambon change into voiced approximants at the same place of articulation when these sounds occur on a morpheme boundary, either before the morpheme break or after the break, if morpheme sequencing puts them in intervocalic position (Jang 2008: 6), for example (1):

(1) la-t-ep-mbo
 la-l-ep-o
 lie-RLS-1SG-PAST
 'I slept'

(Digul Wambon, Jang 2008: 6)

The realization of /-ep-mbo/ as [epo] is due to full assimilation of /ᵐb/ to the voiceless /p/ of the preceding suffix followed by geminate consonant elision.

Nasal epenthesis (glossed as LNK in this book) has been formulated as follows by Jang (2008: 7): "In between two vowels across a morpheme or word boundary, when one morpheme ending in a vowel precedes another morpheme beginning with a vowel which is not a part of the inflectional suffixes, a transitional nasal /n/ is inserted between the vowels. The nasal insertion between morphemes that are bound together phonologically which is in connection with affixes and clitics, is obligatory; between separate words it is optional". Consider example (2):

(2) na-ap
     na-n-ap
     my-LNK-house
     'my house'

(Digul Wambon, Jang 2008: 7)

The examples of Greater Awyu languages in this book as a rule give the resulting surface forms, rather than the underlying forms, with some exceptions where relevant. In such cases, the underlying forms are in the first line of the example, with the surface forms placed directly beneath, for example (1) and (2).

2.3 Kombai

2.3.1 Kombai consonant phonemes

Kombai, of the Ndeiram subgroup, has the following consonants (see Table 5):

Table 5: Kombai consonant phonemes (de Vries 1993a: 6).

	bilabial	alveolar	Palatal	Velar
Plosives	ᵐb	ⁿd	ɟ	ⁿg ⁿgʷ
Nasals	m	n		
fricatives	ɸ			x xʷ
Laterals		l		
Vibrants		r		
semi-vowels	w ɥ		j	

Notice the absence of voiceless stops. The Kombai /r/ is the initial and medial reflex of proto Awyu-Dumut *t which has /s/ reflexes in some Awyu and Dumut languages, e.g. proto Awyu-Dumut *turu 'ear' with reflex /suru/ 'ear' in Aghu, but /ruro/ 'ear' in Kombai (Wester 2014: 25, 27). Proto Awyu-Dumut *k and *p have the fricative reflexes /x/ and /ɸ/ in Kombai (Wester 2014: 26, 28, for example *pi>fi 'name'). The rounded velars seem to be a Kombai innovation. The phonemes /ᵐb/, /ɸ/ and /x/ have lateralized allophones in free variation with the non-lateralized allophones in all positions, e.g. [jaᵐboma] 'ill', [jaᵐbˡoma] 'ill' (de Vries 1993a: 130). During the release of the lateralized pre nasalized plosives some air is channeled along the sides of the tongue, giving a short but distinct lateral twist to the sound.

2.3.2 Kombai vowel phonemes

De Vries (1993a: 9) reports contrasts between nasal vowels and oral vowels (see Table 6), for example *a* 'house' and *ã* 'breast'. However, phonologically there are underlying stem final nasals that are realized as nasalization on the vowel, since Kombai does not allow consonants in word final position. When suffixes or clitics beginning with a vowel are attached to these stems, the underlying nasal surfaces, e.g. *lã* 'woman', *lan=a* 'woman=CONN'. Oral underlying final consonants also show up when there is a suffix or clitic which follows the stem in the phonological word (3) and (4):

(3) *momoɸ=o   lã*
     uncle=MOD wife
     'uncle's wife'

(4) *momo   bo-me*
     uncle DUR-come[RLS.NON1SG]
     'Uncle is coming.'   (Kombai, de Vries 1993a: 10)

Table 6: Kombai vowel phonemes (de Vries 1993a: 7).

ɪ y		ɯ u
ɛ		o
	a	

The final consonant /ɸ/ of *momoɸ* 'uncle' is deleted (4). This final /ɸ/ of the word *momoɸ* has been retained before the connective =*o* in (3). Notice that Kombai, of the Ndeiram subgroup, has a synchronic phonological rule of word final consonant deletion, whereas the languages of the Awyu subgroup have undergone a diachronic process of final consonant deletion: the deleted C have gone from the synchronic system and do not show up in any context, with the possible exception of final nasals in Aghu (van den Heuvel 2016: 11).

Besides final C deletion, Kombai has a number of other phonological processes that operate on morpheme- and word boundaries, such as vowel harmony (across both word and morpheme boundaries, de Vries 1993a: 12) and nasal epenthesis, two processes that occur in one form or another in all Greater Awyu languages.

2.3.3 Kombai syllables, words, stress

There is one syllable type in Kombai (C)V. The canonical word form is (C)V.(CV) Kombai has contrastive stress in the form of a pitch accent on the prominent syllable.

2.4 Korowai

Korowai represents the Becking-Dawi branch of the Greater Awyu family in this overview of phonological patterns. (Tables 7 and 8) The following summary is based on van Enk and de Vries (1997: 54–61).

Table 7: Korowai consonant phonemes (van Enk and de Vries 1997: 55).

	bilabial	alveolar	palatal	velar
voiced plosives	b	d	ɟ	d
voiceless plosives	p	t		k
prenasalized plosives	ᵐb	ⁿd		ⁿg
Nasals	m	n		
Fricatives	ɸ	s		x
Laterals		l		
semi-vowels	w ɥ		j	

2.4.1 Korowai consonant phonemes

Korowai has implosive allophones of the voiced stops /b/ and /d/ that freely vary with the egressive pulmonic allophones. Just like Kombai, Korowai has lateralized allophones, restricted in Korowai to the velar voiceless fricative phoneme /x/. The fricative phonemes have a voiced realization in intervocalic position.

2.4.2 Korowai vowel phonemes

Table 8: Korowai vowel phonemes (van Enk and de Vries 1997: 60).

	front	central	Back
Close	i y		u
half-close	e		o
half-open	ɛ	a	ɔ

2.4.3 Korowai syllables, words, stress

Korowai has one syllable type: (C)V(C). These syllables may be combined into words with the result that VV (but not VVV) clusters are formed, as well as medial CC clusters. Word stress is a contrastive pitch accent. Although CC clusters are allowed and do occur (e.g. *pyxmo* 'to throw'), CC clusters at morpheme boundaries in phonological words undergo consonant cluster reduction on a grand scale (C1+C2>C2) and on a lesser scale of the type (C1+C2>C1). Merging and subsequent fortition to /t/ occurs when two laterals occur on both sides of a morpheme break: *l+l>t*, e.g. *gil-laxul> gitaxul* 'an old bivouac'. Korowai shares nasal epenthesis in intervocalic conditions at morpheme breaks with all other Greater Awyu languages. With Dumut languages it shares the change from voiceless stop to voiced approximant whenever morpheme sequencing puts a voiceless stop in intervocalic conditions, e.g. *saxu-tena>saxulena* 'little banana'.

2.5 Conclusion

Symmetrical five vowel systems are both in Trans New Guinea languages (Pawley and Hammarström 2018: 85) and globally the most common pattern (Dixon 2010 vol. I: 8).[5] Digul Wambon follows that pattern but Greater Awyu languages tend to have more than the expected five vowels. The close front rounded vowel /y/ is a typologically rare vowel, both within New Guinea and globally (Foley 2000: 368). Wester (2014: 39) reconstructs the *y for proto Awyu-Dumut *y (Wester 2014: 39). Aghu is the only language of the Awyu subgroup that retained the /y/. *y became /u/ in the other Awyu languages (Wester 2014: 39). In the Dumut subgroup the /y/ is retained from proto Dumut only in Mandobo whereas it changed into /i/ in Yonggom Wambon and Digul Wambon (Wester 2014: 38). Wester (2014: 38) gives examples such as proto Dumut */aryn/ 'thorn' with the reflexes /arin/ 'thorn' in Yonggom Wambon, /alin/ 'thorn' in Digul Wambon and /oryn/ 'thorn' in Mandobo.

The vowel /y/ also occurs in Korowai, of the Becking-Dawi branch and in Kombai (Ndeiram subgroup). Therefore the vowel /y/ is probably retained from proto Greater Awyu.

Aghu is relatively complex in its vowel system, with oral and nasal vowels, long and short vowel phonemes and the addition of the close rounded vowel /y/ which makes the basic vowel system an asymmetrical six vowel system. These complications resulted from compensation for the (diachronic) process of final consonant deletion that took place in the Awyu subgroup. Kombai "repaired" the Aghu asymmetry by adding not just the /y/ but also the unrounded close back vowel /ɯ/. Korowai distinguishes half-open and half-close front and back vowels, and has the /y/, resulting in an eight vowel system.

The relatively simple consonantal systems of Greater Awyu languages are of a type found in many Trans New Guinea languages, with between 11 and 15 consonants, multiple series of plosives, two or three nasals in bilabial, alveolar or velar positions, semivowels /j/ and /w/, and very small classes of rhotics and fricatives (Pawley and Hammarström 2018: 82). The contrast between voiceless stops and voiced, prenasalised ones, is also very common in Trans New Guinea languages (Pawley and Hammarström 2018: 82). The Awyu subgroup lost this prenasalization feature of voiced stops. Korowai, of the Becking-Dawi branch, has a three way contrast of oral voiced stops, prenasalized voiced stops and voiceless stops, not so common in New Guinea according to Foley (2000: 369). It occurs for example in languages of the Lower Sepik family. Marindic-

---

5 This section is based on de Vries (2017: 945–946).

Jaqajic languages, neighbors of Greater Awyu languages, also have this three-way distinction.

Greater Awyu (C)V(C) syllable types also conform to the generally speaking simple phonotactics of Trans New Guinea languages (Pawley and Hammarström 2018: 87).

The complexity and distinctive character of Greater Awyu phonologies resides in the phonological rules that operate on morpheme- and word boundaries, from vowel harmony to nasal epenthesis, intervocalic voicing and fricativization and in the phonetic realizations of phonemes. For example, Korowai has lateralized and implosive realizations of those. Both Korowai and Kombai have lateralized allophones of voiceless fricatives.

Chapter 3
Morphology

3.1 Introduction

This chapter gives an overview of the main patterns of morphology found in Greater Awyu languages. Wester (2014) provides detailed typological overviews of the morphology of the Awyu-Dumut branch with regard to the major word categories of nouns, adjectives, pronouns, verbs and demonstratives and she reconstructs proto Awyu-Dumut morphology for these categories. This chapter summarizes her findings for Awyu-Dumut languages, deals with minor categories left untreated or not discussed in full by Wester (2014), viz. adverbs, imperatives, secondary demonstratives, reflexive and reciprocal pronouns, quantifiers and numerals. This chapter also describes Becking-Dawi morphology, comparing it in pattern and matter with the morphology of the Awyu-Dumut branch.

My analysis of Awyu-Dumut syntax (especially clause combinations) and information structure is different from Wester (2014) and this influences the analysis of parts of the Awyu-Dumut morphology, especially the interpretation of switch reference morphology, postpositions, conjunctions and connectives.

Morphologies of Papuan language families, especially bound verb morphologies, tend to form the relatively stable core of inherited characteristics that set language families apart and define their boundaries, even in contexts of intense language contact and multilingualism. This is certainly true of the Greater Awyu language family and the families that surround it: the boundaries between the Asmat-Kamoro, Greater Ok, Greater Awyu and Marindic-Jaqajic families are very sharp in terms of their morphologies, in patterns and matter and much less so in terms of syntax and discourse (see chapters 4 and 5). For example, the verb morphology of the Greater Awyu family, with four forms per paradigm based on the distinction speaker (1st person) versus non-speaker (conflating 2nd and 3rd person), with realis and irrealis as basic distinction, with three verb types, in combination with shared morphemes to realize these patterns, distinguishes the family very clearly from all its neighbors (de Vries, Wester and van den Heuvel 2012).

Verbs dominate Greater Awyu morphology, grammar and discourse. Greater Awyu verbs marginalize other word classes because speakers prefer to carry out their tasks with the use of verbs. For example, Greater Awyu languages have sets of six personal pronouns that can be used for maintaining participants in discourse but speakers strongly prefer to do that through verbal agreements and switch reference instead.

The most important strategy available to speakers of Greater Awyu languages for using verbs rather than other word classes is a morphological one: all these languages have a very productive compounding scheme to verbalize members of other parts of speech, by compounding the stems of the verbs *mo* 'to do' and *ke* 'to be(come)' with roots of other word classes (see §3.6.1.1). Demonstratives, nouns, numerals, adjectives and question-words are routinely turned into verbs by *mo* and *ke* compounding and these verbs are then used as mini clauses in strings of chained clauses with a range of semantic and pragmatic functions. For example, rather than using an adverb of manner to modify a verb, speakers verbalize an adjective and then use the verbalized adjective as head of a medial mini clause that fulfills the same function as a manner adverb:

(5) *Jaxov=e   matet-mo   ka-l-e-mbo?*
    3PL=CONN good-do[SS] go-RLS-NON1PL-PAST
    'Did they travel well?'
    (Digul Wambon, de Vries and de Vries-Wiersma 1992: 9)

We find a verbalized demonstrative *emo* 'to do that' in example (6c) as head of a mini clause. It functions as a discourse conjunction that links two clause chains in connected discourse, a type of linkage called generic verb linkage. Generic verb linkage is an alternative to tail-head linkage of clause chains that is used by speakers to make the scope of the anaphoric connection more general, for example when speakers want to summarise the story as a whole and point back to that story rather than the immediately preceding clause chain (de Vries 2005: 376; de Vries 2019). Example (6a)-(6c) is part of a Yonggom Wambon text from Drabbe (1959: 145). Tail-head linkage connects (6a) and (6b) and generic verb linkage connects (6b) and (6c):

(6a) *Kamenwon i-no   ra -ku-r-an.*
     bullroarer swing.round-SS.SIM hold -go-RLS[NON1SG]-PAST
     'He was swinging around the bullroarer.'

(6b) *Ra-ku-r=a   te   ko- ndarama-r-an*
     hold-go-RLS[NON1SG]=SEQ CNJ go-stick-RLS[NON1SG]-PAST
     'He held (it) and stuck (it) in a *segepotop* sago palm.'

(6c) E-mo-ro   te   rira-r=a
that-do-SS CNJ   go.down-RLS[NON1SG]=SEQ
kem   ku-r-an.
downstream go-RLS[NON1SG]-PAST
'He did that and then went away downstream.'

(Yonggom Wambon, Drabbe 1959: 145)

Although verbs in this way marginalize closed word classes, they also diachronically provide the same small closed word classes with new members, when verbs used as conjunctions or numerals, or question-words, become very frequent, lose verbal characteristics and end up as petrified invariant members of minor closed word classes.

For example, verbs of motion used as conjunctions meaning 'and; next' may freeze into petrified verbs and thus supply the small closed class of conjunctions with new members. Digul Wambon *nda-kono* originally meaning 'coming-going' and *kono* 'going', were medial verb forms, restricted to same subject and simultaneity conditions. They are now used in all contexts as invariant discourse conjunctions glossed as 'next; further' (de Vries and de Vries-Wiersma 1992: 74–75).

The chapter starts with a discussion of nouns (§3.2), followed by adjectives (§3.3), personal pronouns (§3.4), deictics and demonstratives (§3.5) and verbs (§3.6). The section on verbs discusses the verbal morphology of two Greater Awyu languages in detail, Yonggom Wambon, of the Awyu-Dumut branch and Korowai, of the Becking-Dawi branch. §3.7 deals with question words, §3.8 with quantifiers, §3.9 with numerals, §3.10 with adverbs and §3.11 with postpositions, conjunctions and connectives.

3.2 Nouns

Greater Awyu noun morphology is simple (Wester 2014: 49–64) as is the rule in Trans New Guinea languages (Pawley and Hammarström 2018: 90). The two branches, Awyu-Dumut and Becking-Dawi, have exactly the same patterns of noun morphology but they differ partly in the morphemes that they use to realize the patterns. There are three patterns of affixation that involve nouns: possessive pronominal prefixes (§3.2.1), plural suffixes with kinship nouns (§3.2.2) and derivational suffixes to derive verbal nouns (§3.2.3). These verbal nouns play a key role in periphrastic constructions of Greater Awyu languages, especially in the areas of negation, aspect and modality (van den Heuvel 2016). Greater Awyu nouns form both endocentric and exocentric compounds with other nouns (§3.2.4).

3.2.1 Possessive pronominal prefixes

Greater Awyu languages have a set of six possessive pronominal prefixes that may be prefixed to nouns irrespective of their semantic type (e.g. alienable or inalienable nouns). Aghu and Kombai have only dedicated possessive pronominal forms for 1SG and 2SG and use personal pronouns to express possession in the rest of the paradigm (Wester 2014: 73). Kinship nouns are hardly found without possessive prefixes, sometimes merging with the stems (Wester 2014: 57).

Possessive pronominal prefixes of Becking-Dawi languages correspondclosely to those reconstructed for proto Awyu-Dumut by Wester (2014: 74). The following table gives the possessive forms of Greater Awyu languages and proto Awyu-Dumut. I have added Tsaukambo data (from Baas 1981) and a row of tentative proto Greater Awyu possessive prefixes.

Proto Greater Awyu *k remained *k in proto Awyu-Dumut but it has reflexes /k/, /x/, /g/, /ⁿg/ or zero in Awyu-Dumut languages (Wester 2014: 28). The forms of the possessive prefixes of Table 9 follow from the regular sound changes in Awyu-Dumut languages summarized in Table 2.7 of Wester (2014: 28). In the Becking-Dawi language Korowai, *k became /x/ in all positions in the word, e.g. Korowai *xomu* 'to die'[6] and corresponds to proto Awyu-Dumut *küm* 'to die'. Korowai *xul* 'sky', proto Awyu-Dumut **kut* 'sky'. Korowai *xél* 'flower', proto Awyu-Dumut **ket* 'flower'. Korowai *xabéan* 'head', proto Awyu-Dumut **kaiban* 'head'. Korowai *xal* 'skin', proto Awyu-Dumut **kat* 'skin'.[7] Korowai *xai* 'to go', proto Awyu-Dumut **ko/ka* 'to go'. Incidentally, the preceding examples also show the correspondence between proto Awyu-Dumut word final *t and Becking-Dawi final lateral /l/.

Medial proto Awyu-Dumut *k: proto Awyu-Dumut **wakot* 'moon', Korowai *waxol* 'moon'. Final proto Awyu-Dumut *k: **muk*, Korowai *mux* 'hair'; **ok*: *ax* 'water' (de Vries, Wester and van den Heuvel 2012: 294). The form of Korowai personal and possessive pronouns also show this general Becking-Dawi fricativization of *k: for example, proto Awyu Dumut **nVkV-* 'our' and Korowai *noxu-* 'our' (§3.4.1).

Data from Korowai exemplify Greater Awyu possessive prefixation. They show vowel harmony. Vowel harmony is a general Greater Awyu phenomenon, not restricted to possessive prefixes (§2.1.1). Affixes may assimilate to stems in

---

[6] In a number of Greater Awyu languages the stem of the verb 'to die' is combined with the stem of the derivational verb *mV* 'to do' (§3.6.1), e.g. Korowai *xomu* 'to die', Kombai *xumo* 'to die', Mandobo *kümo/ küma* 'to die'. Pawley (2005: 85–88) proposes a proto Trans New Guinea etymon *kumV-.

[7] Pawley (2005: 85–88) proposes a proto Trans New Guinea etymon *(ŋg,k)a(nd,t)apu 'skin'.

Table 9: Possessive pronominal prefixes in Greater Awyu languages (Wester 2014: 73).

	1SG	2SG	3SG	1PL	2PL	3PL
Dumut subgroup						
Yonggom Wambon	na-	ⁿgo-	ya-	naⁿgo-	ⁿgaⁿgo-	yaⁿgo-
Digul Wambon	na-	ⁿga-	ya-	nexo-	noxo-	yaxo-
Mandobo	ne-ne-	ⁿgo-ne	e-ne-	noⁿgü-ne-	neⁿgi-ne-	yeⁿgi-ne-
Awyu subgroup						
Aghu	na-	ga-	–	–	–	–
Pisa	na-	ga-	ena-, ewa-	nuna-	guna-	yoxona-
Shiaxa	na-	ga-	wa-	naxa-	gaxa-	yaxa-
Yenimu	na-	ga-	wa-	niga-	giga-	yaxa-
Ndeiram subgroup						
Kombai	na-	ⁿgu-	xe-	naⁿgu-	naⁿge-	yano-
Becking-Dawi subgroup						
Korowai	nV-	gV-	yV-	noxu-	gexené-	yexené-
Tsaukambo	nV-	–	yV-	–	–	–
Proto Awyu-Dumut	*na-	*ⁿga-	*ya-, *wa-	*nVkV-	*ⁿgVkV-	*yaka-
Proto Greater Awyu	*na-	*ⁿga	*ya-	*nVkV-	*ⁿgVkVne-	*yakana-

vowel quality and the other way around and it tends to occur as an unpredictable, speaker-dependent form of vowel variation (see Drabbe 1957: 7) for Mandobo vowel harmony and van den Heuvel (2016: 22–23) for Aghu vowel harmony). However, in a number of specific affixes in Greater Awyu languages vowel harmony has become obligatory and predictable. The singular forms of Korowai possessive prefixes show systematic vowel harmony that assimilates the position (front, central, back) of the vowel of the possessive prefix to the position of the vowels of the noun stem or to the place of articulation of the initial consonant.[8]

---

[8] V = /a/ with central vowel in first syllable of noun stem; V = /o/ with back vowel in first syllable of noun stem and before stem initial /w/; V = /e/ with front vowel in first syllable of noun stem and before front consonants (bilabial and alveolar), irrespective of the quality of the vowels in the following stem (van Enk 1997 and de Vries 1997: 67).

(7) na-xabéan
    1SG-head
    'my head'   (Korowai, van Enk and de Vries 1997: 67)

(8) no-wayo
    1SG-thumb
    'my thumb'   (Korowai, van Enk and de Vries 1997: 67)

The possessive pronouns of Korowai may take the postpositional clitic =xa and then form independent possessive pronouns:

(9) 1SG   na=xa   'mine'
    2SG   ga=xa   'yours'
    3SG   ya=xa   'his/hers/its'
    1PL   noxu=xa   'ours'
    2PL   gexené=xa   'yours'
    3PL   yexené=xa   'theirs'

(10) If=è   na=xa.
     this=CONN   mine=CONN
     'This is mine.'   (Korowai, van Enk and de Vries 1997: 68)

3.2.2 Plural suffixes with kinship nouns

Kinship nouns are an exceptional subclass of nouns in Greater Awyu languages, morphologically and pragmatically. They are highly frequent, not only because kinship is the foundation of social organization in these clan communities but also because the use of proper names of people is generally avoided, certainly in addressing people (Stasch 2009: 77). Instead, kinship nouns are used. We will return to the cultural pragmatics of kinship terms as a key part of Greater Awyu person reference systems in chapter 6. Some kinship dyads are close and intimate (e.g. mother's brother-sister's son), others are highly taboo (e.g. mother-in-law and son-in-law), distant and marked by avoidance behavior and this affects the use of kinship terms. The plural forms of kinship nouns are used in singular reference for taboo or avoidance relations, such as the mother-in-law/son-in-law dyad (Stasch 2009: 86).

Morphologically, kinship nouns are also exceptional, because they are the only nouns that take plural suffixes and they are obligatorily (or at least almost always) possessed. Furthermore, kinship nouns in Dumut languages have special address forms ending in *-op* or *-ap*, derived from the reference form (e.g. Yonggom Wambon *nati* 'father' (reference) and *nati-op* 'father' (address)) (Wester 2014: 55). Korowai has a vocative suffix *-o* that optionally occurs with kinship nouns used to address people (van Enk and de Vries 1997: 129).

There is occasionally full reduplication of nouns to express plurality but that strategy is used sparingly in Greater Awyu texts and seems to be restricted to a number of kinship nouns (and a few other nouns denoting humans and nouns denoting houses), and then only when the context is ambiguous and the speaker wants to resolve that ambiguity (Drabbe 1959: 16; Wester 2014: 54). Adjectives do have plural forms in Greater Awyu languages, mostly based on reduplication, to express the plurality of the nouns they modify (see §3.3).

The two branches of the Greater Awyu family use rather different plural suffixes. The suffixes that expresses plurality of kinship nouns in all Awyu-Dumut languages are reflexes of the proto Awyu-Dumut suffix **-ŋgV*, with **-ŋgu(i)* for proto Dumut and **-gi* for proto Awyu languages, for example Mandobo *ŋgu*, Digul Wambon *-ŋgui* and Aghu *-gi* (Wester 2014: 56).

(11) *na-nin-ŋgui*
      1SG-older.brother-PL
      'my older brothers'   (Digul Wambon, Jang 2008: 70)

Digul Wambon is the only language of the Awyu-Dumut branch that has two other plural suffixes that are not a reflex of the proto Awyu-Dumut suffix * *-ŋgV*. The kinship noun *mbut* 'brother-in-law' takes *-alile* as plural suffix and *net* 'older brother' takes *-na*:

(12) *na-net-na*
      1SG-older.brother-PL
      'my older brothers'
                    (Digul Wambon, de Vries and de Vries-Wiersma 1992: 40)

(13) *na-mbut-alile*
      1SG-brother.in.law-PL
      'my brothers-in-law'
                    (Digul Wambon, de Vries and de Vries-Wiersma 1992: 40)

Some languages share the plural suffixes of kinship nouns with a few other nouns that denote humans beings (e.g. Wambon, Jang 2008: 70; Korowai, van Enk and de Vries 1997: 66), for example with clan names that are used in person reference, with the noun for 'person' and with demon terms that are used metaphorically to denote foreign persons (see chapter 6).

The only language of the Becking-Dawi branch that we have data for on kinship plurals, Korowai, does not use a form that corresponds to the proto Awyu-Dumut kinship plural suffix * -ŋgV. Instead, it uses five different plural suffixes (stem + -dém, stem + -alin, stem + -xül, stem + -él, stem + -aŋgol), a plural prefix m-, special plural forms and reduplicated forms. The plural forms are unpredictable and have to be specified per kinship noun. Some kinship nouns have two or three plural forms. Examples (Korowai, van Enk and de Vries 1997: 65–66):

(14) mbolop 'husband's father'
mbolof-alin/mbolo-mbolop 'husband's fathers'
ban 'wife's parent'
ban-dém/ban-alin/ 'wife's parents'
ban-aŋgol
ni 'mother'
ni-xül 'mothers'
mom 'maternal uncle'
mom-él 'maternal uncles'
mbam 'child'
mbam-mbam 'children'
abül 'son'
abü-dem/ m-abün 'sons'

Van den Heuvel and Fedden (2014: 11–12) notice that the Korowai plural suffix -él corresponds to the proto Greater Ok kinship plural suffix *-Vl, with reflexes such as -il (and -al) in Telefol, Oksapmin and Tifal. They also noted that Digul Wambon is the only Awyu-Dumut language with two irregular kinship plural suffixes besides the regular one that corresponds to the proto Awyu-Dumut suffix *-ŋgV, viz. -na (12) and -alile (13).The last one, -alile, is similar both to Korowai -alin and Greater Ok *-Vl.

Since both Korowai and Digul Wambon border on Greater Ok languages and since no other Greater Awyu language has these suffixes, Korowai and Digul Wambon probably borrowed -él and -alile from a Greater Ok language, according to van den Heuvel and Fedden (2014: 11–12). Marriages across language boundaries are very frequent and clans in border areas tend to have a high degree of marriage-related multilingualism (see chapter 6). Notice that the kinship plural formations of Korowai are highly irregular and have to be stored per kin term. It seems a distinct possibility that speakers borrowed specific kinship terms as a whole, including plural suffixes (van den Heuvel and Fedden 2014: 11–12).

3.2.3 Derivation of (verbal) nouns

Greater Awyu languages have a productive derivation of nominal infinitives or verbal nouns from verbs. Jang (2008: 66) compares them to English gerunds, Drabbe (1959: 86) calls them *infinitief* and van den Heuvel (2016: 54) calls them verbal nouns "to express that these forms are derived from verbal roots but: (i) have very few verbal properties left, especially because they cannot, on their own, serve as the head of a main verbal clause; (ii) share a number of distributional properties with nouns; (iii) also have some idiosyncratic properties which make them different from other nouns".

This subclass of verb-derived nouns plays an important role in the grammars of Greater Awyu languages, for two reasons. First, Greater Awyu languages do not allow clauses to function as core arguments in clauses unless they are first reduced to verbal nouns (see §4.5 Clause combinations). The second reason for the significance of verbal nouns in Greater Awyu languages is their role in periphrastic constructions of modality and aspect, often with auxiliary verbs of doing (*mo*) and being (*ke*).

These patterns will be exemplified by data from Aghu as analyzed by van den Heuvel (2016: 53–61). The use of verbal nouns to enable core arguments to denote events is illustrated by (15)-(18).

(15) efe te büsiü asin oman oxo
 3SG FOC house buildII.VN ignorant COP
 'He cannot build houses' (Aghu, Drabbe 1957: 15)

(16) ga n-ongã jafi oxo
 2SG LNK-cutII.VN beautiful COP
 'Your carving (carved work) is beautiful' (Aghu, Drabbe 1957: 15)

(17) efe tamaŋ ge de
 3SG writeII.VN FOC COP
 'It is his writing.' (Aghu, Drabbe 1957: 15)

Van den Heuvel (2016: 58) remarks that (16) also shows that verbal nouns can be possessed in the same way as other nouns, with the possessive linker *n-*. Van den Heuvel (2016: 54) describes the semantics of the verbal nouns as follows: "If we take a verb with a basic lexical meaning X, a verbal noun formed from lexeme X usually refers to 'the activity or event of X-ing'. With certain verbs, however, the verbal noun may also refer to what Drabbe calls the result of a process (1957: 15), or to what could tentatively be called the 'effected object' or 'affected subject'".

Verbal nouns or nominal infinitives are based on secondary stems in Dumut languages (if a verb has a secondary stem) and on irrealis stems in Awyu languages. The distinction between primary and secondary stems has eroded in the Dumut subgroup and there are many irregularities in verb stems (Wester 2014: 89). Becking-Dawi languages do not have multiple verb stems. In the Dumut subgroup, Mandobo has *-rop* (21), Yonggom Wambon *-nop* and Digul Wambon *-mop* as nominalizer (18). For example, Digul Wambon *en-* (primary stem)/*ande-* (secondary stem) 'to eat' and *ande-mop* 'the eating; food'. The verb *hetak-* (primary stem)/*hetko-* (secondary stem) has *hetko-mop* 'the seeing' (18).

Aghu (Awyu subgroup) forms verbal nouns by nasalizing the final vowel of the verb stem (van den Heuvel 2016: 53–54). When Aghu verbal nouns are augmented with *-a*, they acquire the aspectual sense of 'about to do something' (van den Heuvel 2016: 58). Kombai (Ndeiram subgroup) has a realis verbal noun (realis stem+ *-no*) and an irrealis one (irrealis stem + *-ni*).

Korowai has *-un* as suffix attached to its verbal nouns. Loughnane and Fedden (2011: 27) reconstruct *-Vn* as a proto morpheme for verbal nouns in Proto–Ok-Oksapmin and Korowai may well have borrowed verbal nouns from its Ok neighbours, also taking their nominalizer, since Greater Ok languages have a consistent use of close reflexes of *-Vn* throughout the family (van den Heuvel and Fedden 2014: 9–10).

Greater Awyu languages use verbal nouns in constructions that express negation of events (19), the (in)ability to do something (15), impossibility to do something, intention to do or not to do something, or the wish that something should not happen (21). Verbal nouns also play a key role in constructions that express a range of aspectual meanings, for example phasal aspects, of being about to do something (22), or the imminent start of a process (20), the end of an event (23), or durative, habitual and iterative aspects (24).

The auxiliary verbs of doing, being and posture verbs are often used to assist verbal nouns in the expression of these modal and aspectual meanings (20) and (22). Consider these examples of verbal nouns in Greater Awyu languages:

(18) *Nuk oi hetko-mop=sixi ndave-l-epo.*
     I   pig see.II-NOM=for come-RLS-1SG-PAST
     'I have come to see the pig.'
                              (Digul Wambon, de Vries and de Vries-Wiersma 1992: 41)

(19) *Joxo de baxen=de xo.*
     3PL FOC sitII.VN=NEG COP
     'They are not here.'   (Aghu, Drabbe 1957: 16a)

(20) *a aw=akĩ e m-oxe*
     rain FOC already=rain.II.VN
     'It is starting to rain already.'   (Aghu, Drabbe 1957: 15)

(21) *No küma-rop nda gen.*
     1SG die.II-VN NEG be[IRR.NON1SG]
     'Let me not die/I should not die.'   (Mandobo, Drabbe 1959: 104)

(22) *Doü ade-ni ma-de*
     sago eat-VN.IRR do-1SG[IRR]
     'I shall eat sago in a moment.'   (Kombai, de Vries 1993a: 17)

(23) *nu dépo-n=ga lefaf.*
     I smoke-VN=CONN finished
     'I have stopped smoking.'   (Korowai, van Enk and de Vries 1997: 93)

(24) *Nu dépo-n=ga wé-ma-lé.*
     I smoke-VN=CONN continuous-do-[RLS]1SG
     'I smoke all the time.'   (Korowai, van Enk and de Vries 1997: 93)

3.2.4 Noun compounds

Noun compounds come in two types in Greater Awyu languages: endocentric ones, where one noun modifies another (25)-(28) and exocentric ones, where two nouns are of equal status (29)-(34) (Wester 2014: 51–52; van Enk and de Vries 1997: 66; de Vries 1993a: 34).

Greater Awyu endocentric compounds consist of a modifying noun with main stress, followed by the head noun (25) but Aghu (26)-(27) and Mandobo also have endocentric compounds with the head noun first and the modifying noun second, with primary stress in the noun compound on the second noun stem of the compound (Wester 2014: 51). The latter case concerns compounds from taxonomies of trees, plants or animals where the head noun denotes a generic category (for example tree or bird or marsupial) and the second noun the species (26)-(27).

(25) xawí-sip
yearbird-beak
'beak of the yearbird; penis gourd'
(Korowai, van Enk and de Vries 1997: 66)

(26) kuso-ba'xi
marsupial-kangaroo
'kangaroo'
(Aghu, Drabbe 1957: 4)

(27) kuso-maxi'ko
marsupial-fieldmouse
'fieldmouse'
(Aghu, Drabbe 1957: 4)

(28) mbir=e=ragai
feast=LNK=fish
'fish that one takes along for food during travel to a feast'
(Yonggom Wambon, Drabbe 1959: 118)

In exocentric compounds, the coordinate nature and the equality of the two noun stems is reflected:
(i) in the stress pattern, with each member receiving the same stress (Wester 2014: 51; Drabbe 1959:12, 117);
(ii) in the fact that the order of the two noun stems is irrelevant (at least it varies across Greater Awyu languages in pairs such as (29) and (30));
(iii) in the use of the conjoining clitic =o in (some) exocentric compounds of Yonggom Wambon (33)-(34) which contrasts with the use of the modifier-head clitic =e in (some) endocentric compounds of Yonggom Wambon (28).

Exocentric compounds are common in Trans New Guinea languages (Pawley and Hammarström 2018: 126), especially in the domain of kinship.

(29) momo-laŋge
mother's brother-sister's son
'family; relatives'
(Kombai, de Vries 1993a: 34)

(30) raŋgen-mom
sister's son-mother's brother
'family; relatives' (Mandobo, Wester 2014: 52)

(31) yum-defol
husband-wife
'(married) couple' (Korowai, van Enk and de Vries 1997: 66)

(32) ni-até
mother-father
'parents' (Korowai, van Enk and de Vries 1997: 67)

(33) itir-o-kurup
cassowary-CNJ-wild.pig
'big game' (Yonggom Wambon, Drabbe 1959: 117)

(34) ŋgin-o-kerop
head-CNJ-eye
'face' (Yonggom Wambon, Drabbe 1959: 117)

3.3 Adjectives

Adjectives are a small, open word class in Greater Awyu languages (Wester 2014: 49–50; van Enk and de Vries 1997: 69). Adjectives take adjectival suffixes in some Awyu-Dumut languages: in Yonggom Wambon (-*op*, -*matan*, -*mban*, Drabbe 1959: 118), Aghu (-*axa*) and Kombai (-*xe*) (Wester 2014: 50). Drabbe (1959: 118) writes that some Yonggom Wambon adjectives must take these adjectival suffixes, other adjectives do so optionally and yet others can only take some of the available adjectival suffixes, while yet others occur with all three of them.

To express comparisons, Greater Awyu speakers juxtapose two clauses with comparee and standard expressed as parallel subjects, the parameter is intensified in the first clause and negated in the second clause, as in the following Korowai example:

(35) *If-e=xa   abül=efè   xoŋgél=xayan, waf-e=xa   abül*
    this-LNK=MOD man=TOP   man=TOP   that-LNK=MOD man

be-xoŋgé-tebo-da.
NEG-big-be[RLS.NON1SG]-NEG
'This man is bigger than that man.' (Lit. 'this man is very big; that man is not big') (Korowai, van Enk and de Vries 1997: 71)

Superlative meanings may be contextually derived from the use of adjectives with strong meanings and intensifying adverbs:

(36) *Yanop mup=xayan*
    man   very.good=very
    'the best man' (Korowai, van Enk and de Vries 1997: 71)

Dumut languages, Korowai (37) and Kombai have partial or complete reduplication of adjectives to express plurality of the noun which they modify (Wester 2014: 49). In addition, some adjectives in Greater Awyu languages have special plural forms, e.g. Yonggom Wambon *ndoi* 'empty' with plural form *ndomboroi* 'empty (PL)' (Drabbe 1959: 118).

(37) *Mbam   afo-afop*
    Child thin-thin
    'skinny children' (Korowai, van Enk and de Vries 1997: 71)

Drabbe (1959: 118) writes that in Yonggom Wambon all adjectives have plural forms. There are several ways to produce plural forms of adjectives in Yonggom Wambon: partial reduplication, complete reduplication, irregular special plural forms and partial reduplication in combination with the plural infix *-mbV-*. The meaning of the reduplicated plural formations is not to express degrees of intensity ('very skinny') but to express that the head noun of the phrase has plural referents (37). Degrees of intensity are expressed by intensifying adverbs in the adjective phrase, see §4.2.4.

3.4 Personal pronouns

3.4.1 Basic forms

Greater Awyu languages have six free personal pronouns (Table 10) (Wester 2014: 66; de Vries, Wester and van den Heuvel 2012: 274, 298). They may take the same postpositions and connectives that nouns take. In some languages,

Table 10: Greater Awyu personal pronouns (from Wester 2014: 66).

	1SG	2SG	3SG	1PL	2PL	3PL
Dumut						
Yonggom	nup	ⁿgup	yup	naⁿgup	gaⁿgup	jaⁿgup
Digul Wambon	nuk	ⁿgup	nexep	noxop	goxop	yaxop
Mandobo	nöp	ⁿgöp	ege	noⁿgüp	neⁿgip	jeⁿgip
Awyu						
Aghu	nu	gu	efe	nügu	gügu	yoxo
Pisa	nu	gu	eki	nugu	gugu	yoxo
Shiaxa	no	go	ewe/ege	noxo	goxo	yoxo
Yenimu	nu	gu	ewe/egi	ugu	gugu	yoxo
Ndeiram						
Kombai	nuf	guf	xe	nagu	nage	ya
Wanggom	nu?	gu?	?	naⁿgu	naⁿgi?	?
Becking-Dawi						
Korowai	nup	gup	yup	noxup	gexenép	yexenép
Tsaukambo	nu	gu	yu, kabu	nau, nahu	gau	yau, kayano
Komyandaret	nonu	gonu	ye	nau	gagu	?
Proto Dumut	*nup	*ⁿgup	*yup, *eke	*nakup	*ⁿgakup, *nakip	*yakup
Proto Awyu	*nu	*gu	*eke	* nüku	* güku	*yaku
Proto Awyu-Dumut	*nup	*ⁿgup	*yup, *eke	*nakup	*ⁿgakup, *nakip	*yakup
Proto Greater Awyu	*nup	*ⁿgup	*yup	*nakup	*ⁿgVkup	*yVkup

I added a row of tentative proto Greater Awyu pronouns to Table 4.1 of Wester (2014: 66).

there are separate paradigms of pronouns with subject function (=S&A), e.g. Mandobo (Drabbe 1959: 10) or object function (e.g. Korowai, van Enk and de Vries 1997: 69). Possessive pronominal prefixes, formally closely related to personal pronouns, have been discussed in §3.2.1.

In the Becking-Dawi language Tsaukambo, the Becking-Dawi fricativization of the proto Greater Awyu velar stop (*k>*x) was followed by further lenition to [h] and in some words [h] further reduced to zero in intervocalic position (de Vries 2012b: 185). This is reflected in the Becking-Dawi pronoun forms: Korowai 1PL *noxup*, Tsaukambo *nahu* and *nau*. Proto Greater Awyu velar stop *k was retained in proto Awyu-Dumut (proto Awyu-Dumut 1PL **nakup*). In the Awyu-Dumut languages, proto Awyu-Dumut *k has medial reflexes /k/, /g/, /x/ and /ᵑg/ and the pronouns of Table 10 have the forms predicted by the regular sound changes of Wester (2014: 28).

3.4.2 Emphatic forms of personal pronouns

In line with the general tendency for Greater Awyu verbs to relieve other word classes from their tasks (§3.1), Greater Awyu speakers tend to prefer verbal means (agreements, switch reference) over personal pronouns to track given participants. The relative infrequency of personal pronouns makes them rather salient when they do occur (Wester 2014: 74). This may explain the fact that personal pronouns often take focus clitics in Greater Awyu languages (§4.4.3) and that Dumut languages developed separate paradigms of emphatic personal pronouns (38).

The emphatic forms in the Dumut subgroup are based on the noun for intestines *ot* (Jang 2008: 72). The intestines represent the seat of emotions and thoughts, the inner person or self in Greater Awyu languages as in many other Papuan communities (de Vries 2013: 121). By prefixing the possessive pronouns to the noun *ot* 'intestines; gut', emphatic forms of personal pronouns developed that mean 'myself, himself', for example Mandobo *na-n-ot* (1SG-LNK-gut 'my gut', Drabbe 1959: 10). The form of the emphatic pronouns in Digul Wambon (see (38)) are explained by Jang (2008: 72) as based on the personal pronouns, followed by the noun *ot* 'intestines' and the focus clitic =*ke*. Vowel harmony affects the vowels of the personal pronouns. The change from /p/ to voiced bilabial approximant /v/ also is a regular sound change in Digul Wambon (Jang 2008: 5; §2.2.3). Therefore an emphatic form such as 2SG emphatic *ᵑgovotke* is derived with regular sound changing processes from *ᵑgup-ot=ke*.

This explanation does not work for the 1SG emphatic form of Digul Wambon, since the first singular personal pronoun is *nuk*, not *nup*. The final /k/ of the 1SG personal pronoun is a puzzling and remarkable deviation from the /p/-final pattern of personal pronouns in Dumut languages (Wester 2014: 68). It seems likely that the emphatic 1SG form retained an older form of the 1SG pronoun, *nup* which is consistent with the proto forms for Dumut languages (Table 10), a form that later changed into *nuk* but was preserved in the emphatic paradigm.

(38) Emphatic pronouns of Digul Wambon (de Vries and de Vries-Wiersma 1992: 41)
SG 1 *novotke*
   2 *ᵑgovotke*
   3 *nexovotke*
PL 1 *noxovotke*
   2 *ᵑgoxovotke*
   3 *jaxovotke*

3.4.3 Reflexive and reciprocal pronouns

Greater Awyu languages derive reflexive forms from the personal or possessive pronoun set, by adding reflexive suffixes, e.g. Digul Wambon adds *-ta* to the personal pronouns:

(39) Digul Wambon reflexive pronouns (de Vries and de Vries-Wiersma 1992: 42)
SG 1 *nuk-ta*
   2 *ᵑgu-ta*
   3 *nexo-ta*
PL 1 *noxo-ta*
   2 *ᵑgoxo-ta*
   3 *jaxo-ta*

(40) *Jaxov=e   jaxo-ta-n=e   ox-o-map=ka   heta-knde.*
     3SG=CONN 3SG-RFL-LNK=CONN water-GEN-reflection=in see-[RLS]NON1PL
     'They see themselves in the mirror.'
                        (Digul Wambon, de Vries and de Vries-Wiersma 1992: 42)

Korowai adds a reflexive suffix *-pa (n)* to its possessive pronominal prefixes to derive reflexive forms (van Enk and de Vries 1997: 68):

(41) *Nu ne-pa   imo-p.*
     1SG 1SG-self see-1SG.INT
     'I want to see myself.'   (Korowai, van Enk and de Vries 1997: 68)

Kombai reflexive pronouns are formed by suffixing *-ra* 'self' to personal pronouns:

(42) *Xo   mene   xe-ra   ba-fera.*
     Man   this   3SG-RFL DUR-see[RLS.NON1SG]
     'This man is seeing himself.' (Kombai, de Vries 1993a: 35)

The suffix *-ra* 'self' is not only used in reflexive conditions but may also express focus with personal pronouns (and nouns):

(43) *Xe-ra   xwui   fa.*
     he-FOC   transgression do[RLS.NON1SG]
     'HE stole.'   (Kombai, de Vries 1993a: 35)

When subject and object are coreferential, Aghu uses the emphatic forms of the personal pronouns (with the emphatic marker *ku*) as subject, in combination with the word *nikiaxamu* 'back' as object (van den Heuvel 2016: 179):

(44) *nu   ku   nikiaxamu   ügeme-de.*
     I   EMP   back   chop-RLS[1SG]
     'I chopped myself.'   (Aghu, Drabbe 1957: 7)

Reciprocal action between A and O is expressed by reciprocal pronouns in O position in Greater Awyu languages, *koto-mu* in Aghu, *xuro-xuro* in Kombai (de Vries 1993a: 48) and *xolo-xolop* in Korowai (van Enk and de Vries 1997: 48), *ŋgotap* in Yonggom Wambon, all cognate words (see Wester 2014: 25–30 for the sound correspondences between the velars /k/, /x/, /ŋg/ and the alveolars /t/, /l/, /r/ and for the loss of final consonants in the Awyu subgroup, in Kombai final C is realized as zero).

(45) *kotomu   o-xe-nã*
     RECIP   say-RLS.NON1-NON1PL
     'they said to each other'   (Aghu, Drabbe 1957: 23)

Yonggom Wambon has a reciprocal construction where reduplication plays an even more important role. Not only the reciprocal pronoun (*ŋgotap* or *kowae* 'each-other') is reduplicated but so is the bare verb stem and the whole phrase then functions as O of the verb *mo* 'to do' that is used in all Greater Awyu languages in periphrastic constructions with a range of grammatical functions:

(46) *ngotap i   ngotap i   mo-gon-in*
     RECIP   hit RECIP   hit do-RLS-NON1PL
     'They hit each other.'   (Yonggom Wambon, Drabbe 1959: 140)

When used once the word *ŋgotap* is used as an adverb meaning 'in return, in exchange, in compensation, in pay-back'. The notion of exchange and reciprocality are often referred to in Greater Awyu texts and they play a key role in many cultural practices (van Enk and de Vries 1997: 48; Stasch 2009) Korowai has a verb *xolopa-mo* 'to reciprocate' derived from *xolop* 'in return' and *pa* 'also' that is used to refer to these cultural practices of exchange, compensation and retribution (van Enk and de Vries 1997: 48).

(47) Taget   ŋgotap   jaga-r-an.
     kauri.shell in.return give-RLS[NON1SG]-PAST
     'He gave kauri-shells in return.'   (Yonggom Wambon, Drabbe 1959: 139)

3.5 Deictics and demonstratives

3.5.1 Introduction

Greater Awyu languages have three deictic roots with spatial-temporal meanings related to the location of the three grammatical persons: speaker-related ('here with me, the speaker, now'), addressee-related ('there, then, with you there') and third person-related ('over there, away from both you and me') (van Kessel 2011). Wester (2014: 141–147) describes deictics and demonstratives in the Awyu-Dumut branch and reconstructs three deictic roots for proto Awyu-Dumut *me* or *ne* for the near deictic, *ep* for the far deictic and *kop* for the distant deictic (Wester 2014: 146).

The Becking-Dawi branch (represented by Korowai) has the same three-way deictic system but has partly different deictic roots: *ip* for the speaker-oriented deictic, *wap* for the addressee-related deictic and *xop* for the distant one. The last one is cognate with the Awyu-Dumut distant deictic (with the Korowai velar fricative /x/ corresponding to proto Awyu-Dumut velar stop /k/, de Vries, Wester and van den Heuvel 2012: 294).

These deictic roots may occur in Greater Awyu languages on their own, functioning as adverbs of time and place in the clause (48) or as independent demonstratives (49), as in these Korowai examples[9]:

---

[9] The deictic roots lose their final /p/ when used without connectives or postpositional clitics.

(48) I   le-ba-lé.
      here   come-COM-[RLS]1SG
      'I have come here.'   (Korowai, van Enk and de Vries 1997: 72)

(49) I   mbaxa?
      this   what
      'What is this?'   (Korowai, van Enk and de Vries 1997: 73)

However, the deictic roots more often combine with case clitics and connectives in Greater Awyu languages to form deictic adverbs, for example Digul Wambon *ep=ka* in (52), demonstrative modifiers in noun phrases, such as *ifexa* in (38) in Korowai or in Digul Wambon *evo* in (50) and (51) and independent demonstratives, for example Digul Wambon *eve* in (50) and (51).

The deictic roots are also input for a process of deriving deictic verbs in Greater Awyu languages by creating compounds of the verb stem *mo* 'to do' and the deictic roots. For example, in his description of Yonggom Wambon Drabbe (1959: 122) mentions *mene-mo-* 'to do like this' and *emo-* 'to do like that, to do thus'. These deictic verbs are used in Yonggom Wambon as discourse conjunctions with the meaning 'and; next', for example *emoro* in (6c). Van Enk and de Vries (1997: 86) report the same type of derived deictic verbs for Korowai (*wa* 'that'; *wa-mo-* 'to do that/thus'; *i* 'this'; *i-mo-* 'to do this/in this way'). The medial SS form *imonè* of the Korowai deictic verb *imo-* developed into a time adverb meaning 'now' (van Enk and de Vries 1997: 86).

Yonggom Wambon has an additional derivation of deictic adjectives by suffixing the adjectival suffix *-op* to the deictic roots (Drabbe 1959: 121). The result are deictic adjectives like *ew-op* 'like that' and *mene-wop* 'like this', for example *jet menewop* 'a bird like this'.

3.5.2 Demonstratives, definiteness and topicality

Demonstratives imply definiteness and are used as definite articles in some Greater Awyu languages. For example, Drabbe (1959: 18) reports that the Mandobo demonstrative *mbo* 'that' often "completely functions as our definite article" and no longer functions as a distal deictic (see discussion in Wester 2014: 148–149).[10]

---

[10] My translation, in Dutch "geheel en al de functie heeft van ons bepaald lidwoord".

Demonstratives also acquire topicality functions that are no longer deictic, a development that is not uncommon in Trans New Guinea languages (Haiman 1978; Reesink 1987: 233; de Vries 1995). The bridge between the demonstrative function and the topicality function is topic-comment constructions with extra-clausal themes or topics that Greater Awyu speakers very often use (see §5.6). Compare (50) and (51):

(50) Ev=o   kap,   ev=e   na-mbap=nde.
     that=MOD man   that=CONN 1SG-father=COP
     'That man, that is my father.'   (Digul Wambon, de Vries 1995: 526)

(51) Ev=o   kav=eve, v=eve, ev=e   na-mbap=nde.
     that=MOD man   that=CONN 1SG-father=COP
     'That man, that is my father.'   (Digul Wambon, de Vries 1995: 526)

In topic-comment constructions such as (50) and (51) speakers frequently use the independent demonstrative *eve* 'that' in the comment clause as an anaphoric demonstrative pronoun which resumes the extra-clausal topic in the comment clause. Such resumptive demonstratives cliticized to the preceding extra-clausal theme phrase, lost their deictic nature and became a theme or topic clitic, creating the need for another resumptive demonstrative in the comment clause: compare the first *=eve* (topic clitic) and the second *ev=e* as resumptive demonstrative pronoun in (51). From this bridging context, demonstrative-based topic markers spread to other contexts, for example to mark clauses as topics, (52):

(52) Ep=ka   mba-l-eva-mbo-n=eve,   sanov=e
     there=CIRC sit-RLS-1PL-PAST-LNK=TOP   little.finger=CONN[11]
     ilo-ka-l-eva-mbo.
     descend-go-RLS-1PL-PAST
     'After we had stayed there, we went downriver on Monday.' (Lit. 'given that we stayed there')
                                  (Digul Wambon, de Vries and de Vries-Wiersma 1992: 87)

---

11 Body part nouns are also used as numerals in Greater Awyu languages (§3.9); the noun for little finger has the numeral meaning 'one' and when the syntactive connective *=e* (§4.4.1) is attached to the nouns for the fingers and the wrist, they function as peripheral arguments (time adverbials) in the clause that denote the days of the week, except Sundays ('we went downriver on (day) one (=Monday)').

3.5 Deictics and demonstratives

The loss of deictic meaning of the demonstrative-derived topic clitics is shown by the use of far deictic-based topic clitics with first person pronouns and by compounds of proximal and distant demonstrative-based topic markers in Digul Wambon (53):

(53) Nux=eve   nombo-n=eve   ndayo-nge   ka-l-ep-o-n=o
     1SG=TOP   this-LNK=that(TOP) oar-be[SS]   go-RLS-1SG-PAST-LNK=CNJ
     'as far as I am concerned, I went by canoe and. . .'
                                           (Digul Wambon, de Vries 1995: 525)

Similar developments of deictics into topic markers took place in the other Dumut languages, e.g. Mandobo *mbo* 'that' (54) and Yonggom Wambon *ewe* 'that' (55) (Wester 2014: 150–153). The demonstrative based markers occur with both extra-clausal themes and intraclausal topics in Greater Awyu languages, both glossed as TOP, although their pragmatic function differs somewhat. Extra-clausal themes denote the domain of relevance for the subsequent utterance(s). Intraclausal topics denote entities about which the clause predicates (de Vries 1993b).

(54) Nda-j=o   ŋgo-aŋgen   mbo   ŋgo-gamben=o   Kimitponop
     No-LNK=FOC   your-wife   TOP   your-mate=FOC   Kimitponop
     matero   ŋgo-aŋgen   mbo   tima-gen.
     get.up   your-wife   TOP   took-RLS[NON1SG]
     'Well, as for your wife, your mate Kimitponop has taken your wife.'
                                              (Mandobo, Drabbe 1959: 60)

(55) In-gin-in=ewe=nga,   ut-ken-ep.
     eat-RLS- NONPL=TOP=CIRC   enter-RLS-1SG
     'When they were eating, I went in.'   (Yonggom Wambon, Drabbe 1959: 134)

Interestingly, Yonggom Wambon may use both the postposition =*nga* 'in, at, on, with'[12] that marks the semantic role circumstance of inanimate peripheral arguments (time, place, instrument, manner), as well as the pragmatic marker =*ewe* that marks the clause *in-gin-in* in (52) as a thematic background clause ('given that they were eating, I came in'). This clustering of a semantic postposition and a pragmatic one is exceptional in Greater Awyu languages, where arguments are either unmarked or marked for one type of relation to the verb (§4.4).

---

[12] When marking the A core argument, *nga* is recruited to mark the ergative or perhaps more aptly called agentive argument (§4.3.1 and §4.4.2).

3.5.3 Demonstratives and verbs of coming and going

Wester (2014: 146–147) suggests that the reconstructed proto Awyu-Dumut distant deictic *kop has its origin in the Proto Awyu-Dumut verb *ko 'to go (away from deictic center)' and that the proximate deictic root *me originates from the Proto Awyu-Dumut verb of coming *me (towards deictic center). This diachronic derivational relation with deictic motion verbs can also be seen in the sets of secondary demonstratives that are derived from motion verbs of ascending, descending and crossing in Awyu-Dumut languages. But Becking-Dawi languages do not seem to derive their secondary deictics from directional verbs (van Kessel 2011: 33).

For example in Yonggom Wambon, secondary demonstratives are derived from motion verbs by addition of a demonstrative suffix -p, the same -p that we find in many reflexes of primary deictics in Greater Awyu languages. Drabbe (1959: 122) gives four Yonggom Wambon verbs of motion that form input for such derived, complex deictics: *tut-/turu-* 'to go up' (river, hill); *ri- /riro-* 'to go down' (river, hill), *un-/ondo-* 'to cross; go to the other side (of river)' and *ut-* 'to go in or out of a space'. These motion verbs depict motion away from the deictic center, the speech act location. (Yonggom Wambon has primary and secondary verb stems, Drabbe 1959: 126). To reverse the deictic orientation towards the utterance location, compounds are formed with the verb stem *ma-* 'to come (towards the utterance location)': *ma-tut-* 'to come up', *ma-ri-* 'to come down', *m-un-* 'to come across' and *m-ut-* 'to come in or out of a space'.

By adding -p or -re to these compound verbs with *ma-*, elevational proximate demonstratives and adverbs are formed, for example *ma-ri-re* 'this down here'. To form distal elevational demonstratives and adverbs, the verb root *ko* 'to go away' combines with the motion verbs *tut-/turu-*, *ri-* and *un-* and the suffix -p or -re is added, e.g. *ko-turu-p* '(that) up there' and *k-uŋgo-re* 'that across' (56):

(56) Enop k-uŋgo-re   ri-wa-n-in
     tree DST-cross-DEM   cut-1PL-LNK-FUT
     'We will cut that tree across on the other side.'
                                        (Yonggom Wambon, Drabbe 1959: 122)

Rivers and streams are the basis of spatial orientation and more generally highly significant in cultural geography and metaphorical practices (see §6.10 and Stasch (2001: 34–52) about the spatial and social iconicity of streams in Korowai society). This explains the frequency of stream-based elevational verbs and elevational adverbs in Greater Awyu texts (going/coming upstream/downstream, going/coming across stream, going down toward and up from stream), as bare stem or stem plus SS suffix verbs in SS clauses or as part of serial verb constructions.

3.6 Verbs

Verbs are the heart of Greater Awyu languages. They are morphologically by far the richest class of words: they express person, number, mood, modality, tense, aspect, negation, interclausal temporality (simultaneity and sequence) and switch reference. This section first gives an overview of Greater Awyu verb systems (§3.6.1) and then zooms in on the verb systems of Yongggom Wambon (§3.6.2) and Korowai (§3.6.3), each representing a branch of the Greater Awyu family.

3.6.1 Overview of Greater Awyu verb systems

3.6.1.1 Derivation of verbs

Speakers strongly prefer the use of verbs for all sorts of linguistic tasks, even where other word classes are available for that task (see §3.1). To keep verbs in that preferred role, Greater Awyu languages have very productive systems of verbalization, centered around the verbs *mo/ma* 'to do' and/or *ke* 'to be(come)'. Korowai does not have a form of the intransitive *ke* verb but only has *mo* that as an independent verb means 'to do'. But as derivational element the verb stem *mo* can be used in Korowai to derive both transitive and intransitive verbs, from adjectives, question-words, nouns, demonstratives, e.g. *leléal* 'glad' and *leléal-mo-* 'to be glad', *manop* 'good', *manop-o* (<*manop-mo-*) 'to cure' *i* 'this', *i-mo-* 'to do this', *texén* 'cause, reason', *texén-mo-* 'to intend', to mean, to want'.

These *mo* and *ke* verbs have three main functions in Greater Awyu languages. The first function is as auxiliary verbs in various grammatical domains, for example negation (57)-(58), conditionals (59) and aspect (60)=(24):

(57) *Me-nok   mo-t-ip.*
     come-NEG.VN do-RLS-1SG
     'I did not come.'   (Yonggom Wambon, Drabbe 1959: 140; Wester 2014: 136)

(58) *Me-nok   ki-t-ip.*
     come-NEG.VN be-RLS-1SG
     'I did not come.'   (Yonggom Wambon, Drabbe 1959: 140)

(59) Rawa-r-an ke-t ki-n-in=ŋga,
    take-RLS[NON1SG]-PAST be-RLS[NON1SG] be-LNK-FUT.NON1SG=CIRC
    na-luk
    IMP[SG]-say
    'If you have taken it, say so.' (Lit. you took (it), if it is the case, if it will be the case, say!) (Yonggom Wambon, Drabbe 1959: 142)

(60) Nu dépo-n=ga wé-ma-lé.
    I smoke-VN=CONN continuous-do-[RLS]1SG
    'I smoke all the time.' (Korowai, van Enk and de Vries 1997: 93)

The second function of the *mo* and *ke* verbs is the very productive procedure of deriving verbs from roots of other word classes by forming compound verb stems, e.g. to verbalize adjectives (*wagae-mo-* in (61), deictics (62), nouns (e.g. Digul Wambon *taxet* 'kauri shell' and *taxi-mo-* 'to buy/sell') and question words (63). This verbalization procedure is one of the strategies that speakers use to distribute elements out of clauses over chained mini clauses, argument distribution, see §5.5), for example the manner argument in (61) ('firmly') is not expressed in the same clause as the verb which it modifies (*rapken* 'he held') but given its own mini clause. Similarly, the question-word in (63) is given its own clause and not expressed in the same clause that is questioned:

(61) Wagae-mo rap-ken.
    good-do[SS] hold-RLS[NON1SG]
    'He held it firmly.' (Yonggom Wambon, Drabbe 1959: 132)

(62) E-mo waepmo-gen.
    that-do[SS] walk-RLS[NON1SG]
    'Thus/in that way he walked.' (Yonggom Wambon, Drabbe 1959: 121)

(63) Fene-mo-ra xe xone=xa
    how-do-and[SS] he get[RLS.NON1SG]=Q
    'How did he get it?' (Kombai, de Vries 1993a: 44)

The third function of *mo* and *ke* verbs is to integrate standard Indonesian and Papuan Malay verbs and adjectives within Greater Awyu grammars by the same derivational procedure that turns members of Greater Awyu word classes into verbs, by forming compound verb stems with *mo* and *ke*, e.g. Indonesian *belajar* 'to learn' and Digul Wambon *belajatmo-* 'to learn' (de Vries and de Vries-

Wiersma 1992: 14), Indonesian *istirahat* 'pause' and Korowai *isila-ma* 'to have a pause; to rest' (93).

Since *mo* and *ke* can turn anything anytime into a verb, it comes as no surprise that the lexica of all Greater Awyu languages contain many verbs ending in *mo* or *ke*, including verbs derived from roots that no longer function independently, e.g. there is a Korowai verb *imo-* 'to see' but not a root *i*.

3.6.1.2 Serial verbs

Serial verb consructions (SVC) enable series of verbs to function as a single syntactic head of the clause. Serial verbs are a common phenomenon in Greater Awyu languages, and in Trans New Guinea languages in general (Pawley and Hammarström 2018: 116). Serial verbs must share core arguments, cannot be separated from each other by the insertion of a conjunction and are tightly integrated under one intonation contour. The Greater Awyu serial verbs are of the type called "compact SVCs" by Pawley and Hammarström (2018: 116): "In compact SVCs the verb roots are always contiguous and specify sub-events of a tight-knit semantic unit, typically translatable in English by a single verb or verb plus particle, e. g. Kalam *d ap* (get come) 'bring', *d am* (get go) 'take', *am d ap* (go get come) 'fetch', *d nŋ* (touch perceive) 'feel', *ñb nŋ* (eat perceive) 'taste', *tb tk* (cut sever) 'cut off'. Individual roots cannot be modified".

The unpublished Korowai field dictionary of Stasch (n.d.) contains over 300 serial verbs, very many of them based on the verbs of ascending and descending from a tree house, for example *ai xa-fen* (descend go-1PL.ADH), *ai loxte-* 'descend and disappear' (figuratively used for 'to die', said of infants). The texts in chapter 9 also show many serial verb constructions of types well-known from other Trans New Guinea languages where rather generic motion verbs and verbs of holding are combined with more specific verbs of breaking, splitting, cutting and so on to describe subevents of frequent and easily recognizable cultural practices of daily life. The daily routine of providing the house with firewood is denoted by *in küomo ro me-* 'firewood break hold come' in chain (3) of the Mandobo text §9.2.2. This makes the generic verbs of coming, going, hitting, and holding very frequently occurring in texts of Greater Awyu languages.

SVCs are often used in Trans New Guinea languages as the functional equivalent of valency changing derivational morphology in other languages (Pawley and Hammarström 2018: 111) and the Greater Awyu languages are no exception. Compare for example the intransitive Mandobo verb *ndogo* 'to go across a river' and the transitive serial verb construction *ro ndogo* 'to take someone across a river' (literally 'hold go across'). Sometimes up to four verbs are involved in a serial verb construction, for example Mandobo *kotet orü giamo ro me-* 'to bring brushwood', literally 'brushwood chop break hold come' (Drabbe 1959: 58).

3.6.1.3 Three verb types
Greater Awyu languages distinguish three morphologically distinct types of verbs: two types of independent verbs and one type of dependent verbs (de Vries 2010: 329; de Vries, Wester and van den Heuvel 2012: 277). The first type of independent verbs are fully inflected verbs with three suffix slots, for modality, subject person-number and tense, in that order e.g. *rawaran* and *kinin* in (59). The second independent verb type, semi-inflected verbs, has two suffix slots after the stem, one for modality (realis/irrealis) and one for subject person-number, e.g. *mo-t-ip* (do-RLS-1SG) in (57).

There is one type of dependent verb forms, medial same subject verbs. These verbs are non-finite and consist of a bare verb stem, e.g. *wagaemo* in (58), or a verb stem plus a suffix that marks switch reference relations and/or relations of temporal or conceptual distance, e.g. *i-no* (swing-SS.SIM) in (65a).

3.6.1.4 Realis and irrealis
The realis and irrealis distinction is the most fundamental distinction of the verb system of Greater Awyu languages (de Vries, Wester and van den Heuvel 2012: 277; Wester 2014: 87). This makes Greater Awyu languages members of "a widely scattered minority of Trans New Guinea languages, such as Dani (Barclay 2008), in the far west, the Awyu-Dumut languages in the southwest (Wester 2014) and Duna (San Roque 2008), in the highlands of Papua New Guinea" (Pawley and Hammarström 2018: 100).

Tense is secondary to modality (realis and irrealis) in Greater Awyu languages (Wester 2014: 105; van Enk and de Vries 1997: 96–97). Just as in languages of the Dani family (Barclay 2008) tense suffixes can optionally be added to (ir)realis forms of Greater Awyu languages. The Awyu-Dumut branch has a cross-linguistically very rare pattern of irrealis as formally unmarked (69) and realis as marked with a suffix, contradicting the statement by Dixon (2012: 25) that "if one term may have zero realization, or a zero allomorph, this is always realis". The Becking-Dawi branch marks irrealis forms with a suffix and leaves the realis forms unmarked.

The distinction between realis and irrealis is expressed both in verb stems and in verb suffixes in the Awyu-Dumut branch (Wester 2014: 88), whereas in the Becking-Dawi branch (represented by Korowai), it is only expressed in suffixation.

The Awyu subgroup has realis and irrealis stems for its verbs. Dumut languages have primary and secondary stems. The primary stems are realis stems but the secondary stems are used for both realis and irrealis, thus blurring the distinction (Wester 2014: 90). De Vries and de Vries-Wiersma (1992: 23–24) observe that Digul Wambon verbs have one basic or primary stem and up to three unpredictable tense- or mood related suppletive stems. The basic stem is the shortest and some of the derived stems reflect derivation rules that lost their productivity, revealing an older system of vowel additions to stems, for example *hetak-* 'to see' (basic stem), *hetaxa-* 'to see' (past stem), *hetaxo-* (future stem); *ndak-* 'to give', *ndaxa-* (past stem) and *ndaxo-* future stem. The primary stem is no longer a realis stem in Digul Wambon, because of the many irregularities in the stem system. For example *en-* 'to eat' has a suppletive stem *ande-* which is used in past and future tense forms and in the plural imperative. The imperative singular of *en-* has its own suppletive stem *na-* (de Vries and de Vries-Wiersma 1992: 24).

3.6.1.5 Switch reference

Switch reference marks identity or non-identity of subject referents[13] in the transitions between clauses that make up the clause chain. In Greater Awyu languages switch reference is local, that is, switch reference marking of a clause monitors whether there is (dis)continuity of subject reference with respect to the next clause in the chain. The switch reference marked clause is the marking clause and the clause that follows it and that is monitored for subject (dis)continuity is called the reference clause.

Switch reference and clause chaining play a key role in the morphology and syntax of mountain Trans New Guinea languages but it is not restricted to Trans New Guinea (Roberts 1997, e.g. Manambu, Ndu family, Aikhenvald 2008). Pawley and Hammarström (2018: 99) claim that the largest concentration of switch reference marking languages, – and with the highest complexity-, is New Guinea, the Trans New Guinea group in particular. It comes as no surprise therefore that early missionary linguists such as Pilhofer (1933) and Drabbe (1957, 1959) understood and described the basics of clause chaining and switch reference long before modern labels for the same phenomena were invented.

Suter (2018: 137) credits Jacobsen (1967) for the coinage of the term switch reference but notes that "The English technical terms "medial verb" and "final verb"

---

[13] The SS and DS glosses of Greater Awyu data should not be taken to mean that switch reference operates on switches of referents of all syntactic subjects as may be the case in other languages with switch reference systems. DS stands in the Greater Awyu glosses for a switch of reference in a subsection of syntactic subjects, namely a switch to a topical subject or a subject with high agentivity, just as in quite a few other Trans New Guinea languages where a switch to non-topical, non-agentive or background subjects in the reference clause does not trigger DS verbs in the marking clause that precedes it in the chain, cf. Roberts (1997: 161–171).

replicate the German terms *Satzinnenform* and *Satzendform* coined by Pilhofer (1928, 1933). Pilhofer variously called the same verb forms *unselbständig* and *selbständig* (i.e. dependent and independent)[. . . . . .] In his Kâte grammar of 1933 he gave a precise description of the syntax of the medial verb forms, distinguishing between *Durchgangsformen* (i.e. same subject forms) and *Wechselformen* (i.e. different subject forms)".

Peripheral Trans New Guinea languages outside the core Trans New Guinea area tend to have either less elaborate forms of clause chaining or no clause chaining at all (Asmat-Kamoro, Marind, Gogodola-Suki, Kiwai, some Chimbu-Waghi languages (Pawley and Hammarström 2018: 99)). In some peripheral Trans New Guinea families long sequences of coordinate mini clauses may occur that functionally look very much like clause chains but lack switch reference and sequence/simultaneity morphology and have no distinction between final and medial verbs (Inanwatan, South Bird's Head family, de Vries 2004).

Greater Awyu languages have less developed systems of clause chaining, with little elaboration of medial or dependent verb morphology, compared to canonical clause chaining systems of languages of the mountain Trans New Guinea type. The only verb type that is unambiguously medial is the non-finite same subject type. There are no dedicated final verbs, since both fully inflected and semi-inflected verbs may occur in final and non-final clauses in the chain. But there is a clear tendency for fully inflected verbs to occur predominantly in final clauses.Although there are no dedicated medial different subject verb types, to function in opposition to the medial same subject forms, most Greater Awyu languages have ways to mark switch of subject referent.

The most common way is to press fully or semi-inflected verbs into switch reference service: when a verb form without a subject person-number slot is used (=medial SS), this signals that the reference clause has the same subject referent as the marking clause. But when the reference clause has a different (topical) subject (DS) from the marking clause, a verb with a subject person-number slot (=fully or semi-inflected verbs) must be used in the marking clause. In itself reanalysing the finite/non-finite opposition medially as a SS/DS switch reference opposition is very common in clause chaining languages. Roberts' (1997: 136) sample of 122 languages of Papua New Guinea with switch reference contains 46 languages with that strategy.

In Greater Awyu languages, when a semi-inflected or fully inflected verb is used medially, this creates a strong expectation that the next clause in the chain will have a different subject, on the basis of frequency patterns in language use. But it is not always clear to what extent in some languages or varieties the high frequency and strong association of the DS/finite and SS/non-finite opposition crossed the boundary between a high frequency pattern in language use and a grammatical category of switch reference in the language system. But perhaps this problem is only a problem if one believes in grammatical categories as essentially different from highly frequent patterns of language use. It seems more realistic to assume that there is a continuum of conventionalization of patterns of language use, without a clear cut-off point after which highly frequent patterns of usage would turn into grammatical patterns that are part of the "language system".

The most likely historical scenario for the emergence of switch reference systems based on reanalysis of finite and non-finite oppositions is economy of expression in head-final languages such as Greater Awyu languages (de Vries 2010). Forces of economy operate on series of conjoined clauses with highly predictable, redundant information, in contexts of high thematic continuity. When the subject is continued from one clause to the next and when the predictable subject is only expressed in person and number suffixes on the verb (the default in Greater Awyu languages), speakers will leave out the redundant subject person-number slot. Similarly, when the tense conditions are continued from clause to clause, speakers will delete the tense suffix, leaving tense to be expressed in the final clause, the head of the clause chain. Daniels (2014: 400) sees important parallels to the development in Dumut languages in two Sogeram languages (Nend and Manat): "The first sentence becomes dependent on the second for its tense information, but is not subordinate to it structurally [. . . . . . .] this is similar to the change that De Vries (2010) discusses in the Dumut family, although in that case the process created a new switch reference system, whereas here it recruited new morphology for a switch reference system that already existed".

When conjoined clauses that denote events which share the same participants, time span and location, i.e. in conditions of maximal thematic closeness and predictability, speakers will maximally apply redundancy reduction strategies (de Vries 2010). Therefore, partial or complete stripping verbal forms of subject person-number and TAM coding would be expected to occur at first only in conditions of maximal thematic continuity. Wester (2014: 176) draws attention to an interesting observation by Drabbe (1950: 110) that Pisa, of the Awyu subgroup, only uses its "stripped" medial SS verbs in precisely such conditions of maximal thematic continuity: when not only the subjects remain the same but also the time frame (simultaneity) and when the two events are closely related, conceptually close. This leads Wester (2014: 176) to the hypothesis that Pisa may well represent the very first stage of emerging clause chaining in Greater Awyu languages, where non-finite SS medial verbs not only require subject continuity but full thematic continuity. All other Greater Awyu languages use reduced medial SS verbs in both simultaneity and sequence conditions. Evidence for a gapping-like historical scenario of reducing verbal morphology in conjoined clauses comes from the fact that conjoining conjunctions remain in place to connect the clause with reduced, dependent verb form to the next clause in the chain. Also, where Greater Awyu languages have developed dedicated medial same subject forms, their switch reference and/or temporality affixes (sequence versus simultaneity) can often be shown to be conjoining conjunctions that were reanalysed as suffixes of medial verbs (de Vries 2010).

Once there are reduced same subject verbs, speakers will initially use both independent verbs and reduced verbs in same subject conditions but gradually independent verbs will be pushed out of SS conditions and become associated with different subject conditions (de Vries 2010). The first contexts where independent verbs are pushed out of SS contexts will be contexts of full thematic continuity (simultaneity, conceptual closeness) and only in later stages speakers will start using reduced SS verbs in sequential conditions (Wester 2014: 182).

Various Greater Awyu languages seem to be at various stages of emergent clause chaining and switch reference. Kombai is close to the final stage, where the presence of any independent verb in a series of conjoined clauses almost always implies a switch of subject reference. In the Dumut chain (Mandobo, Yonggom Wambon, Digul Wambon), the situation is more complex and open for various interpretations.

Yonggom Wambon allows independent verbs in subject continuity contexts, for example *rakura* in (6b) and *rirara* in (6c). The fact that independent verbs frequently occur in same subject conditions, means that the strength of the association between independent verbs and different subject transitions is still weak. Therefore, it is not clear to what extent this switch reference use of independent verbs is fully grammaticalized in this dialect. Various interpretations are possible.

Wester (2014: 179–184) argues that independent verbs in all Dumut languages, including Yonggom Wambon, signal DS when used before another conjoined clause but that there are two specific grammatical conditions where independent verbs can occur before clauses with same subjects: (i) when one event is completed before the next event and the conceptual relation between the two events is not close (Wester 2014: 180) and (ii) when a clause is followed by a clause that gives a specification of the first clause (Wester 2014: 178). It is doubtful whether the occurrence of independent verbs in SS conditions is limited to these two circumstances in all Dumut languages. Yonggom Wambon, for example, also uses independent verbs in subject continuity conditions, when the two events not only share the same subject but also the same time span (simultaneity) and where the two events are conceptually one, for example (76).

De Vries (2010) argues that there is a strong frequency association in language use between independent verbs and DS conditions in Yonggom Wambon but that this frequency association in language use has not yet hardened into a grammatical rule at the end of the conventionalisation continuum. Yonggom Wambon has dedicated same subject verbs (non-finite) but lacks fully grammaticalized coding of different subject: when two conjoined consecutive verbs have different subjects, independent verbs must be used but when independent verbs are used, it is still grammatical for them to have the same subjects in the next clause.

The limited number of Digul Wambon texts available to us show a consistent use of *t*-forms (independent verbs with a realis suffix -*t* and a person-number slot) as a signal of different subject but all other independent verb types can be followed by clauses with same subjects (and different subjects: they are switch reference neutral). When the realis *t*-forms of Digul Wambon occur in final clauses, they are just realis marking verbs but when they occur in conjoined sequences of clauses, they signal realis *and* different subject. The optional conjoining clitic =*o* is obligatory in non-final use of *t*-forms. When the *t*-forms occur in final clauses, they do never take the conjoining clitic =*o*. The formation [stem+ -t + person-number + -*o*], therefore, has become exclusively associated with medial different subject conditions and has become a realis different subject verb, at least in the texts available to us (de Vries 2010).

In other words, Digul Wambon is different from other Greater Awyu languages such as Kombai, where *all* independent verb types, if they occur before another clause in a conjoined sequence, became strongly associated with different subject conditions, a development that makes the very presence of a subject person-number slot a signal of different subject, in opposition to non-finite verbs that are same subject. In Digul Wambon, the grammaticalization of switch reference does not focus on the distinction between non-finite (SS) versus finite (DS, all independent verbs). Rather, the grammaticalization of switch reference centers around one particular type of independent verbs, namely semi-inflected verbs with the -*t* realis suffix.

All other independent verb types of Digul Wambon are switch reference neutral and may occur medially in clause chains under subject continuity conditions, in contrast to *t*-forms. Digul Wambon indeed allows fully inflected verbs in conjoined sequences of clauses with same subjects, for example *kalevambo* in de Vries and de Vries-Wiersma (1992: 93).[14] The semi-inflected realis verbs (with the

---

14 *Lap-nda-no   alep-top   ilo-ka-l-eva-mbo=nde   alep=kup*
take-come-LNK-SIM canoe-inside descend-go-RLS-1PL-PAST=CONN canoe=with
ukhu-mbelo   xali-ndave-l-eva-mbo.
put.in-SS.SEQ   carry-return-RLS-1PL-PAST
'We brought (the pig) down to the canoe and having put (the pig) in the canoe we returned'.
(Digul Wambon, de Vries and de Vries-Wiersma 1992: 93)

modality suffix -*kend*) similarly are switch reference neutral and may occur in same subject and different subject conditions. Convergence with languages that lack clause chaining and switch reference could have triggered speakers to re-introduce fully inflected verbs of final clauses medially in conjoined clauses, a development away from canonical switch reference.

Independent verb forms including fully inflected verbs (64) and especially semi-inflected realis verbs (with the realis suffix -*kend*), are frequently found preceding medial SS forms of verbs of motion and verbs of finishing or stopping which are used to express aspectual and temporal interclausal relations: when one event went on (with durative aspect) until the next event started or when one event has finished before the next (Jang 2008: 60; Wester 2014: 100–101). Consider (64):

(64) *ngerkaji-ke-l-eva-mbo-n=o*   *kutip-ke-lo*
chainsaw-be-RLS-1PL-PAST-LNK=CNJ night-be-SS
ko-xe-n=o   *nda-tulo*   *la-l-eva-mbo*
go-RLS[NON1SG]-LNK=CNJ come-ascend[SS] lie-RLS-1PL-PAST
'We continued sawing until the night fell and we went up (the house) and slept.'   (Digul Wambon, de Vries and de Vries-Wiersma 1992: 90)

The switch reference systems of Greater Awyu languages only track subjects which are discourse topics (see §4.5.2). Switches to different grammatical subjects with referents of low topicality cannot be marked by DS. In (64) there is continuity of the topical subject 'we' and there are multiple switches to non-topical referents of grammatical subjects, viz. the subjects of *koxeno* 'it went on' and *kutipkelo* 'it became dark'. Before such switches to non-topical subjects we find clauses with either switch reference neutral independent verbs or medial "false" same subject forms in Greater Awyu languages (see §4.5.2), as in (64). Wheater clauses, experiential clauses, but also aspectual clauses that are part of aspectual or temporal constructions (such as independent verb plus *koxeno* 'until' or independent verb plus *kitmbelo* 'after') have inanimate subject referents of low topicality that do not persist in the discourse and that are never preceded by DS forms.

The second way to mark switch reference in Greater Awyu languages is with switch reference conjunctions which cliticize to independent verbs. Korowai (65a/b) and Aghu (66)-(67) are examples of the second type.

(65a) *Nu lép-telo=do*   *yu be-lai-da.*
1SG ill-be[RLS.NON1SG]=DS 3SG NEG-come[RLS.NON1SG]-NEG
'I am ill but he does not come.'
        (Korowai, van Enk and de Vries 1997: 108)

(65b) *Yu   mbaxa-mol-mo=daxu   xomilo?*
      3SG what-do-do[RLS.NON1SG]=SS die[RLS.NON1SG]
      'Why did he die?' (Lit: What occurred to him and he died?)
                                      (Korowai, van Enk and de Vries 1997: 109)

(66) *è-nu=ku   da-de*
     eat-RLS[1SG]=SS.SEQ   come-RLS[1SG]
     'I first ate and then came here.'   (Aghu, Drabbe 1957: 37)

(67) *tam-oxo=ne   xo-de*
     write-RLS.NON1[SG]=DS.SEQ   go-RLS[1SG]
     'He wrote and I went.'   (Aghu, Drabbe 1957: 38)

Aghu is interesting since it may attach switch reference conjunctions as clitics (SS and DS) to independent verbs (like Korowai) but the presence of semi-inflected verbs (without any switch reference clitics) in a conjoined clause also strongly implies switch of subject reference in the next clause (van den Heuvel 2016: 313–332). Therefore, Aghu seems to employ the type of switch reference found in the Becking-Dawi branch as well as the type found in the Awyu-Dumut branch. Aghu's switch reference clitics occur only with semi-inflected verbs, only occur in conditions of sequentiality of the two consecutive events and are relatively rare in texts (van den Heuvel 2016: 313–332). Aghu speakers prefer the use of the other switch reference system, with medial verbs without subject person-number slot marking SS and conjoined independent verbs marking DS, i.e. they prefer the Awyu-Dumut system over the Becking-Dawi system.

The strong association in Aghu between different subject conditions and one type of independent verbs, the semi-inflected verbs with two slots, is also found in other Awyu-Dumut languages, for example Digul Wambon, where the realis *t*-forms have a similar very strong frequency association with DS conditions. This is a natural outcome of the behavior of speakers: the tensed three slot fully inflected verbs tend to be far less frequent than the semi-inflected two slot verbs and when the tensed verbs occur, they tend to occur in the final clauses of sentences, paragraphs or whole texts. In Yonggom Wambon this tendency is so strong that tensed verbs have become final verbs (de Vries 2010).

3.6.1.6 Subject person and number
Greater Awyu verb paradigms consist of four forms each: 1SG, NON-1SG, 1PL and NON-1PL. The verb paradigms express two oppositions: speaker (marked by a suffix) and non-speaker (zero marked) and singular (zero marked) versus plural

(marked by a suffix). The systematic conflation of second and third person in all verb paradigms is a striking characteristic which sets the Greater Awyu language family apart from its neighbors (de Vries, Wester and van den Heuvel 2012: 296; Wester 2014: 77). Greater Awyu languages being pro-drop languages, this implies that independent verb forms such as *rira-r=a* in (6c) out of context may mean 'you(SG), he, she, went down' (Wester 2014: 74).

This Greater Awyu 2/3 syncretism is very systematic, in singular and plural, and occurs in all verb paradigms and this is typologically uncommon, also in Papuan languages where it occassionaly occurs in much more restricted forms (Cysouw 2003: 131–132). There is one exception to Greater Awyu 2/3 conflation: the Korowai adhortative paradigm distinguishes second and third person (see §3.6.3.3 and de Vries, Wester and van den Heuvel 2012: 296).

3.6.1.7 Tense

There is a lot of variation in the tense systems of Greater Awyu languages, in the distinctions that are made, in the affixes used and in the positon of the tense affixes in the verb (Wester 2014: 105–116).[15] Whereas the Awyu subgroup has four past tenses (hodiernal past, a hesternal past, a distant past and an historical past, Wester 2014: 112), Kombai, of the Ndeiram subgroup, does not have a past tense (de Vries, Wester and van den Heuvel 2012: 283). The Dumut subgroup has one general past tense. Drabbe (1959) and de Vries and de Vries-Wiersma (1992) distinguished a present tense for Dumut languages. However, Wester (2014: 93–100) convincingly argued that the present tense forms of Dumut languages (and the Non-future tense of Kombai) express realis modality.

The Dumut subgroup, as well as Kombai (Ndeiram subgroup) and Aghu, of the Awyu subgroup, have future tense (Wester 2014: 113). Some languages use constructions with the verb *mo/ma* 'to do' to create specific tenses, e.g. immediate and remote future tenses of Kombai and Digul Wambon (Jang 2008: 34; de Vries 1993a: 17; Wester 2014: 115).

Korowai, of the Becking-Dawi branch, differs strongly from the Awyu-Dumut branch in terms of its tense system (van Enk and de Vries 1997: 96–101): *-méma* and *-(fe)lu/-lulo* are (optionally) suffixed to both realis and irrealis verb forms. When *-méma* is added to realis forms, the result is an immediate past and when suffixed to irrealis forms the result is an immediate future form. Suffixing *-(fe)lu/-lulo* to realis verbs results in yesterday's past form and adding *-(fe)lu/-lulo* to irrealis verbs creates a tomorrow's future paradigm. Also, Korowai has a tense suffix *-baxa* that only occurs with realis forms and this creates a hodiernal past form.

---

15 This section on tense and aspect is based on de Vries (2017).

Tensed, fully inflected forms are marked verb forms, relatively infrequent in texts of Greater Awyu languages. Speakers prefer to use just semi-inflected verbs (realis or irrealis, without tense suffix) to refer to past or future events when the context leaves no doubt about the time setting. This also explains the association between tensed forms and the final clause of a multi-clause sentence, or the final clause of a paragraph or story as a whole in Greater Awyu texts: the final clauses contain the tense setting for all preceding realis or irrealis forms. Wester (2014: 106) observes that five of the nine Aghu stories published by Drabbe (1957) have a historical past at the end, setting the time frame for the medial SS verbs and the untensed independent realis and irrealis verbs in the whole story. Tensed verbs in Yonggom Wambon seem to occur only in final clauses of multi-clause sentences, where they express the tense of the untensed two-slot verbs and medial verbs in the *voorzinnen*, the term Drabbe uses for the preceding clauses in the conjoined string of clauses (Drabbe 1959: 133). This points towards the development of fully inflected verbs into final verbs in this dialect. In the neighboring Digul Wambon dialect tensed verbs occur both in final and non-final clauses.

3.6.1.8 Aspect

Greater Awyu languages distinguish durative, completive, iterative-habitual and phasal aspects. Rather than by an aspect slot in the verb, Greater Awyu languages express these aspects by a combination of derived stems, periphrastic constructions involving posture verbs, auxiliary verbs of doing and being and verbal nouns (Wester 2014: 117–126). However, Korowai, of the Becking-Dawi branch and Kombai, of the Ndeiram subgroup, have aspect slots in the verb, Kombai a prefix and Korowai a suffix, both expressing the durative and completive contrast (de Vries 1993a: 28–29; van Enk and de Vries 1997: 92–94).

3.6.2 Verbs in Yonggom Wambon

After the general overview of the Greater Awyu verb system in §3.6.1, I will now discuss verbal morphology of two languages in more detail, one of each branch, Yonggom Wambon (Awyu-Dumut) and Korowai (Becking-Dawi). These languages are relatively well-documented and for both we have a good corpus of texts. The verbal forms of Yonggom Wambon were described by Drabbe (1959). Consider the verbs in (68a)–(68d):

(68a) *Ketmon i-no=te mando-na-n-in*
 dance swing-SIM=CNJ come-IRR.NON1PL-LNK-FUT
 'They will come (while) dancing.' (Yonggom Wambon, Drabbe 1959: 134)

(68b) *Iŋ-gen-ep=te kim-gen.*
 hit-RLS-1SG=CNJ die-RLS[NON1SG]
 'I killed him.' (Lit. 'I hit and he died') (Yonggom Wambon, Drabbe 1959: 134)

(68c) *Tat-mo raga-r-an.*
 bad-do[SS] speakII-RLS[NON1SG]-PAST
 'He spoke badly.' (Yonggom Wambon, Drabbe 1959: 132)

(68d) *Rawo-ro me-gen-ep*
 hold-SS come-RLS-1SG
 'I took (it) and came.' (Yonggom Wambon, Drabbe 1959: 133)

The verbs occurring in (68a)-(68d) illustrate the three main types of verb forms in Greater Awyu languages: same subject verbs (*tatmo, rawaro, ino*), fully inflected verbs (*ragaran, mandonanin*) and semi-inflected verbs (*megenep, kimgen, iŋgenep*).

3.6.2.1 Same subject verbs

There are three types of medial SS verb forms in Yonggom (Drabbe 1959: 132–133): bare verb stem (*tatmo* in (68c)), verb stem+ *-no* (*ino* in (68a)), verb stem + *-ro* (*rawo-ro*, (68d)).

Medial SS verbs do not express subject person-number, modality or tense; they are dependent on the first independent verb to their right for their interpretation in terms of subject person-number, modality and tense. They do express that the next clause in the chain has the same subject referent. When followed by the suffix *-no*, the temporal relation to the next clause is one of simultaneity. One would expect the suffix *-ro* to express sequence but according to Drabbe (1959: 132) both stem+ *-ro* and the bare stem can occur in simultaneity and sequence conditions.

It is important to notice that clauses headed by these medial same subject verbs are conjoined to the next clause, they are not a constituent of the next clause. This is shown by the (optional) occurrence of the conjoining conjunction (=)*te* (phonologically conditioned allomorphs =*t*, =*nde*). The element (=)*te* is used both to coordinate noun phrases (69) and to conjoin clauses (70) in Yonggom Wambon (de Vries 2010: 330).

(69) *Ka-gup te ra-ra-mun de munotit t*
man-PL COORD woman-woman- PL COORD child. PL COORD
in-gin-in.
eat-RLS-NON1PL
'The men, women and children are eating.'
(Yonggom Wambon, Drabbe 1959: 145)

(70) *Sumo Te ko-gen.*
lift[SS] COORD go-RLS[NON1SG]
'He lifted (it) up and went.' (Yonggom Wambon, Drabbe 1959: 134)

The "coordinate-dependent" (Foley 1986: 177) type of clause linkage of (70), with conjoining conjunctions linking dependent clauses to independent clauses and with switch reference and temporality distinctions expressed on medial verbs, as in (68a)-(68d), is characteristic of clause chaining languages. The term "coordinate", with its implication of syntactically equivalent members of the coordinate structure and where each clause can independently select its tense (e.g. English 'John worked yesterday and Bill will work tomorrow'), is perhaps not fully adequate to denote this type of chaining linkage with medial verbs that cannot stand on their own. All clauses that precede the final clause of the chain are under the scope of the tense of the final clause.

De Vries (2010) argues that the medial SS verbs of Greater Awyu languages are the result of reduction of independent verbs in conditions of subject continuity. That explains the presence of conjoining clitics with medial SS verbs as in (70). And it also explains the form of various medial SS suffixes in Greater Awyu languages which were interclausal conjunctions that first cliticized and then integrated in the reduced verbs as medial suffixes (de Vries 2010: 341). For example, the Yonggom Wambon medial verb suffix *-no* that signals simultaneous relations with the next verb in same subject conditions (e.g. *i-no* in (68a) can be explained as derived from the conjoining clitic =*o* that cliticized to the verbs (with the nasal linker separating =*o* and the stem final vowel): *i-n=o* (swing-LNK=CNJ>*i-no* swing-SS.SIM). The Digul Wambon same subject and sequence medial suffix *-mbelo* was derived from the anteriority conjunction *mbet* 'first'/'and then', combined with the conjoining clitic =*o* (de Vries 2010).[16]

---

[16] The final /t/ of *mbet-* changes into /l/ when it finds itself in intervocalic position due to morpheme clustering, see Wester (2014: 23) for this and other common morphophonemic processes in Awyu-Dumut languages.

3.6.2.2 Fully inflected verbs

(71) 1SG   *etagarewan*
             etaga-t-ep-an
             see-RLS-1SG-PAST
             'I saw'

    NON1SG *etagaran*
             etaga-t-an
             see-RLS[NON1SG]-PAST
             'he/she, it, you saw'

    1PL   *etagarewanan*
             etaga-t-ew-an-an
             see-RLS-1-PL-PAST
             'we saw'

    NON1PL *etagarinan*
             etaga-t-in-an
             see-RLS-NON1PL-PAST 'they/you (PL) saw'

Fully inflected verbs in Yonggom Wambon consist of a verb stem followed by a modality slot (realis *-t* or *-ken* or irrealis, zero-marked), a subject person-number slot and finally a tense slot. The tense suffixes are *-an* for past tense and *-in* for future tense. Drabbe (1959: 128) mentions a third tense expressed by *-ken* that he describes as a present tense that is also used as narrative tense in stories about the past. The cognate forms of Digul Wambon have also been analyzed as present tense forms with narrative functions by de Vries and de Vries-Wiersma (1992: 25). Wester (2014: 93–100) reanalyzes the *ken*-forms of Dumut languages including Yonggom Wambon as realis forms (see §3.6.2.3). This is a Past paradigm of Yonggom Wambon fully inflected verb forms of the verb *etaga* 'to see' (Wester 2014: 107, based on Drabbe 1959: 130):

    Yonggom Wambon phonemes /p/ and /t/ are realized as [w] and [r] in intervocalic conditions in morpheme sequencing. The four forms are based on two distinctions: speaker versus non-speaker (zero-marked) and singular (zero-marked) versus plural, as in all Greater Awyu languages. Wester (2014: 85) reconstructs proto Awyu, proto Dumut and proto Awyu Dumut subject person-number markers.

3.6.2.3 Semi-inflected verbs

The realis paradigm in Yonggom Wambon is based on primary stems and the irrealis paradigm on secondary stems, if a verb has multiple stems. Irrealis is formally unmarked and realis is marked by *-t*. Realis forms are used when an event has been actualized and they may refer to events in present and past. Irrealis forms are used for events or actions that have not (yet) been actualized and they occur in adhortative, intentional and future conditions. Just like the past tense marker *-an* may be added to realis forms to explicitly mark the past tense, the tense suffix *-in* may be added to the irrealis forms to mark future tense. Consider the paradigms of these two semi-inflected verbs (Yonggom Wambon, Drabbe 1959: 128–129):

(72)   Realis   Irrealis
 1SG   *etagarep*   *majop*
         etaga-t-ep   majo-p
         see-RLS-1[SG]   come.down-1[SG][IRR]
         'I saw/I see'   'I want to/will come down'
 NON1SG *etagat*   *majon*
         etaga-t   majo-n
         see-RLS[NON1SG]   come.down-[IRR]NON1[SG]
 1PL   *etagarewan*   *majowan*
         etaga-t-ew-an   majo-w-an
         see-RLS-1-PL   come.down-[IRR]1-PL
 NON1PL *etagarin*   *majonan*
         etaga-t-in   majo-n-an
         see-RLS-NON1PL   come.down-NON1-[IRR]PL

Wester (2014: 94–95) distinguishes a second realis paradigm in Yonggom Wambon (and in the other Dumut languages) with realis suffix *-ken*, besides the realis paradigm with the suffix *-t* of (69). The *ken*-forms are viewed as present tense forms by Drabbe (1959: 128). Both analyses have their pros and cons. Wester (2014: 99) admits that she has not found a clear functional difference between *t*-forms and *ken*-forms in Yonggom Wambon and therefore the question remains why Yonggom Wambon would have two realis paradigms with very similar uses and meanings. The *t*-forms of Yonggom Wambon, just like the Digul Wambon *t*-forms and the Korowai realis forms, have a key property that the *ken*-forms do not have: a tense suffix can be added to them, turning them into tensed realis forms, with a modality and a tense slot. This cannot be done with *ken*-forms in any Dumut language and this follows naturally from assuming that *-ken* marks a present tense in Yonggom Wambon that functionally overlaps with the realis *t*-forms. On the other hand, Drabbe (1959: 133) gives examples of the use of *ken*-forms where their tense reading is controlled by a tensed form in the final clause, inconsistent with *-ken* as present tense marker:

(73) Iŋ-gen-ep   kima-r-an.
     hit- PRES(?)-1SG die-RLS[NON1SG]-PAST
     'I killed him.' (lit. I hit and he died.')

(Yonggom Wambon, Drabbe 1959: 133)

The Yonggom Wambon semi-inflected verbs (realis *t*-forms and irrealis zero-forms) are independent forms that may occur in conjoined clause sequences, when the subject remains the same *anderewa* in (74a) (see also *rakura* in (6b) and *rirara* in (6c)), when there is a switch of topical subject reference, *taembarin* in (75) and in aspectual and temporal constructions with relator verbs as auxiliaries *andera* in (74b), where there is a switch to a non-topical subject, a context where Greater Awyu languages demand either medial SS verbs or switch reference neutral independent verbs (§4.5.2). Notice that *t*-forms in Yonggom Wambon have a different grammatical place than in Digul Wambon: Digul Wambon *t*-forms specialized in non-final context as DS verbs, unlike Yonggom Wambon, where *t*-forms are switch reference neutral independent verbs (see §3.6.1.4).

(74a) *Ande-r-ew=a   mbumo-gon-ep=te   me-gen.*
      eat.II-RLS-1SG=SEQ finish- RLS-1SG=CNJ come-RLS[NON1SG]
      'I ate and then I finished it and he came.' ('After I had eaten he arrived.')

(Yonggom Wambon, Drabbe 1959: 136)

(74b) *Ande-r=a   mbumo=te   me-gen.*
      eat.II-RLS[NON1SG]=SEQ finish[SS]=CNJ   come-RLS[NON1SG]
      'After he had eaten, he came.'   (Yonggom Wambon, Drabbe 1959: 136)

(75) *Naerop taemba-r-in   kima-r-an*
     Naerop shoot-RLS-NON1PL   die-RLS[NON1SG]-PAST
     'They shot Naerop and he died.'

(Yonggom Wambon, Drabbe 1959, Wester 2014: 179)

The clitic =*a* of *ander=a* in (74b) was analyzed by Drabbe (1959: 134) as a sequence conjunction but =*a* may very well be a more general conjoining conjunction. Since sequence conditions occur more frequently than simultaneity conditions in narrative texts, it stands to reason that Drabbe found it often in sequence contexts but it occurs also in simultaneity contexts, for example (76):

(76) Tuma-r-in=a   woŋopon ke-ge-gon-in.
     chop-RLS-NON1PL=CNJ long.time be-be-RLS-NON1PL
     'They kept chopping (the canoe) for a long time.'
                                        (Yonggom Wambon, Drabbe 1959: 183)

3.6.2.4 Imperative, interrogative and prohibitive mood

Yonggom Wambon, like other Awyu-Dumut languages, has suppletive imperative stems. It derives imperative stems by prefixing an element *na-* or *n-* and suffixing *-n* to a primary or secondary stem (Drabbe 1959: 130; de Vries, Wester and van den Heuvel 2012: 287). An alternative way is to add the imperative stem *nok* of the auxiliary verb *mo* 'to do' to a (secondary) verb stem. By adding a plural suffix *-nin*, plural imperatives are formed. There are many irregularities in the formation of imperative forms. Some examples:

(77) verb stem   mba-, mbage- 'to sit'   en- ande- 'to eat'
     Imperative SG   na-mbo-n   n-an
                     mbage-nok   ande-nok
     Imperative PL   na-mbo-nin   n-an-in

Prohibitives (Drabbe 1959: 141) are formed by adding the prohibitive suffix *-tit* to a secondary verb stem. The plural suffixes *-na* and *-an* surround *-tit* to pluralize the prohibitive. In line with Greater Awyu 2/3 syncretism the prohibitive forms have 2nd and 3rd person readings. Some examples of prohibitive forms:

(78) jo-tit
     call-PROH[SG]
     'you (SG) must not call/let him not call'
                                        (Yonggom Wambon, Drabbe 1959: 141)

(79) jo-na-tir-an
     call-PL-PROH-PL
     'you (PL) must not call him, do not call him'/'do not let them call'
                                        (Yonggom Wambon, Drabbe 1959: 141)

Yes/no-questions are formed by cliticising *=to(n)* to verb forms. Question word questions optionally have the question clitic *=kuji* attached to the last word of the sentence (Drabbe 1959: 140).

3.6.2.5 Negation

Yonggom Wambon negates verbal predicates periphrastically by suffixing the negative nominalizer *-nok* to verb stems which are then arguments of the auxiliaries *mo* 'to do' or *ke* 'to be' (Drabbe 1959: 140; Wester 2014: 136). This negative nominalizer suffix is unrelated to the imperative stem *nok* of the auxiliary verb *mo* 'to do' discussed in §3.6.2.4

(80) *me-nok   mo-t-ip*
     come-NEG.VN do-RLS-1SG
     'I did not come.'   (Yonggom Wambon, Drabbe 1959: 140)

(81) *me-nok   ki-t-ip*
     come-NEG.VN do-RLS-1SG
     'I did not come.'   (Yonggom Wambon, Drabbe 1959: 140)

The primary stem *me* 'to come' is used in the negative verbal nouns of (80)-(81) but from the secondary and tertiary stems of verbs negative verbal nouns may also be formed, without differences in meaning, e.g. *me-*, *mende-* and *mando-* 'to come' (*me-nok*, *mende-nok*, *mando-nok*, all meaning 'the not coming').

Nominal and adjectival predicates are negated by the negative copula *tomba*, with allomorph *domba* after predicates ending in a nasal (Drabbe 1959: 124):

(82) *Nuw=e   mberon domba.*
     1SG=CONN small   NEG.COP
     'I am not small.'   (Yonggom Wambon, Drabbe 1959: 124)

Copula clauses with locative-existential function are negated by *ndoi* (Wester 2014: 135):

(83) *Menep=e   kagup ndoi*
     1SG=CONN   small NEG.COP
     'Now there are no men.'   (Yonggom Wambon, Drabbe 1959: 147)

The Dumut languages, including Yonggom Wambon, are not very representative for negation strategies of Greater Awyu languages (Wester 2014: 138–139). The other groups, including Becking-Dawi, all employ reflexes of a proto Greater Awyu pre verbal negator **pV-* combined with a post verbal negator **-ndV*.

3.6.2.6 Aspect

Durative aspect is periphrastically expressed in Yonggom Wambon in ways that we find in all Greater Awyu languages and indeed in many other languages of the world, with posture verbs (Wester 2014: 117; Drabbe 1959: 141). Reflexes of the proto Greater Awyu verb *mba* 'to sit' are used to express duration in all Greater Awyu languages, except Pisa which uses both the posture verb of lying down and of sitting (Wester 2014: 119). The aspectual auxiliary verb of sitting is preceded by a medial same subject verb form. In Yonggom Wambon, it is the medial SS simultaneity form *verb stem+ -no*:

(84) Mirip   mari-no   mbage-r-an.
     rain   come.down-SS.SIM   sit-RLS[NON1SG]-PAST
     'It was raining.'   (Yonggom Wambon, Drabbe 1959: 141)

An alternative strategy, again found throughout Greater Awyu languages, is to use an invariable aspectual adverb following or preceding an independent verb. This aspectual adverb is derived from the verb of sitting and cliticizes to the clause final verb. Yonggom uses *mbon* that follows independent verb forms:

(85) Mirip   majo-n-in=mbon.
     rain   come.down-LNK-NON1SG[IRR]= DUR
     'It will be raining.'   (Yonggom, Drabbe 1959: 141)

Iterative aspect in Yonggom follows the general Greater Awyu pattern of deriving iterative verb stems by reduplicating the verb stem and adding the stem of the auxiliary verb of doing *mo* (Wester 2014: 121–122; Drabbe 1959: 126), e.g. *en-* 'to eat', *en-en-mo* 'to eat repeatedly'. Habitual stems are derived by reduplicating the verb stem, adding the habitual suffix *-op*, followed by the auxiliary verb stem *mo*. The derived habitual verb precedes the verb of sitting in this habitual periphrastic construction (Drabbe 1959: 141):

(86) Ndun=e   yugup ra -me   en-ene-y-op-mo   mbage-t.
     sago=CONN   3SG   take-come   eat-eat-LNK-HAB-do   sit-RLS[NON1SG]
     'The sago, he is the one who brings and eats it.'
                        (Yonggom Wambon; Drabbe 1959: 154–155; Wester 2014: 122)

Completive aspect is expressed in Yonggom Wambon as in other Greater Awyu languages with verbs that mean 'to finish', 'to not do something (=to stop doing something)' or 'to put down something'. Yonggom Wambon uses, according to Drabbe (1959: 136), the verbs *mbumo-* 'to finish', *ndoimo-* 'to stop' (an activity, lit. 'to not do') and *oro-* 'to lay down something':

(87) Ande-w=a   mbumo   te   ka-j-ip.
     eat.II-[IRR]1SG=SEQ finish[SS] CNJ   go-LNK-[IRR]1SG
     'After I have eaten, I want to go.'   (Yonggom Wambon, Drabbe 1959: 136)

Such aspectual verbs belong to a group of verbs in Greater Awyu languages that were called relator verbs by de Vries and de Vries-Wiersma (1992: 74), because they combine the expression of aspectual meanings with the expression of interclausal relations in clause chains. Sometimes this relational interclausal function becomes the main function and this opens the way for grammaticalization into interclausal conjoining conjunctions when such verbal forms petrify into invariable discourse conjunctions, for example *kono* 'going', *nda-kono* 'coming-going' in Digul Wambon (de Vries and de Vries-Wiersma 1992: 74) and *xenè* 'going' in Korowai. Yonggom uses motion verbs as relator verbs that express that the first action or event went on until another event or state commenced, meaning 'until':

(88) Mbage-p   ka-n   werepmo-j-i
     sit-[IRR]1SG go-[IRR]NON1SG   be.healthy-LNK-[IRR]1SG
     'I want to stay/ I stay until I am recovered.' (Lit. I want to stay and it will go on and I will be healthy)   (Yonggom Wambon, Drabbe 1959: 135)

3.6.3 Verbs in Korowai

Korowai is the only language of the Becking-Dawi branch about which we have enough data to make a comparison with Awyu-Dumut verbs possible. The overall pattern of the Korowai verb system is the same as found in Awyu-Dumut languages: we find the same three basic verb types, the realis-irrealis distinction as central to the system, conflation of 2nd and 3rd persons in verb paradigms and the same pattern and matter of negating verbs (de Vries, Wester and van den Heuvel 2012: 299).

3.6.3.1 Three verb types

Korowai has medial same subject verbs (bare verb stem or stem plus SS suffix *-nè*), semi-inflected verbs with two suffix slots: a person-number and modality slot (realis or irrealis) and three slot verbs that add a tense suffix or aspect prefix to semi-inflected verbs. The latter two types are independent verbs. The letter *e* represents a non-phonemic transitional schwa, the *è* represents a half open vowel phoneme /ɛ/ and the letter *é* represents a half closed vowel phoneme /e/. Consider this section of a Korowai text with the three verb types:

(89) *Xof-e=xa   xomilo=do   mél*
     that-LNK=MOD die[RLS.NON1SG]=DS earth
     laimexo-baxa-ti=xa   abül lu-falé.
     bury-HOD-NON1PL[RLS]=MOD man   ascend-appear[RLS.NON1SG]
     'that man who died and whom they buried earlier today went up and appeared'   (Korowai, van Enk and de Vries 1997: 158)

The verbs *xomilo* and *falé* are examples of semi-inflected verbs, with *xomilo* linked to the next clause by the switch reference clitic conjunction =*do*; *laimexo-baxa-ti* is a fully inflected verb and *lu* a medial same subject verb.

3.6.3.2 Same subject verbs and switch reference
Korowai has just one medial same subject verb form that consists of the bare verb stem, such as *damilmo* in (90), or the verb stem plus the same subject suffix -*nè*, such as *le-nè* in (90).

(90) *mé-bol   damilmo le-nè   lu-ba-lé*
     earth-hole open[SS] come-SS ascend-COM-[RLS]1SG
     'I opened the grave and after I had gone up (the tree house stairs)'
                                   (Korowai, van Enk and de Vries 1997: 109)

Korowai has another way to code subject continuity (SS) between consecutive conjoined clauses. Clauses with independent verbs can be conjoined to other clauses asyndetically but in the majority of cases speakers attach a switch-reference clitic to the independent verb to indicate whether the next clause has the same subject or a different subject. If such a clitic is absent, the independent form is switch reference neutral. These are the switch reference conjunctions of Korowai:

(91) =*do(n)*   different subject
     =*daxu(l)* same subject
     =*aŋgu*   same subject/intentional
     =*tofexo*   different subject/adversative

The clitics =*do(n)*, (92), =*(le)lexu* (95) and =*daxu(l)* (93) are functionally unmarked and occur frequently. The clitics =*aŋgu* (92) and =*tofexo* (94) are marked and only occur in intentional and adversative contexts (van Enk and de Vries 1997: 110).

(92) *Ge-lal=to   fédo-m=do   fo-p=aŋgu   ne-mom*
your-daughter=FOC give-2SG.IMP=DS take-1SG.INT=SS *my-uncle*
xolop-fuda-mo-p.
replace-compensate-do-1SG.INT
'You must give your daughter and I want to marry her and I want to replace my uncle (=you must give your daughter to me as a compensation-gift for my (dead) mother's brother).'
(Korowai, van Enk and de Vries 1997: 110)

(93) *waf-è   xülo   xe-nè Démbol xandun=ta=fexo*
there-CONN upstream go-SS Démbol stonebank=at=CIRC
isila-ma-lè=daxu   beba-lè=fexo   wa-fosü   xe-nè
rest-do-[RLS]1PL=SS sit-[RLS]1PL=until MED-downstream go-SS
xo-sü   xa-lé.
DST-downstream go-[RLS]1PL
'And there we went upstream until we rested on the stones of the Dembol river and from there we went downstream.'
(Korowai, van Enk and de Vries 1997: 72)

(94) *Xaxul   nu ne-mom   dodépa- lé=lofexo   be-lai-da.*
Yesterday I 1SG-uncle call-[RLS]1SG=DS.ADV NEG-come[NON1SG.RLS]-NEG
'Yesterday I called my uncle but he did not come.'
(Korowai, van Enk and de Vries 1997: 110)

(95) *i   waxol fa=ləlexu*[17]   *xa-xə-te*
this moon appear[IRR.NON1SG] go-IRR-NON1PL
'This moon will appear first and then they'll go' (from the unpublished field notes of Rupert Stasch)

Stasch (in personal communication) observed that speakers in conversations regularly end an utterance with a verb that is affixed for switch reference, a non-canonical use of DS clauses, (96) (see Sarvasy 2015 for non-canonical chain

---

[17] Rupert Stasch brought =*(le)lexu* to my attention. The examples in his notes seem to indicate that the conjunction is used in anteriority conditions.

final use of switch reference marked clauses in Nungon). The utterance is an answer to a previous question why the man had moved to a different place. When Greater Awyu speakers use Papuan Malay, they frequently use the conjunction *jadi* 'therefore' or *baru* 'and; next' in similar contexts when speakers for whatever reasons want to leave inferences, conclusions or consequences implicit. For example:

(96) nə=lidop-telo=do
     1SG=one-be[RLS.NON1SG]=DS
     'I was the only one left'   (Korowai, notes of Rupert Stasch)

3.6.3.3 Semi-inflected verbs

Whereas in the Awyu-Dumut branch we find the cross-linguistically rare marking of realis forms, with the irrealis as the unmarked member of the distinction (zero-marked), Korowai of the Becking-Dawi branch, has unmarked realis forms and marked irrealis forms (with the irrealis suffix *-xa*, allomorphs *-xe* and *-axa* (97), both paradigms with phonologically conditioned changes to the verb stems (van Enk and de Vries 1997: 90–91). The Realis paradigm of *alo-* 'to stand' and the Irrealis paradigm of *lai-* 'to come' are given in (97).

(97)   Realis   Irrealis
    1SG   ale-lé   la-xe-lé
            stand-[RLS]1SG   come-IRR-1SG
    NON1SG alo   la-xé
            stand[RLS.NON1SG]   come-IRR[NON1SG]
    1PL   ale-lè   la-xe-lè
            stand-[RLS]1PL   come-IRR-1PL
    NON1PL ale-té   la-xe-té
            stand-[RLS]NON1PL   come-IRR-NON1PL

Besides the general irrealis paradigm of (97), Korowai and Tsaukambo, both of the Becking-Dawi branch, have a special adhortative paradigm (with imperative and intentional readings) that corresponds to the irrealis paradigm of the Awyu-Dumut branch (72). But whereas its Awyu-Dumut counterpart has a broad irrealis meaning (with adhortative and intentional readings in certain contexts, but never imperative readings since Awyu-Dumut languages have dedicated imperative forms), the Korowai paradigm has only adhortative meanings (with imperative readings in 2nd person forms and intentional readings in

1st person forms). The Becking-Dawi adhortative paradigm differs from the Awyu-Dumut irrealis cognate paradigm because it does not conflate 2nd and 3rd persons (unlike all other Greater Awyu verb paradigms).

(98) adhortative paradigm of *lu-* 'to enter' in Korowai and irrealis paradigm for *tami-* 'to cut a canoe' in Yonggom Wambon (Drabbe 1959: 128):

		Korowai	Yonggom Wambon
SG	1	*lu-p*	*tami-p*
		enter-1SG[ADH]	cut.canoe-[IRR]1SG
	2	*lu-m*	*tami-n*
		enter-2SG [ADH]	cut.canoe-[IRR]NON1SG
	3	*lu-n*	*tami-n*
		enter-2SG [ADH]	cut.canoe-[IRR]NON1SG
PL	1	*lo-f-un*	*tami-w-an*
		enter-1-PL[ADH]	cut.canoe-1-[IRR]PL
	2	*lo-m-un*	*tami-n-an*
		enter-2-PL[ADH]	cut.canoe-[IRR]NON1SG
	3	*le-tin*	*tami-n-an*
		enter-3PL[ADH]	cut.canoe-[IRR]NON1SG

Wester (2014: 85) reconstructs the proto Awyu-Dumut subject person-number suffixes *-ep* (1SG), *-en* (NON1SG), *-epan* (1PL) and *-enan* (NON1PL). The plural suffixes can be subanalyzed as *-ep-an* and *-en-an*, with *-ep* marking first person and *-an* plural. The Korowai first person marker *-p* and the plural suffix *-Vn* in the adhortative paradigm clearly continue Greater Awyu subject person and number suffixes that we find in Awyu-Dumut verb paradigms and in proto Awyu-Dumut (de Vries, Wester and van den Heuvel 2012: 296). It is likely that the Korowai adhortative paradigm was the old irrealis paradigm (just as it still is in the Awyu-Dumut branch) that was replaced by a competing irrealis paradigm with *-xa* as irrealis marker.[18] The close relationship between the adhortative and irrealis in Korowai is shown by the fact that the negative forms of the adhortative paradigm (104) also function as irrealis negative forms, i.e. the opposition irrealis vs. adhortative is neutralized in the negative forms. Adhortative (and imperative)

---

18 De Vries, Wester and van den Heuvel (2012: 286) reconstruct an interrogative clitic *=ka (yV) for proto Awyu-Dumut. Kombai has a question clitic *=ka* and in the Awyu subgroup we find Aghu with its question clitic *=ka(yo)*. Mandobo (Dumut subgroup) has *=keya* and Yonggom Wambon *=kuyi*. There could very well be an etymological relation with the interrogative clitic as the basis for the irrealis suffix.

paradigms are "universal in Trans New Guinea languages with TAM morphology" (Pawley and Hammarström 2018: 101).

3.6.3.4 Three-slot verbs: tense and aspect

Just as in the Awyu-Dumut branch, the realis and irrealis forms of Korowai can be expanded with one more slot (van Enk and de Vries 1997: 96–100). The third slot comes right after the verb stem before the modality slot and the person-number slot and it contains either a tense suffix or an aspect suffix.

Realis, irrealis and adhortative forms may optionally be expanded with the suffixes -*méma* 'a moment ago/in a moment' (99)-(100) and -*(fe)lu/-lulo* 'yesterday/tomorrow' (101)-(102), indicating degrees of remoteness in time from the moment of speaking.

(99) *i-méma-lé*
see-IMM-[RLS]1SG
'I (just) saw (a moment ago)' (Korowai, van Enk and de Vries 1997: 97)

(100) *dépe-mémo-xa-lé*
smoke-IMM-IRR-1SG
'I will smoke in just a moment.' (Korowai, van Enk and de Vries 1997: 98)

(101) *alo-felu-té*
stand-NEAR-[RLS]NON1PL
'they/you(PL)stood' (yesterday, recently)
(Korowai, van Enk and de Vries 1997: 99)

(102) *dépa-lulo-xa-té*
smoke-NEAR-IRR-NON1PL
'they/you will smoke tomorrow/ in the very near future'
(Korowai, van Enk and de Vries 1997: 100)

The suffix for near future or recent past can also be added to the adhortative (imperative, intentional) paradigm:

(103) *dépa-lulo-p*
smoke-NEAR-1SG[ADH]
'I want to smoke tomorrow/let me smoke tomorrow'
(Korowai, van Enk and de Vries 1997: 100)

The suffix -*baxa* can only be added to realis forms, it indicates that the event occurred (earlier) today, (104).

(104) *alü-baxa-li*
    cook-HOD-1SG
    'I cooked (earlier today)' (Korowai, van Enk and de Vries 1997: 98)

The aspect suffixes -*ba*, marking completive and -*mba*, for durative, can only occur in realis forms and they are mutually exclusive with tense suffixes:

(105) *dépo-mba-lé*
    smoke-DUR-1SG
    'I am/was smoking.' (Korowai, van Enk and de Vries 1997: 92)

(106) *dépe-ba-lé*
    'I have smoked.' (Korowai, van Enk and de Vries 1997: 92)

Apart from the morphologically expressed completive and durative aspects, Korowai employs periphrastic constructions with verbal nouns, reduplicated derived verbs and auxiliary verbs to express durative, habitual and iterative meanings and phasal aspects (marking the onset and end of an action, see van Enk and de Vries 1997: 93–94).

3.6.3.5 Negation

Korowai independent verb forms are negated by prefixing *be-* and suffixing -*da* to the verb forms (de Vries, Wester and van den Heuvel 2012: 297):

(107) *dépa-te*
    smoke-[RLS]NON1PL
    'they smoke(d)' (Korowai, van Enk and de Vries 1997: 101)

(108) *be- dépa-te-da*
    NEG-smoke-NON1PL[RLS]-NEG
    'they did/do not smoke' (Korowai, van Enk and de Vries 1997: 101)

Tsaukambo, another Becking-Dawi language, uses *(bo)-V-nda*, with an optional negative prefix (de Vries 2012b: 174). The Becking-Dawi negation pattern and matter correspond to the proto Awyu-Dumut negation **pe-V-(nde)* reconstructed by Wester (2014: 140).

The adhortative (intentional, imperative) paradigm is negated as follows:

(109) SG 1 *be-dépo-pelé-da* 'I do not want to smoke/I shall not smoke'
     NON 1 *be-dépo-n-da*
     PL 1 *be-dépo-pelè-da*
     NON 1 *be-dépa-tin-da*

When the imperative meaning is relevant, the negative prefix *be-* is absent and the negative imperative adverb *belén* is added:

(110) *dépo-n-da*   *belén*
     smoke-2SG[ADH]-NEG NEG.IMP
     'Do not smoke!'   (Korowai, van Enk and de Vries 1997: 101)

(111) *dépa-tin-da*   *belén*
     smoke-2PL[ADH]-NEG NEG.IMP
     'Do not smoke!(PL)'   (Korowai, van Enk and de Vries 1997: 101)

The finite negative forms of (112)-(113) may be replaced by verbal nouns, optionally linked to *belén* by the connective *=xa*:

(112a) *dépo-n*   *belén*
      smoke-VN NEG.IMP
      'Do not smoke!'   (Korowai, van Enk and de Vries 1997: 102)

(112b) *dépo-n=xa*   *belén*
      dépo-ŋga   *belén*
      smoke-VN=CONN NEG.IMP
      'Do not smoke!'   (Korowai, van Enk and de Vries 1997: 102)

3.6.3.6 Conclusion

Korowai, of the Becking-Dawi branch, has the same verb system as the languages of the Awyu-Dumut branch. The specific intentional-adhortative paradigm, including its subject person-number suffixes and verb negation do correspond in matter and pattern to Awyu-Dumut languages. However, there are also striking differences. Korowai does not have suppletive verb stems, it has a different set of subject person-number suffixes, it has both a general irrealis paradigm and a specific intentional-adhortative paradigm and it expresses past and future tenses with the same set of tense suffixes (interpreted as past tenses in realis forms and as future tenses in irrealis forms) (de Vries, Wester and van den Heuvel 2012: 299).

3.7 Question words

Words used to question who did something, where, when, what and how in Greater Awyu languages belong to various word classes. The first word class are verbs and given the tendency to carry out linguistic tasks preferably with verbs (see §3.1), we would expect at least some question words to be either full verbs or petrified verb forms in Greater Awyu languages. And this is indeed what language descriptions report in all subgroups, in various degrees (Aghu, Drabbe 1959: 27; Digul Wambon, Jang 2008: 20; Kombai, de Vries 1993a: 44; Korowai, van Enk and de Vries 1997: 77). Here are some examples from Kombai and Korowai:

(113) *Fene-mo-ra*   xe   *xone=xa.*
how-do-and[SS] 3SG get[RLS.NON1SG]= Q
'How did he get it?'   (Kombai, de Vries 1993a: 44)

(114) *Yu   mbaxa-mol-mo=daxu   xomilo*
3SG what-do-do[NON1SG.RLS]=SS die[NON1SG.RLS]
'Why did he die?' (Lit: What occurred to him and he died?)
                                   (Korowai, van Enk and de Vries 1997)

The second tendency is for question words to function as adjectives in noun phrases (when=what day, why=what reason, who=what person, what=what thing and so on). Kombai is one of the Greater Awyu languages to use that strategy:

(115) *Gu   narof=o   ro   bo-fera=xa?*
2SG   what=CONN thing DUR-see[RLS.NON1SG]= Q
'What are you looking at?'   (Kombai, deVries 1993a: 43)

Most Greater Awyu languages have a very small closed class of question words that are not verbs or adjectives, usually question words for who and what. Intonation and, optionally, focus clitics mark the informational saliency of the question phrase but the question phrase does not move to clause initial position. Consider this Kombai example

(116) Gu   naluf=a   afo-n-e=xe?
      2SG   what=FOC   take-NON1SG[IRR]-LNK=Q
      'What do you want to take?'   (Kombai, de Vries 1993a: 42)

3.8 Quantifiers

Greater Awyu languages have a small, closed class of quantifiers that occur after adjectives in the noun phrase (117). Jang (2008: 96) observes that in Digul Wambon either a numeral quantifier is present or a member of the small class of quantifiers that consists of *tembet / mbumba* 'null, empty', *ndiknde / mandak* 'a little', *lali* 'several, some', *ndaghit* 'many' and *mighup* 'all'.

(117) maxü   muyiyano   biduma
      dog   big.PL   many
      'many big dogs'   (Kombai, de Vries 1993a: 39)

(118) En   kaklap   ndagheti   lulepo.
      en   kaklap   ndaghet-ndi   lu-te-mbo
      tree   solid   many-FOC   cut-RPAST.1SG
      'I cut many solid trees.'   (Digul Wambon, Jang 2008: 96)

3.9 Numerals

Numerals do not belong to the word category of quantifiers as they are nouns. Greater Awyu languages, with the exception of the Awyu subgroup, have extended body tally part systems of counting (Laycock 1975; de Vries 2014). This type of numeral systems occurs only in a limited area of central New Guinea and in the adjacent part of Australia (Lean 1992). Body part tally systems do not operate on base and derived numbers and they form a closed set of numerals. The languages of the Awyu subgroup do not have extended body part tally systems based on hands, arms and head but hands-and-feet systems (127), just as their Marindic neighbors where the hand (5) is a base number (e.g. 6 is hand and one).

Counting in extended body part tally systems commences with the little finger of the left hand until the thumb is reached, then goes up the arm to a highest point on the head and then goes down again via the other arm until the little finger of the right hand is reached, the highest number in these closed numerals systems, e.g. 23 in Kombai. The nouns that denote the body parts function also as numerals, for example the Korowai noun *piŋgup* means 'middle finger' but when in a compound noun with the noun *anop* 'amount' it is used as a numeral modifier in a noun phrase with the meaning 'three':

(119) *gol piŋgu-anop*
 pig index.finger-amount
 'three pigs' (Korowai, van Enk and de Vries 1997: 74)

The numeral use of the body part tally nouns in Greater Awyu languages is distinguished from the other uses, in various ways. First, conventional gestures must be performed with the numeral use. The middle finger and index finger are stretched out and held tightly together and speakers touch the body part involved. Second, when used in noun phrases as numeral modifiers, this is morphologically coded in various ways, Dumut languages must use the comitative suffix *-kup* to mark the body part noun as a numeral modifier (122), Becking-Dawi languages form compound nouns with the noun *anop* (119).

The extended body part systems in the Greater Awyu family are a kind of add-on to an elementary system that is not body part based and has just the numbers one and two (as in Korowai), one, two and three (as in Mandobo) or one and two as base numbers, with three (two-one) and four (two-two) as derived numbers in a binary system (Kombai). We will illustrate the three types of numeral systems that occur in Greater Awyu languages (elementary binary non-body part based stem, extended body part tally system, hands-and-feet system) with data from Wambon dialects and from Aghu[19]:

(120) Numerals from Digul Wambon (de Vries and de Vries-Wiersma 1992: 44–48) and Yonggom Wambon, Drabbe 1959: 123)

	Digul Wambon	body part	Yonggom Wambon	body part
1	sanop	little finger	omae	–
2	sanopkunip	ring finger	irumo(n)	–
3	taxem	middle finger	itipmo	–
4	hitulop	index finger	kurugut(kup)	index finger
5	ambalop	thumb	aŋgu(kup)	thumb
6	Kumuk	wrist	kumuk(kup)	wrist
7	mben	lower arm	mben(kup)	lower arm
8	Muyop	elbow	ŋgambin(kup)	inside of elbow

---

[19] The next section is taken from de Vries 2014: 333–336 (Kenon and Yonggom Wambon numerals) and 338–340 (Aghu numerals).

3.9 Numerals

9	javet	upper arm	jawet(kup)	upper arm	
10	malin	shoulder	mak(kup)	shoulder	
11	ŋgokmit	neck	ŋgombenmit(kup)	neck	
12	Silutop	ear	turutop(kup)	ear	
13	kelop	eye	kerop(kup)	eye	
14	kalit	nose	ambotop(kup)	nose	

The nose is the turning point in the Wambon dialect continuum (that includes the varieties called Digul Wambon and Yonggom Wambon). In other Greater Awyu languages the crown of the head is the turning point. After the nose, counting goes down again via the right-hand side of the body, by forming compounds with the noun *em* 'other side' in Digul Wambon and *ajam* 'other side' in Yonggom Wambon as first and modifying noun stem. This addition of *ajam* 'other side' is optional in Yonggom Wambom where a connective ligature links the noun stems. Drabbe (1959: 123) writes that the numerals for 25, 26 and 27 do not use the *ajam* 'other side' compound, as one would expect. 25 and 26 are compounds with the noun *it* 'hand/arm' and *wamip* 'middle' for 25 and with *waŋgop* 'ring finger' for 26. The body part noun *segek* 'little finger' denotes 27. Notice that these three body parts are not used for 1, 2 and 3 in the Yonggom dialect.

(121)

	Digul Wambon	body part	*Yonggom Wambon*
15	em-kelop	other side eye	(ajam-e-)kerop(kup)
16	em-silutop	other side ear	(ajam-e-)turutop(kup)
17	em-ŋgokmit	other side neck	(ajam-e-)ŋgombenmit(kup)
18	e-malin	other side shoulder	(ajam-e-)mak(kup)
19	em-javet	other side upper arm	(ajam-e-)jawet(kup)
20	e-muyop	other side elbow	(ajam-e-)ŋgambin(kup)
21	e-mben	other side lower arm	(ajam-e-)mben(kup)
22	em-kumuk	other side wrist	(ajam-e-)kumuk
23	em-ambalop	other side thumb	(ajam-e-)aŋgu(kup)
24	em-hitulop	other side index	(ajam-e-)kurugut(kup)
25	em-taxem	other side middle finger	it-wamip(kup)
26	em-sanopkunip	other side ring finger	it-waŋgop(kup)
27	em-sanop	other side little finger	segek(kup)

In the numeral use of the words, conventional gestures must accompany the use of the number words: the fingers are bent and the parts of the arm and head are touched with the outstretched middle finger and/or index finger. When the body part nouns are used as numeral modifiers in noun phrases, the suffix *-kup* must be added, a suffix with a basic comitative function that is also used in noun coordination and with the meaning 'also' (§4.2.7). E.g. Digul Wambon:

(122) *Ap   hitulop-kup*
 house index.finger-with
 'four houses'

Together with the touching and bending gestures, the obligatory affixation with *-kup* distinguishes the numeral use of these nouns from their other uses.

The body part nouns *sanop* 'little finger', *sanopkunip* 'ring finger' cannot be used as numeral modifiers in noun phrases in Digul Wambon:

(123) **ap   sanop-kup*
 house little.finger-with
 'one house'

Instead, two numeral modifiers are used in Digul Wambon that reveal an elementary system of numerals that are not based on body parts and that do not take *-kup*:

(124a) *ap   ndominuk*
 house one
 'one house'

(124b) *ap   ilumo*
 house two
 'two houses'

The non-body part based numerals for 'one' are also used in some Greater Awyu languages to express indefinite-specific reference, sometimes in combination with dedicated specificity markers, e.g. in Korowai (van Enk and de Vries 1997: 75).

To say 'three houses' the Digul Wambon form *ilumtaxemo* is used, composed of *ilumo* 'two' and *taxem* 'middle finger.'

(125) *ap   ilum-taxemo*
 house two-middle finger
 'three houses'

Yonggom Wambon has alternative numbers that Digul Wambon lacks. Yonggom Wambon speakers may also use *kumuk-kumuk* 'wrist-wrist', i.e. 'six-six' for 12. Yonggom Wambon has Muyu, a Greater Ok language with a base 6 system, as its eastern neighbour. Drabbe (1959: 123) remarks that this seems to suggest influence from Muyu. Counting systems travel easily in New Guinea (Laycock 1975) and South New Guinea is well-known for its sometimes highly elaborate senary systems connected to cultural practices of ritualised yam counting, e.g. in the Kolopom and Yam families(Evans et al. 2018: 690).

Counting systems are easily borrowed, combined and discarded in the New Guinea context because they are tightly connected to, and reflections of, changing contexts of language contact, multilingualism, trade networks, political integration in nation-states and of religious and ritual practices. Therefore, most if not all, counting systems of New Guinea described in older sources (including my own descriptions of Greater Awyu numeral systems) have been wholly or partially replaced by counting systems and numerals of English, Tok Pisin, Indonesian and Papuan Malay. Döhler (2016: 106) observes for example that the Komnzo speech community, with its elaborate senary system used in ritual yam feast contexts and its traditional restricted system that counted to four or five, nowadays mostly use English numerals. The Greater Awyu similarly used a bodypart tally system alongside a restricted system of counting to four that was not based on body part nouns and that served almost all daily needs of counting. When varieties of Indonesian entered the Greater Awyu area, the higher body part tally numerals (body parts above the upper arm) were the first to disappear, followed by the lower parts of arm and hands, then the restricted systems were discarded.

Drabbe (1959: 123) observes that Yonggom Wambon speakers also use a base 5 and base 10 system parallel to the body part system. They count on the five fingers to 5, repeat that once and the second time they call *aŋgu* 'thumb', they say *tikmae* (=*tig omae*=rattan string one). This way of counting has to do with the fact that shell-money or dog teeth money comes in groups of ten shells or teeth on strings of rattan fibre. Having reached *tikmae* 'ten', people count two times to *aŋgu* 'thumb/five' after which they say *tig irumon* 'twenty' (literally two strings). Having reached 30, they say *kagaw itipmon* where *kagap* is a another word denoting 'ten' and *itipmon* 'three'. Speakers count until 100 (=*kagap mak*, where *mak* 'shoulder' is the body part numeral 'ten', ten times ten).

(126) *Taget kagaw aŋgu rap-ken-ep.*
 kauri-shell ten thumb take-RLS-1SG
 'I got 50 kauri-shells.' (Yonggom Wambon, Drabbe 1959: 123)

The Awyu subgroup differs from the other Greater Awyu subgroups because they have hands-and-feet systems of counting and numerals, with hand/5 and body/20 as base, as in Aghu numbers (Drabbe 1957: 28):

(127) Aghu numerals

	Numeral	corresponding body part
1	Fasike	–
2	okuomu/okuoma	–
3	okuomasike	–
4	sigiane/sigianému	little finger
5	bidikimu/bidikuma	Hand
6	bidikuma-fasike	hand-one
7	bidikuman-okuoma	hand-two
8	bidikuman-okuomasike	hand-three
9	bidikuma-sigiane	hand-little finger
10	bidikuma-bidikuma	hand-hand
11	kito wodo	big toe
12	kito wodo womu	toe next to big toe
13	kito efe womu	toe in the middle
14	kito sigia womu	toe next to little toe
15	kito sigia	little toe
	kitikumu	foot
	kitifikumu	the one foot
16	afi-kito wodo	the other big toe
17	afi-kito wodo womu	the other toe next to big toe
18	afi-kito efe womu	the other toe in the middle
19	afi-kito sigia womu	the other toe next to little toe
20	aghù-bigi	person-bone
21	aghù-bigi fasike	person-bone one
22	aghù-bigi okuomu	person-bone two
30	aghù-bigi bidikuma-bidikuma	person-bone hand-hand

3.10 Adverbs

Even if we use a broad definition of adverbs as modifiers of constituents other than nouns (Schachter and Shopen 2007: 20), we end up with a very small, closed sets of adverbs in Greater Awyu languages. If Greater Awyu speakers want to modify adjectives, they just take other adjectives that mean 'true', 'big' or 'small' and use them without any formal changes to modify adjectives (see §3.3). Independent demonstratives that mean 'this (one)'or 'that one' can be used to modify clauses, to express where or when an event happens, again without formal changes and then mean 'here' or 'now' or 'there' and 'then'. To modify verbs speakers prefer mini clauses headed by a verbalized adjective (128):

(128) *Mbon-mo   na-gap*
     slow-do[SS] IMP-walk
     'Walk slowly!'   (Yonggom Wambon, Drabbe 1959: 132)

Aghu is exceptional because it has a large class of adverbs that end in *-mu* (van den Heuvel 2016), derived from adjectives or verbs. The *-mu* derivational suffix is most probably a fossilized form of the verb *mo/mV* 'to do' (van den Heuvel 2016) that still occurs in many Awyu-Dumut languages as a verb and is used to derive verbs from adjectives, deictics and nouns (see §3.6.1.1). These *mo*-derived verbs are then used to modify other verbs, as in Digul Wambon (5).

The few dedicated adverbs of Greater Awyu languages comprise no more than a handful of usually short words that may modify both verbs and entire clauses and have meanings such as 'just', 'already', 'only', 'again', 'also'. Consider these examples from Aghu and Digul Wambon:

(129) *Hitulov=e   osi   ka-l-eva-mbo.*
     index=CONN again go-RLS-1PL-PAST
     'On Thursday (=indexfinger=4=fourth day) we went again.'
             (Digul Wambon, de Vries and de Vries-Wiersma 1992: 53)

(130) *Mase   xo-xe-ne   i-ge.*
     already go-NON1.RLS[SG]-DS lie-NON1.RLS[SG]
     'He has gone already and it is lying'> 'his footsteps are there' (Aghu, van den Heuvel 2016)

3.11 Postpositions, conjunctions and connectives

Greater Awyu languages have small, closed sets of postpositions (to express grammatical relations of arguments in clauses), conjunctions (to link nouns in coordinate noun phrases, clauses in sentences and sentences in connected discourse) and connectives (with specific syntactic functions). These elements will be described in chapter 4 on syntax since the description of their roles and meanings is completely dependent on the analysis of syntactic patterns of Greater Awyu languages.

Chapter 4
Syntax

4.1 Introduction

This chapter describes major patterns of syntax in Greater Awyu languages. The description is incomplete because the available descriptions give limited information on syntax. The texts that we do have exhibit a strong tendency for noun phrases to consist of a head noun with at most one modifier and for clauses to consist of a verb with at most one (core or peripheral) argument. To keep phrases and clauses syntactically simple, speakers routinely distribute elements of phrases and clauses over series of mini phrases and mini clauses (see §5.5).

The first section is about the syntax of noun phrases, including relative clauses (§4.2). Then clause structure is discussed (§4.3), followed by a section on the grammatical functions of postpositions (§4.4). The final section is about clause combinations (§4.5).

4.2 Noun phrases

4.2.1 General overview of noun phrase structure

Greater Awyu nouns can be modified by other nouns, by adjectives, quantifiers, numerals, demonstratives and clauses. The unmarked order is head noun followed by one or more modifiers but Greater Awyu languages allow modifiers in prenominal position, as a marked choice. The markedness of the prenominal area of noun phrases is shown by restrictions that apply in the prenominal position but not in the post nominal position in a number of Greater Awyu languages. For example in Digul Wambon, in the postnominal area there are multiple modifier slots, although speakers rarely produce such complex noun phrases spontaneously. But in the prenominal area there is room for just one modifier (Jang 2008: 89). That single prenominal modifier slot can be filled by any type of modifier, for example by a demonstrative modifier (132), a possessor noun (137), a relative clause (130) or a numeral modifier (135). Once the prenominal slot is filled, for example with *evo* 'that' in (132), other modifiers have to move to the area after the head noun, for example *ambalopkup* 'five' in (132). Phrases with two modifiers in the prenominal area are rejected (131):

(131) *ev=o   ambalop=kuv=o   kap
      that=MOD thumb=with=MOD man
      'those five men' (Digul Wambon, de Vries and de Vries-Wiersma 1992: 55)

(132) ev=o   kap ambalop=kup
      that=MOD man thumb-with
      'those five men' (Digul Wambon, de Vries and de Vries-Wiersma 1992: 55)

Another proof of markedness of the prenominal position in the noun phrase is that some Greater Awyu languages must mark the prenominal modifier with a genitive or an attributive clitic, whereas the same modifiers occur (only) unmarked in postnominal position. This is for example the case in Korowai and Digul Wambon. Compare (133) which speakers reject because the postnominal modifier is marked by =o, with (134), where the postnominal modifier occurs unmarked and with (135), where the same modifier, now prenominal, must take the modifier-head clitic =o.

(133) *ev=o   kap ambalop=kuv=o
      that=MOD man thumb=with=MOD
      (Digul Wambon, de Vries and de Vries-Wiersma 1992: 56)

(134) ev=o   kap ambalop=kup
      that=MOD man thumb=with
      'those five men' (Digul Wambon, de Vries and de Vries-Wiersma 1992: 56)

(135) ambalop=kuv=o   kap
      thumb=with=MOD   man
      'five men' (Digul Wambon, de Vries and de Vries-Wiersma 1992: 56)

The reason for this markedness of the prenominal position of modifiers could be that speakers prefer to place modifiers appositionally, semantically modifying the preceding noun and intonationally integrated in the noun phrase but syntactically more or less juxtaposed to the noun. Because of the high frequency of this strategy to prefer loosely juxtaposed post nominal modifiers, that order conventionalised to a point that the post nominal modifiers lost their syntactic independence and became a post nominal modifier integrated also syntactically in the noun phrase.

The modifier-head connective =o of Digul Wambon cliticizes to the last word of the modifying constituent in the noun phrase and marks the preceding constituent as a modifier of the noun that follows the clitic, whatever its categorial status (demonstrative (136), numeral phrase (135), possessor phrase (137), or relative clause (138)).

(136) [[ev]=o   [lan]]
      that=MOD   Woman
      'that woman' (Digul Wambon, de Vries and de Vries-Wiersma 1992: 55)

(137) [[Ahituv]=o [-n-ap]]
      that=MOD   -LNK-house
      'the house of Ahitup' (Digul Wambon, de Vries and de Vries-Wiersma 1992: 55)

(138) [[ŋguw=e   alip=ka   ŋgaluma-t-po-n]=o   [kaw]=e]
      2SG=CONN yesterday=in   meet-RLS-PAST-LNK=MOD   man= CONN
      na-net=ndi.
      my-older.brother=COP
      'The man you met yesterday is my older brother.' (Digul Wambon, Jang 2008: 105)

When there are multiple modifiers in the Digul Wambon postnominal area, they occur in the order numeral, adjective, quantifiers and demonstrative, according to Jang (2008: 89). For other Greater Awyu languages we do not have enough information to state in which order the various noun modifiers occur, because the texts of these languages do not have "maximal" noun phrases, that is, with all modifier positions filled.

The grammatical function of the noun phrase in the clause may be marked by postpositions that (often) cliticize to the last word of the noun phrase. These will be discussed below (§4.4). We will first discuss the syntactic properties of a number of specific types of modifiers within noun phrases in more detail.

4.2.2 Possessor nouns as modifiers

Possessor nouns precede the possessed nouns in Greater Awyu languages. Unlike most other types of modifiers, prenominal position is the unmarked (and only) position for possessor nouns, with prosodic prominence on the head noun, the possessed entity and often without any formal marking either of the possessive relation or of the modifier-head relation (Wester 2014: 53). For example, possessor and possessed nouns are simply juxtaposed in some Greater Awyu languages such as Kombai, Korowai (139) and Aghu (140). In others, such as Digul Wambon, simple juxtaposition is exceptional and as a rule a genitival marker (141), or a general modifier-head clitic links the possessor noun to its head (142).

(139) y-afé   Dulexül
      his-older.brother Garden
      'the garden of his older brother' (Korowai, van Enk and de Vries 1997: 174)

(140) Neto   xasi
      father spear
      'father's spear' (Aghu, van den Heuvel 2016: 150)

(141) Ahitup-ko   -n-ap
      Ahitup-GEN   LNK-house
      'Ahitup's house' (Digul Wambon, de Vries and de Vries-Wiersma 1992: 57)

(142) [[Ahituv]=o [-n-ap]]
      that=MOD   -LNK-house
      'Ahitup's house (Digul Wambon, de Vries and de Vries-Wiersma 1992: 55)

The available Greater Awyu texts so far only provided examples of bare nouns rather than noun phrases in the possessor slot, probably due to the strong tendency to avoid syntactic complexity.

The possessor slot in a noun phrase can also be filled by a free personal pronoun as in Aghu (143), or a free possessive pronoun, as in Aghu and Mandobo.

(143) nu   n-amu
      1SG -LNK-meat
      'my meat' (lit. the meat of me) (Aghu, Drabbe 1957: 7; van den Heuvel 2016: 151)

However, rather than using free pronouns in the syntactic possessor slot, Greater Awyu languages prefer possessive pronominal prefixes that fill a morphological slot in the noun word (§3.2.1).

4.2.3 Noun phrases and compound nouns

Greater Awyu languages all have very productive noun compound formation (see §3.2.4). It can be difficult to distinguish between noun phrases with an attributive noun modifying a head noun and noun compounds in Greater Awyu languages that use simple juxtaposition in possessive noun phrases. There are three differences between a noun compound and a noun phrase.

The first is that in noun phrases it is possible to insert a 3SG or 3PL possessive prefix (or sometimes a third person free personal pronoun or free possessive pronoun, as in Aghu (144) between the possessor and possessed noun):

(144) neto   efe   büsiü
      father 3SG   house
      'father's house' (lit. 'father his house') (Aghu, van den Heuvel 2016: 150)

The second way to differentiate a possessive noun phrase from a compound noun in some Greater Awyu languages is the possibility to insert a possessive marker between the two nouns in a noun phrase, sometimes cliticizing to the possessor noun, for example *na* in Pisa, Aghu and Mandobo and *=ko* in Digul Wambon:

(145) u   gater   ete   komo   ŋgun-owon   ge   na-ŋgaŋo, yeŋgine
      pig leftovers CONN   put   burn.magically-1PL   be   say-CAUS   3PL.POSS
      n-anemo   na   gate   komo   ŋgun-on
      LNK-son.in.law   POSS   leftovers put   burn.magically-[RLS]NON1PL
      'Thinking 'let us burn the pig's leftovers', they burn their son-in-law's leftovers' (Mandobo, Drabbe 1959: 29; Wester 2014: 53)

Wester (2014: 53) points to the three different types of possessive noun phrases of Greater Awyu languages represented in this Mandobo example (145): the simple juxtaposition *u gater* 'the leftovers of the pig', a noun phrase with the possessor slot filled by a free pronoun *yeŋgine nanemo* 'their son-in-law' and finally a noun phrase with the possessor phrase linked to the head noun by the possessive marker *na*, *yeŋgine nanemo na gatet* 'the leftovers of their son-in-law'.

The third difference between a compound noun and a possessive noun phrase, reported for Yonggom Wambon, Digul Wambon and Korowai, is the general modifier-head connective that must occur between the possessor noun and the head noun in phrases. Jang (2008: 70) gives the following examples: (146) is a possessive noun phrase and (147) a compound noun.

(146) [[ŋgulum]=o   [n-ambat]]NP
      teacher=MOD   LNK-head
      'the teacher's head' (Digul Wambon, Jang 2008: 70)

(147) [ŋgulum-ambat]N
      teacher-head
      'the head teacher' (Digul Wambon, Jang 2008: 7)

4.2.4 Adjectives

Adjectives follow the noun which they modify in Greater Awyu languages (148) but Korowai, of the Becking-Dawi branch, allows (some) adjectives in prenominal position when they function attributively (149).

(148) maxü   muyiyano biduma
      dog   big.PL   many
      'many big dogs' (Kombai, de Vries 1993a: 39)

(149) manop xaim
      good   treehouse
      'a good tree house' (Korowai, van Enk and de Vries 1997: 69)

Adjectives may express plurality of the head noun through plural forms, derived by reduplication, or by irregular special forms in Greater Awyu languages (see §3.3).

Adjectives may be modified by adverbs that express a high or low degree of the quality denoted by the adjective. These adverbs of degree form an adjectival phrase with the adjectives. Sometimes the adverbs of degree cliticize to the adjective. Normally adverbs follow the adjectives but some intensifier adverbs precede the adjective. Drabbe (1959: 107) mentions *mep* 'purely, wholly' in Mandobo as preceding the adjective:

(150) [[u] HN [[mep] MOD [koneni]] MOD]] NP
      pig   very   big
      'a very big pig' (Mandobo, Drabbe 1959: 107)

Greater Awyu adverbs of degree derive from adjectives with meanings such as pure, true, real (true black=very black) or from adjectives that mean big or small (big black=very black).

Korowai has two adjectives, *talé* 'big' and *tena* 'little' that function both as adjectives (151) and (152) and as augmentative and diminutive adverbs of degree which cliticize to the adjectives they modify (153)–(155):

(151) méan talé
 dog big
 'a big dog' (Korowai, van Enk and de Vries 1997: 70)

(152) méan tena
 dog big
 'a little dog' (Korowai, van Enk and de Vries 1997: 70)

(153) yanop xoŋgé=talé
 person fat=very
 'a very fat person' (Korowai, van Enk and de Vries 1997: 70)

(154) xofilun=talé
 black=very
 'very black' (Korowai, van Enk and de Vries 1997: 70)

(155) xofilun=tena
 black=little
 'a little black; somewhat black' (Korowai, van Enk and de Vries 1997: 70)

Adjectives can occasionally be used as manner adverbs to modify adjectives or verbs without formal changes, for example eŋgoan in the Yonggom Wambon example (156) but Greater Awyu speakers prefer to turn adjectives of manner first into verbs and then use these verbs in medial ss mini clauses which are chained to the clause with the verb that they modify (158).

(156) mbendit eŋgoan roa-r-an
 bow strong make-RLS[NON1SG]-PAST
 'he made a strong bow' (Yonggom Wambon, Drabbe 1959: 107)

(157) eŋgoan timo-nok
 strong hold-IMP[SG]
 'hold it firmly.' (Yonggom Wambon, Drabbe 1959: 107)

(158) wagae-mo rap-ken.
 good-do[SS] hold-RLS[NON1SG]
 'he held it firmly.' (Yonggom Wambon, Drabbe 1959: 132)

4.2.5 Relative Clauses

Nouns can be modified by clauses and Greater Awyu languages use a range of relative clause constructions, from more canonical ones, with the common argument expressed only in the main clause, to relative clause constructions with the common argument expressed only in the relative clause and typologically very rare double headed relative constructions with the common argument expressed both in the relative clause and in the main clause (Dryer 2013).

4.2.5.1 Prenominal relative clauses with the common argument expressed in the main clause

The first type, found in for example Korowai and Digul Wambon, fills the prenominal modifier slot that is linked to the head noun by a general modifier-head clitice, =o in Digul Wambon and =xa in Korowai. The modifier can be a demonstrative, as in (159), a numeral (135), or a possessor noun (142) but it can also be a clause (160):

(159) *If-e=xa*   *abül*
      this-LNK=MOD   man
      (Korowai, van Enk and de Vries 1997: 73)

(160) [*mül-xuf=efè*   *af=efè*   *lamol*   *fu-bo=xa*]
      former-time=TOP then=TOP universe put-[RLS.NON1SG]COM=MOD
      abül=fefè
      man=TOP
      'the man who then, in former times, created the universe'
      (Korowai, van Enk and de Vries 1997: 163)

Examples (159) and (160) have exactly the same structure and the relative clause is just another filler of the prenominal modifier slot in the noun phrase. The common argument of the relative clause and the main clause, *abül* 'the man', is only expressed in the main clause, not in the relative clause.

4.2.5.2 Relative clauses with the common argument only expressed in the relative clause

Korowai has a second type of relative clause that uses the same structure with =*xa* but in the second type the head noun slot is left unfilled and the common argument is expressed only in the relative clause. Compare (160) where clitic =*xa* links the relative clause to head noun *abül* with (161) where the head noun slot is left unfilled. The noun phrase with second reference to the pig in (161), *noxu-gol*, is the predicate of (161).

(161) [*Wa gol ülme-tél=e=xa=fè*]   *noxu-gol*
    that pig kill-NON1PL[RLS]=LNK=MOD=TOP our-pig
    'The pig which they killed is our pig.' (Korowai, de Vries 2006: 826)

The topic marker *=fè* marks the relative clause as an (extra-clausal) theme in (161) that can be paraphrased as 'given (the thing) that they killed the pig, (it is) our pig'. Such clauses may also have adverbial readings ('when they killed the pig') in certain contexts. Notice that I paraphrased (161) with 'the thing', although there is no noun 'the thing' in (161). Instead of leaving the head noun slot unfilled as in (161), Kombai fills the head noun slot with a dummy head noun *ro* 'thing' in such cases (166).

4.2.5.3 Relative clauses with a marked common argument

Jang (2008: 105) notes that Digul Wambon uses both prenominal relative clauses that modify a head noun, with the modifier-head clitic *=o* linking the relative clause modifier to the head (162) and relative clauses with the common argument only expressed in the relative clause itself (163). In the latter relative clause type, the common argument (CA) is marked by the clitic *=a*. In addition, the CA, an O argument, is fronted from its normal position after the A argument. However, an alternative analysis of (163) seems possible where the relative clause does not have an expressed common argument but is a post nominal modifier of the common argument *kava* expressed in the main clause.

(162) [[*ŋguw=e alip=ka   ŋgaluma-t-po-n=o*]MOD [*kaw=e*] HN]]NP
    2SG=CONN yesterday=CIRC meet-RLS-PAST-LNK=MOD man=CONN
    na-net=i.
    my-older.brother=COP
    'The man you met yesterday is my older brother.' (Digul Wambon, Jang 2008: 105)

(163) *Kaw=a   ŋguw=e   alip=ka   ŋgaluma-t-po-n=ewe*
    man=CA 2SG=CONN yesterday=CIRC meet-RLS-PAST[NON1SG]-LNK=TOP
    na-net=i.
    my-older.brother=COP
    'The man you met yesterday is my older brother.' (Digul Wambon, Jang 2008:105)

4.2.5.4 Relative clause constructions with a common argument expressed both in the relative and main clause

Kombai has a typologically very rare relative clause construction (Dryer 2013), because its relative clause construction has the common argument expressed both in the relative clause and in the head noun of the relative noun phrase (de Vries 1993a: 77–80).This double expression can be done with the same noun. Compare (164a) from Kombai.

(164a) [[*Doü adiya-no-n=o*] MOD   [*doü*]] HN, *deyalu-xe*
       sago give-[RLS]NON1PL-LNK=MOD   sago   finished-ADJ
       'The sago they gave, is finished.' (Kombai, de Vries 1993a: 78)

The Mandobo relative clause construction of (164b) may shed light on the development of the Kombai double-headed relative clauses of (164a).

(164b) *Ko-ro itio-gen   do   e-aŋgen omba mbo,   u   omba to*
       go-SEQ see-RLS[NON1SG]   CNJ his-wife other TOP   pig other feral
       ge   mbe gee-r-an,   e-aŋgen mbo ko   u   mbo jo-ro
       be   DUR go-RLS[NON1SG]-PAST   his-wife TOP   go   pig TOP call-SEQ
       me-re   küap jendi-wüop   kiomo-gen.
       come-SEQ   man   road-middle   meet-RLS[NON1SG]
       'He went and saw that his (first) wife, who had been going after the other feral pig, had met a man while she was calling the pig.' (Mandobo, Appendix §9.2.2, (119))

In some Greater Awyu languages we can see how certain grammatical constructions developed out of thematization preferences of speakers (see §5.6), e.g. experiential constructions where the former extra-clausal theme integrated into the following clause as initial topical experiencer. The left-most antecedent of the Kombai double-headed construction could very well be a former extra-clausal theme that integrated as the first constituent of the relative clause, both intonationally (the left-most antecedent is under the intonational contour of the relative clause) and syntactically. This hypothesis seems to receive support from the Mandobo relative clause type where the first antecedent still functions as an extra-clausal theme. Drabbe (1959) uses comma's in his (Mandobo) text editions when there is an utterance-medial pause. The Mandobo relative clause construction of (164b) seems to begin with an extra-clausal theme, bracketed off with a pause, followed by an independent clause, then another medial pause, followed by the second occurrence of the antecedent: 'and that other wife of him, she had been going after the other feral pig, that wife of him had met a man while she was calling the pig'.

It could be that the first antecedent (*eaŋgen omba mbo*) in (164b) and the subsequent relative clause both are juxtaposed utterances, linked not by syntax but by relevance relations, including the link with the subject of the main clause, the second occurrence of the antecedent. The step towards the Kombai type is made when such inference-based, pragmatic relative clause strategies, only marked by medial pauses, become very frequent, leading to syntactic integration in one relative NP. Notice that in Kombai the first antecedent is part of the relative clause and that the relative clause modifier is explicitly marked as a modifier of the head of the relative NP, the second antecedent that is the real syntactic head of the construction.

Rather than a verbatim repetition of the common argument, Kombai often uses a closed set of head noun fillers that classify the referent of the relative NP as male, female or non-human (animals, things), (165).

(165) Yare   gamo xereja b-o-gi-n=o   rumu na-momof=a.
      old.man join work   DUR-do-RLS[NON1SG]-LNK=MOD   Son   my-uncle=COP
      'The old man who is joining the work, is my uncle.' (Kombai, de Vries 1993a: 77)

The common argument is expressed in (165) within the relative clause (the subject argument *yare* 'old man') and as head noun of the relative noun phrase (*rumu* 'son'). When the relative noun phrase refers to a non-human entity, the head noun of the relative NP is *ro* 'thing':

(166) Ai   fali -xa-no   ro   nagu-n-ay=a.
      pig carry go-[RLS]NON1PL   thing our-LNK-pig=COP
      'The pig they took away, is ours.' (Kombai, de Vries 1993a: 79)

This is the closed set of fillers of the head noun slot in the Kombai relative noun phrase:

(167) rumu   'son'
      xuri   'daughter'
      miyo   'child'
      mogo   'man'
      nariya-mogo   'man'
      nariya   'man'
      Ro   'thing'

The same set (167) is used as grammatical head noun in question word phrases of Kombai:

(168) Gu   narof=o   ro   bo-fera=xa?
      2SG what==MOD thing DUR-see[RLS.NON1SG]=Q
      'What are you looking at?' (Kombai, de Vries 1993a: 79)

(169) Gu   yaf=o   rumu-n=a=xe?
      You who=MOD   son-LNK=COP=Q
      'Who are you?' (Kombai, de Vries 1993a: 79)

When kinship terms such as *rumu* 'son' and *xuri* 'daughter' are used in these grammatical roles of being the head of relative noun phrases and question word noun phrases, they come close to being dummy nouns and they lose their lexical meanings and instead bleach into a classifying grammatical meaning, classifying the referents of relative noun phrases as human (*rumu* 'male person', *xuri*, 'female person') versus non-human (*ro*). So in a sense the common argument in the relative clause is the main expression of the CA, with the co-referential classifying head noun being a supportive expression of the CA that mainly serves to provide the noun phrase with a syntactic head.

When the common argument in the relative clause is left unexpressed, the relative noun phrase has a generic reading ('whoever, whatever'):

(170) Xe-lu   xaxe-n=o   rumu
      his-voice   listen[RLS.NON1SG]-LNK=MOD   son
      'Whoever listens to him. . .' (Kombai, de Vries 1993a: 78)

Relative noun phrases with *ro* 'thing' as head noun are often used as fillers of the theme slot that precedes sentences, a slot that may be filled by thematic phrases and thematic clauses. When this is the case, the demonstrative based topic markers *mene* or *mofene* (optionally) mark the thematic clause and the thematic relative clause may receive all sorts of adverbial interpretations. Thematic subordinate clauses that may have both relative and adverbial translation equivalents in English are not only found in Greater Awyu languages but in quite a few other Papuan language families (Foley 1986: 201; Wester 2014: 159).

(171) Uni be-ri-no-n=o   ro,   na-büwogo gamo
      Uni DUR-make-[RLS]NON1PL-LNK=MOD   thing my-parent join[SS]
      ri-no.
      make-[RLS]NON1PL
      'When they were building Uni, my parents also joined the work.' (Kombai, de Vries 1993a: 82)

(172) Xe bo-xu-g-i-n=o   ro   mofene # xwai-migi
      he DUR-ill-RLS-NON1SG-LNK=MOD thing that(TOP) demon-person
      wa-luwa-no   wa-luwa-no   foro-moja-ma-none.
      COM-say-[RLS]NON1PL COM-say-[RLS]NON1PL carry-descend-come-IMP.PL
      'When he was ill, the foreigners had said already: bring him down.'
      (Kombai, de Vries 1993a: 106)

4.2.6 Demonstrative modifiers

Demonstratives are found in Greater Awyu languages in the prenominal modifier slot, as in (174) and in the rightmost slot of noun phrases (173). Although demonstratives have the same form in both positions, they have partly different functions. Prenominally, demonstrative modifiers are always true deictic elements that help the listener to identify and locate the referent of the noun phrase in relation to where the speaker is. Postnominally, they function either as true deictic modifiers of the head noun (173), or as postpositions that express the topical or thematic informational role of the noun phrase (172). See §3.5.2 for the development of topicality functions in Greater Awyu demonstratives. When postnominal demonstrative forms are used as topic markers in Greater Awyu languages, they have a tendency to attach themselves to the last word of the thematic noun phrase as clitics, although this does not occur in Kombai.

(173) Xo   mofene rubu-xe
      man   that   bad-ADJ
      'That man is bad.' (Kombai, de Vries 1993a: 37)

(174) Mofena-n=o   xo   rubu-xe
      that-LNK=MOD   man   bad-ADJ
      'That man is bad.' (Kombai, de Vries 1993a: 37)

4.2.7 Coordinate noun phrases

Greater Awyu speakers often prefer to repeat entire clauses (175) rather than use coordinate noun phrases, as in (176), so coordinate noun phrases are marked. Reesink (1987: 177) also observed that coordinate nouns in Usan tend to be informationally salient. This focality explains why Dumut languages recruited the focus marker =nde as coordinator. When used in coordination, =nde has a general coordinating meaning and can be used in conjunctive (177) and disjunctive contexts (176). In (178) =nde (allomorphs=ndi, =te, =ti) functions as a focus marker.

(175) Matirap-Koŋgorap ja-net   i-r   ande-t,
      Matirap-Koggorap 3SG-older.brother kill-RLS[NON1SG] eat.II-RLS[NON1SG]
      ja-n-ani   i-r   ande-t,
      3SG-LNK-older.sister kill-RLS[NON1SG] eat.II-RLS[NON1SG]
      ja-nan   ambae i-r   ande-t,
      3SG-younger.brother one kill-RLS[NON1SG] eat.II-RLS[NON1SG]
      'Matirap-Konggorap kills and eats his older brother, kills and eats his older sister and kills and eats one of his younger brothers.' (Yonggom Wambon, Drabbe 1959: 153)

(176) Ndu=ndi,   aghup=ti   keladi=ndi   taghimo-p-ta.
      Sago=COORD asparagus=COORD sweet.potato=COORD buy-1SG.INT-ASS
      'I want to buy sago, asparagus and sweet potato.' (Digul Wambon, Jang 2008: 108)

(177) nuk=nde   Kulop=nde
      1SG=COORD Kulop=COORD
      'me and Kulop' (Digul Wambon, de Vries and de Vries-Wiersma 1992: 72)

(178) Jaxov=e   keno=nde taximo-knde?
      they=CONN what=FOC buy-RLS.NON1PL
      'What do they buy?' (Digul Wambon, de Vries and de Vries-Wiersma 1992: 72)

Greater Awyu languages tend to use comitative suffixes as coordinators for closed, exhaustive listing for two members, a very common grammaticalization cross-linguistically (Stassen 2000). The comitative meaning is clearly distinguished from the coordination function because only when the comitative marker is repeated has it coordinative function. Wester (2014: 58) reconstructs a proto Awyu-Dumut comitative marker *-kup 'with' with reflexes in all Awyu-Dumut languages, e.g. Aghu – ko, Digul Wambon – kup and its voiced allomorph =ŋgup, (180)–(181). In these languages the element functions both as comitative and coordination marker (Wester 2014: 58). Aghu is exceptional because ko only functions as coordinator and not or no longer as a comitative (van den Heuvel, p.c.). Becking-Dawi languages follow the same pattern but with different matter. Korowai uses its two comitative clitics =fexo, (179) and =meŋga also as coordinators.

(179) nu=fexo gu=fexo
      I-and   you-and
      'me and you' (Korowai, van Enk and de Vries 1997: 81)

(180) no   ko   eke   ko
      1SG   and   3SG   and
      'me and you' (Aghu, Drabbe 1957: 6)

(181) Belanda-n=o   kav=e   loti=ŋgup   susu=ŋgup
      Dutch-LNK=MOD   person=CONN   bread=COORD   milk=COORD
      en-en-mo-knde.
      eat-eat-do-RLS[NON1PL]
      'Dutch people usually consume bread and milk.' (Digul Wambon, de Vries and de Vries-Wiersma 1992: 71)

When Greater Awyu languages employ a closed set of syntactic clitics that consist of just a vowel (see §4.4.1) and that have various roles as syntactic glue or cohesive devices, they use these also as coordinators, e.g. Yonggom Wambon, Digul Wambon and Kombai. For example, Digul Wambon uses the syntactic clitic =o as a modifier-head clitic in noun phrases (183) and to coordinate nouns (182). When =o occurs repeatedly, on every member of the coordination, it is a coordinator (182). When it occurs once, it functions as a modifier-head clitic (183):

(182) angay=o   kav=o
      dog=COORD   man=COORD
      'the dog and the man' (Digul Wambon, de Vries and de Vries-Wiersma 1992: 72)

(183) angay=o   kav=e
      dog= MOD   man=CONN
      'the man with the dog' (Digul Wambon, de Vries and de Vries-Wiersma 1992: 72)

The clitic =o is in contrast with the clitic =e that marks constituents as arguments of a clause (§4.4.1). Dependent on the context the conjoining vowel clitics have a conjunctive ('and') and a disjunctive ('or') reading and they can be used for both exhaustive and open-ended enumeration:

(184) ui=o   itir=o   ragae=o ra   andonanin=e   taximojip.
      pig=or   cassowary=or   fish=or take   come.NON1PL.FUT=SUB   buy.1SG.FUT
      'If they bring pig, or cassowary, or fish, I will buy it.' (Digul Wambon, de Vries and de Vries-Wiersma 1992: 72)

Kombai has a dedicated disjunctive coordinator *xale* 'or' derived from a noun *xale* 'resemblance', 'likeness' (de Vries 1993a: 49). It is still a noun because the preceding noun is linked to *xale* by a modifier- head connective.

(185) . . .*xogade   lan=a   Xale   xof=o   xale   xumo-ra*. . .
       in.former.times woman=MOD Or   man==MOD or   die-SEQ
       '. . . in former times, when a woman, or a man, died and. . .'
       (lit. in former times when someone like a woman (the likeness of a woman) or like a man (the likeness of a man) died and. . .) (Kombai, de Vries 1993a: 49)

Aghu has an interesting coordination construction just for dyadic kinship relations (van den Heuvel 2016: 159). In this construction the 3SG pronoun *efe* precedes the coordinated kinship nouns:

(186) *efe n-amo   efe n-agã*
     3SG LNK-husband 3SG LNK-wife
     'husband and wife' (Aghu, Drabbe 1957: 7)

Van den Heuvel (2016: 159) observes that "It is important to note that the dyadic construction can be used for dyadic relations only, not for reference to pairs in a non-dyadic relation. In that respect, it can be contrasted to the use of *ko* [. . . .] where the phrase can refer either to a married couple (dyadic) or to a non-married 'man and woman'".

(187) *Lãŋ   go   ku*
     woman COORD man
     'a woman and a man' (Aghu, van den Heuvel 2016: 159)

All Greater Awyu languages other than Aghu prefer exocentric compounds to denote dyadic kinship relations (see §3.2.4).

4.3 Clauses

4.3.1 General overview of clause structure

There are three clause types in Greater Awyu languages, all of them predicate final: transitive, intransitive and copula clauses. In transitive clauses the A argument precedes the O argument (A O V) and the S argument precedes the verb in intransitive clauses (S V).[20] In these regards, Greater Awyu languages reflect the usual Trans New Guinea pattern of unmarked ordering of clause constituents (Pawley and Hammarström 2018: 90).

Both core and peripheral arguments may take syntactic vowel connectives and pragmatic markers but core arguments cannot take the case clitics and relational nouns that express semantic relations of peripheral arguments (§4.4.2). Only core arguments may occur without any marking at all. S and A are treated in the same way by grammatical processes such as subject person-number agreement and switch reference. Some languages have subject (=S and A) pronouns and object pronouns. Nominative alignment is the rule in Trans New Guinea languages (Pawley and Hammarström 2018: 90).

Occasional optional 'ergative' marking of A breaks this basic nominative alignment pattern in some Greater Awyu languages (Digul Wambon, Jang 2008: 75; Yonggom Wambon, Wester 2014: 160). The "ergative" marking of the A argument functions to emphasize the agentivity of the A argument, or to disambiguate A and O, and will be glossed AGT. This occasional form of marking the A differently from S within a fundamentally nominative system has been found in a few other Trans New Guinea language families as well (Dixon 1994: 58; Riesberg 2018 for Yali, Mek family). Cause, reason and instrument markers that occur with peripheral arguments in Greater Awyu language serve as optional ergative or agentive markers, when occurring with the core A argument (Jang 2008:75; Wester 2014: 160).

(188) *Aŋgai=ghot oy=e inen-ghe*
dog=AGT pig=CONN bite-RLS[NON1SG]
'The dog bit the pig.' (Digul Wambon, Jang 2008: 75)

The position of peripheral arguments tends to depend on their semantic function. Peripherals that specify the spatiotemporal setting for the clause as a whole tend to occur in first position, before the S. Peripherals that specify or modify the action denoted by the verb tend to occur right before the verb. However, it is hard to get reliable data on such issues because speakers tend to distribute peripheral and core arguments out of clauses over strings of mini clauses (§5.5).

---

[20] This section is based on de Vries (2017).

4.3.2 Experiential clauses

Both transitive and intransitive clauses have an experiential subtype. The human experiencer is expressed as a clause initial topic follow by either an inanimate S and an intransitive verb (189), or an inanimate A and a transitive verb (190). The verb agrees in subject person-number with the inanimate A (*enop* 'fever' in (190)) or S (*ŋgom* 'blood' in (189)), not with the topic, the human experiencer (*nu* 'me') that is neither subject in (189), because the verb agrees with the inanimate subject *ŋgom* nor object in (190) because objects do not precede subjects in Greater Awyu languages. The only way for objects to precede subjects is by filling the extra-clausal theme slot that is not part of the clause, but in doing so the phrase loses its grammatical relation of object. In the case of Greater Awyu experiential clauses the experiencer is not (or no longer) extra-clausal but intonationally and syntactically integrated in the intransitive experiential clause as the filler of the clause-initial topic slot. This type of experiential constructions occurs in many Trans New Guinea languages (Pawley and Hammarström 2018: 113–114).

(189) *Nu   ŋgom   mut-ken*
 1SG blood descend-RLS[NON1SG]
 'I am bleeding.' (lit. regarding me blood comes down) (Yonggom Wambon, Drabbe 1959: 143)

(190) *nu   enow   i-r-an*
 1SG fever hit-RLS[NON1SG]-PAST
 'I had fever.' (Yonggom Wambon, Drabbe 1959: 143)

It will be argued in §5.6 that such experiential clauses developed out of theme-comment structures that are highly frequent in Greater Awyu texts.

4.3.3 Clauses with posture verbs

A special class of intransitive verbs are posture verbs of sitting, standing and lying because of their role in durative, possessive and existential-locative constructions of Greater Awyu languages. The posture verbs also imply a covert noun classification based on the customary posture culturally ascribed to entities, for example sago and meat 'lie', pigs and trees 'stand' and humans 'sit' (92)–(99).

When used to express durative aspect, the posture verb is preceded by a medial same subject verb form. In Yonggom Wambon it is the medial SS simultaneity form *verb stem+ -no*:

(191)   *Mirip mari-no   mbage-r-an*
       rain come.down-SS.SIM sit-RLS[NON1SG]-PAST
       'It was raining.' (Yonggom Wambon, Drabbe 1959: 141)

The use of posture verbs in possessive constructions is exemplified by Aghu (van den Heuvel 2016: 134):

(192)   *na   n-amse   de ba-xe-nã*
       1SG.POSS LNK-child LOC sit-RLS-NON1PL
       'my children are (sitting) there --> I have children'
       (Aghu, Drabbe 1957: 32)

(193)   *Efe tetabago De   ige*
       3SG thing   LOC lie-NON1RLS[SG]
       'his things are (lying) there -> he has possessions'
       (Aghu, Drabbe 1957: 32)

(194)   *ga   büsiü De   e-ke*
       2SG.POSS house LOC stand-NON1RLS[SG]
       'your house is (standing) there -> you have a house'
       (Aghu, Drabbe 1957: 32)

Locative-existential uses of posture verbs are illustrated by Aghu examples (195)–(199) from van den Heuvel (2016: 132):

(195)   *napi   de ba-xe*
       mother LOC sit-RLS.NON1[SG]
       'mother is present' (Aghu, Drabbe 1957: 32)

(196)   *kesaxe weaxa de   e-dia-nã*
       tree   much   LOC stand-HIST-NON1PL
       'there used to be many trees' (Aghu, Drabbe 1957: 32)

(197)   *wi   de   ie-nan-e*
       pig LOC stand.II- NON1PL-FUT
       'there will be pigs' (Aghu, Drabbe 1957: 32)

(198) dü   de   i-ge
      sago   LOC   lie-RLS.[NON1SG]
      'there is sago' (Aghu, Drabbe 1957: 32)

(199) amu   weaxa   de   aine
      meat   much   LOC   lie.II-NON1SG-FUT
      'there will be a lot of meat' (Aghu, Drabbe 1957: 32)

Notice that even with indefinite S these locative-existential clauses have the normal S V structure of intransitive clauses (198). The dummy locative adverb *de* 'there' or a locative noun phrase must be present in preverbal position when posture verbs function as heads of locative-existential clauses that predicate presence or existence. Posture verbs retain their lexical semantics when used in possessive, locative-existential or durative constructions, in the sense that they express a semantic sub classification of nouns based on customary posture (van den Heuvel 2016: 32). Pawley and Hammarstrom (2018: 115) put the Aghu data in the Trans New Guinea context: "A good many Trans New Guinea languages use verbs of posture 'stand', 'sit', 'lie', and sometimes other verbs like 'hang', 'carry' and 'come' as existential or quasi-copular verbs. Lang (1975) refers to these as '(noun) classifying' verbs because the choice of verb correlates with the size, shape, posture, or composition of the subject nominal referent".

Aghu uses three posture verbs (sit, lie, stand). Asmat, its neighbor, adds 'be in/on the water' and 'be above (eye level)' to the basic sit/lie/stand existential verbs.

(200) *Posture verbs used to refer to a subject's being present in Aghu (from van den Heuvel 2016: 131)*

Type of object	Posture verb used
birds	*ba* 'sit'
living humans	*ba* 'sit' or *e* 'stand'
animals that do not usually creep	*e* 'stand'
'standing things like houses, trees'	*e* 'stand'
creeping animals, like snakes and lizards	*i* 'lie'
'things that are usually in a more or less lying position, so all small things'	*i* 'lie'
fruits on a tree	*i* 'lie'
dead humans or dead animals	*i* 'lie'

4.3.4 Copula clauses

Copula clauses of Greater Awyu languages consist, in the terms of Dixon (2010, II: 159), of a copula subject (CS) followed by a copula complement (CC). The copula complement can be a noun phrase, adjective phrase or a numeral phrase. Copula clauses select a copula from a small set of invariant copulas (205)–(206), or they take a fully inflected copula verb (204). The copula is optional as is shown by (201)–(204) (Drabbe 1959: 124)

(201) *Na-tager   irumon   (de)*
      my-kauri.shell two   (COP)
      'I have two *kauri* shells.' (lit. my shells (are) two) (Yonggom Wambon, Drabbe 1959: 124)

(202) *na-nati   ŋgorowop*
      my-father handsome
      'My father is handsome.' (Yonggom Wambon, Drabbe 1959: 124)

(203) *ewe na-mandup*
      that my-son
      'That is my son'. (Yonggom Wambon, Drabbe 1959: 124)

(204) *oxo   isiom tadi püsiü ki-ke*
      water Very   big   very   become-NON1RLS[SG]
      'The water has become very big.' (Aghu, van den Heuvel 2016: 659)

Yonggom Wambon has an affirmative copula, a negative copula and an interrogative copula:

(205) *na-mandup te*
      my-son   COP
      'It is my son.' (Yonggom Wambon, Drabbe 1959:124)

(206) *na-nati   tomba*
      my-father NEG.COP
      'It is not my father.' (Yonggom Wambon, Drabbe 1959:124)

(207) *juw=e   katoni to?*
      he=CONN stupid COP.Q
      'Is he stupid?' (Yonggom Wambon, Drabbe 1959:124)

4.3.5 Grammaticalization path of nde/te

In Dumut, Ndeiram and Becking-Dawi languages, one copula of the copula set is also recruited to function as focus marker. Compare the Digul Wambon example (208), where =nde is a copula and (209a) and (209b), where =nde is a focus marker. The Korowai examples show the same two functions of the cognate =to (allomorphs =tu and =lo), of copula (210) and focus marker (211):

(208) ŋgup   Gaguov=o   kap=nde?
       2SG   Gaguop=MOD   person=COP
       'You are a person from Gaguop?' (Digul Wambon, de Vries 1986: 29)

(209a) ŋgup   keno=nde heta=xe?
       you(SG) what=FOC see-RLS[NON1SG]
       'What do you see?' (Digul Wambon, de Vries 1986: 16)

(209b) Oi=nde   heta-knde-p.
       pig=FOC see-RLS-1SG
       'I see a pig.' (Digul Wambon, de Vries 1986: 16)

(210) Noxu-yanop=tu.
       our-people=COP
       'It is our people.' (Korowai, van Enk and de Vries 1997: 128)

(211) N-ate=lo   nu   umo.
       my-father=FOC   1SG tell.NON1SG.RLS
       'It was my father who told me.' (Korowai, van Enk and de Vries 1997: 128)

Copula complements tend to be focal and formed the bridge for the copula to add focus marking function (de Vries 1989: 93). In copula clauses, the affirmative copula is still a copula and not a focus marker, as claimed by Wester (2014: 167), because it can only occur on the copula complement, not on the copula subject. In verbal clauses that restriction no longer holds and there the copula element has developed into a focus marker which may occur on any constituent that is in focus in a given context, including subjects, as in (211). We saw in §4.2.7 that in Dumut languages these copula-based focus markers added a further function as coordinators, linking coordinate noun phrases and conjoining clauses.

Wester (2014: 165–168) has a different analysis of =nde and its counterparts in Dumut languages. When it occurs with nouns, she analyzes it as a focus marker, in all its contexts. When it is repeated on every member of a coordinate noun phrase, she concedes that the focus clitic may be analyzed as a coordinator (Wester 2014: 165, note 7), as in:

(212) kagup=te   ra-ra-mun=de
      man[PL]=and woman-woman-PL=and
      'men and women' (Yonggom Drabbe, 1959: 145)

A more substantial difference in both analyses concerns the function of =nde when it connects clauses:

(213a) Ande-r-ew=a   mbumo=te   me-gen-ep.
       eatII-RLS-1SG=SEQ finish[SS]=CNJ come-RLS-1SG
       'I ate and finished (it) and I came.' ('After I had eaten, I came'.)
       (Yonggom Wambon, Drabbe 1959: 136)

(213b) Ande-r-ew=a   mbumo-gon-ep=te me-gen.
       eatII-RLS-1SG=SEQ finish-RLS-1SG=CJN come-RLS[NON1SG]
       'I ate and then I finished it and he came.' ('After I had eaten, he arrived'.)
       (Yonggom Wambon, Drabbe 1959: 136)

The element te/nde is used in both Wambon dialects (Digul and Yonggom Wambon) as a copula ((205) and (208)), as a focus marker (209b), in noun coordination (212), in clause chains connecting clauses (213a)–(213b), at least in my analysis (see §4.2.7 and §4.3.5).

Wester (2014: 165) describes =nde as a subordinator, when it functions with clauses. She has three arguments to support her analysis. First, =nde (allomorph =te after voiceless sounds) occasionally occurs sentence-finally, where it has a focal or assertion-enhancing function (214):

(214) Malin   loxa-t-po;   ap=we
      malin.bird sound-RLS[NON1SG]-PAST house=TOP
      wesat-mo-ni=nde
      sun-do[IRR.NON1SG]-INT=FOC
      'A malin bird had sung, it was at daybreak.' (Digul Wambon, Jang 2008: 127)

This argument is irrelevant because in (214) =nde is not used interclausally as a subordinating clitic but as a focus clitic, one of the functions that it acquired in its grammaticalization path (from copula in nominal clauses to focus marker and to coordinator of nouns and chaining clitic with clauses).

Her second argument is that "the scope of negation and imperatives does not extend over clauses marked by *te*" (Wester 2014: 167). However, she has very little evidence for this, not enough, she admits "to solidify the claim" (Wester 2014: 166).

Her third argument is that "it is not clear how a focus marker would develop into a clausal coordinator in Awyu-Dumut languages" (Wester 2014: 167). However, there is a clear grammaticalization path for that development: =*nde* starts of as copula with nominal predicates (a function it still has), then adds a coordinating function with nouns (noun coordination being informationally salient in Greater Awyu) when focus markers with the coordinated nouns bleached into coordinators. Once the noun coordinating function of =*nde* was well-established and frequently used, its use spread to the chaining of clauses (§4.3.5).

4.3.6 Clauses with invariant existential-locative predicates

To express that someone is present or that someone is present at a location, Greater Awyu languages use intransitive clauses with posture verbs (see (195)–(199) above). However, some grammars report a small, closed set of invariant locative-existential predicative elements, both affirmative and negative, e.g. Yonggom Wambon:

(215) *enanow=e   mbon*
mother=CONN EXIST
'mother is present' (Yonggom Wambon, Drabbe 1959: 124)

(216) *na-matiw=e   ndoi*
my-daughter=CONN NEG.EXIST
'my daughter is absent' (Yonggom Wambon, Drabbe 1959: 124)

Just like the locative-existential intransitive constructions with posture verbs, the locative-existential clauses with invariant markers may have possessive readings (Drabbe 1959: 125):

(217) *na-tager=e   mbon.*
my-money=CONN EXIST
'I have money.' (Yonggom Wambon, Drabbe 1959: 125)

4.4 Postpositions

A closed set of mutually exclusive[21] syntactic (§4.4.1), semantic (§4.4.2) and pragmatic (§4.4.3) postpositions express relations of arguments to the verb in Greater Awyu languages.[22]

4.4.1 Syntactic clitics

Dumut languages, Kombai (Ndeiram subgroup) and Korowai (Becking-Dawi) use a small closed set of syntactic vowel clitics in both phrases and clauses. In phrases, they link nominal modifiers to their heads to signal that the constituent which they cliticize to, is a modifier within a noun phrase (see §4.2.1). In clauses, syntactic clitics link arguments to the verb and they signal that constituents are arguments of the verb (218b). They also function as coordinators with phrases and chaining conjunctions with clauses, see §4.2.7.

The syntactic vowel clitics play a key role in expressing syntactic contrasts, for example Digul Wambon =e marks the demonstrative *ev=e* in (218b) as an independent demonstrative argument in the clause domain, in contrast to the dependent demonstrative *ev=o* marked by =o in (218a) as a modifier in a noun phrase domain:

(218a) *ev=o*   *lan*
          that=MOD woman
          'that woman' (Digul Wambon, de Vries and Wiersma 1992: 43)

(218b) *Ev=e*   *lan*
          that=CONN woman
          'That is a woman.' (Digul Wambon, de Vries and de Vries-Wiersma 1992: 43)

When the modifier-head noun connective =o cliticizes to a clause, it marks that clause as a relative clause (219a). When =e cliticizes to a clause, it marks that clause as an adverbial clause (219b)

---

[21] The Yonggom Wambon topic clitic =*ewe* occasionally co-occurs with the circumstantial postposition =*ka*, see example (55) and discussion in §3.5.2.
[22] This section on postpositions and clitics is based on de Vries (2017).

(219a) ko mba-xe-n=o   kav=eve ev=e na-mbap=nde
       there sit-RLS[NON1SG]-LNK=MOD man=TOP that=CONN my-father=COP
       'The man who sits there, that is my father.' (Digul Wambon, de Vries 1986: 28)

(219b) ndavelepon=e   ev=o   sal=e   noxop Mboma
       come.1SG.PAST LNK=SUB that=MOD day=CONN we   Boma
       ndakndevan=o. . .
       come.1PL.RLS.LNK=CNJ
       'when I returned that day we returned from Boma and. . .' (Digul Wambon, de Vries 1986: 47)

4.4.2 Postpositions expressing semantic roles

Greater Awyu languages have a small set of postpositions and clitics that express the semantic relations of peripheral arguments in clauses. Each of these covers a wide range of different relations. For example, Digul Wambon has a circumstantial case clitic =ka that marks inanimate peripheral arguments: instruments, times (220), locations, source, manner, ablative (Jang 2008: 77). When used with clauses, it marks the clause as a peripheral argument with time function (221). When used with the core A argument, =ka is recruited to serve as an agentive marker (§4.3.1).

(220) Alip=ka   koma-t-mbo
      yesterday=CIRC die-RLS-[NON1SG]PAST
      'He died yesterday.' (Digul Wambon, de Vries 1986: 23)

(221) nux=e andelepo=ŋga   ev=o   kav=e
      I=CONN eat.II. RLS.1SG.PAST=CIRC that=MOD man=CONN
      nde-t-mbo
      come-RLS-[NON1SG]PAST
      'When I ate, that man came.' (Digul Wambon, de Vries 1986: 41)

Nouns play a key role in the expression of the semantic relations of peripheral arguments in Greater Awyu languages, both synchronically as relator nouns (222) and diachronically as input of grammaticalization processes that turned these nouns into case clitics (224), with different varieties within dialect chains showing various stages of the diachronic process.

Synchronically, all Greater Awyu languages have a set of spatial relator nouns that may combine with general circumstantial postpositions, e.g. the Korowai nouns *belüp* 'space under treehouse' and *ün* 'roof ridge' that are used as relator nouns to express spatial notions with *=ta* 'in, at, on', for example *pesau-ün=ta* 'on (top of) the plane', literally 'at the plane roof ridge' (van Kessel 2011: 26). Korowai uses the noun *debüf* 'way, road' similarly as relator noun, e.g. *ale-debüf* 'by canoe' (lit. canoe-way) (van Enk and de Vries 1997: 83), without further marking by a postposition. Digul Wambon uses a wide range of spatial nouns in combination with its general inanimate circumstantial postposition *=ka*, such as *wamip* 'inside', *sinim* 'side', *hitop* 'bottom', *palip* 'top', *kuk* 'front', *kutep* 'outside' (de Vries and de Vries-Wiersma 1992: 59; Jang 2008: 81):

(222) na-yop   sinim=ŋga   mba-knde-p
      my-mother   beside=CIRC   sit-RLS-1SG
      'I sat beside my mother.' (Digul Wambon, Jang 2008: 81)

Yonggom Wambon and Aghu generally avoid the use of generic locative postpositions with their dimensional nouns and prefer to use what Drabbe (1959: 17) calls genitival constructions with the first noun being the possessor and the second the possessed noun, the dimensional noun, e.g. Yonggom Wambon *ran ringgin* 'in proximity of the woman' (lit. the woman's proximity), *mbitip kop* 'in(side) the house' (lit. inside of the house) (Drabbe 1959: 143; van Kessel 2011: 17). Aghu uses the dimensional nouns *gesi* 'proximity', *mo* 'backside', *fü* 'the place underneath something', *betagha* 'outside', *baga* 'border, egde', *womu* 'middle', for example *idi baga* 'alongside the road' (lit. road edge) (Van Kessel 2011: 11; Drabbe 1957: 41). Such relator nouns which are used as postpositions may of course grammaticalize into postpositions. Apart from some bleaching of meaning when an Aghu "postpositional noun" is used with more and more nouns of various semantic domains (e.g. *sama* 'frontside of human body' being used for dishes (dish frontside=upper side of a dish)), there are no strong signs of grammaticalisation such as phonological reduction of the number of syllables, or reduction of vowel qualities to schwa, or lexical stress.

Diachronically, many Greater Awyu languages use a noun that means 'reason' as input for a grammaticalization process which turns the noun into a phonologically reduced, semantically generalized, case clitic to code a wide range of semantic relationships that can be subsumed under the notion of the goal of an action. They use a reflex of a proto Greater Awyu noun **tigin*, e.g. Korowai *texé(n)*, Digul Wambon *si(xin)*, Yonggom Wambon *tigin*, Kombai *ri*. Different languages show different stages of the grammaticalization process from noun to case clitic.

The behavior of modifier-head noun connectives is a diagnostic for the determination of the categorial status of relational nouns in Greater Awyu languages (noun or case marker, see de Vries 1989: 180). When the connectives are obligatory in all contexts, this is an indication that the noun-status is still relevant. When they start to be dropped in certain contexts, especially when this is followed by clitization, phonological reduction and loss of stress, the categorial status is changing in the direction of a case clitic.

We will now illustrate the three main stages of this process: Yonggom Wambon is an example of the first stage, where the 'reason' noun is still a noun. Digul Wambon shows the last stage, where the development ended in a case clitic. Korowai reflects the intermediate stage, where the 'reason' noun loses noun properties, syntactically and semantically but where it has not yet reached the stage of case clitic.

In the Yonggom dialect of Wambon the noun *tigin* 'cause, reason' is the head of the phrase, as shown by the modifier-head connective *=e* of the Yonggom dialect in (223). But in the neighboring Digul Wambon dialect its cognate *=sixi* has become a case clitic (224). In (223) the Yonggom Wambon noun *ran* 'woman' is a possessor noun in a possessive noun phrase with *tigin* 'reason' as head noun ('a woman's reason'). It functions in the prenominal modifier slot of the noun phrase and this is signaled by the syntactic connective *=e*. In (224), in the neighboring dialect Digul Wambon, the cognate *lan* 'woman' is the head noun, as shown by the preceding Digul Wambon modifier-head noun connective *=o and =sixi* is a postpositional clitic marking goal and reason arguments. If *sixi* was the head noun, the connective would have occurred preceding *sixi*. Also, *sixi* has cliticized, has a shorter form *=si* and has a more abstract grammatical meaning, all signs of advanced grammaticalization into a case clitic:

(223) ran=e   tigin=de   Katit pitip   unda-r-in=de
       woman=MOD reason=FOC   Katit house   burn-RLS-NON1PL=CJN
       'because of a woman they burned down Katit's house and. . .'
       (Yonggom Wambon, Drabbe 1959: 148)

(224) Ev=o   lan=sixi   ka-l-e-mbo
       that=MOD   woman=for   go-RLS-NON1PL-PAST
       'Because of that woman they went away.' (Digul Wambon, de Vries 1986: 53)

The Korowai cognate of Yonggom Wambon *tigin* and KenonWambon *=sixin* is *=texé(n).* with allomorph *=lexé(n)* when cliticizing to a word ending in a vowel. It reflects the intermediate stage between (relational) noun and case clitic, because the modifier-head clitic =xa has been dropped in most but not all contexts (van Enk and de Vries 1997: 82–83). In Korowai, as in all other Greater Awyu languages, the reason marker =texé(n) also marks cause (228), recipient (225), reason (226), purpose (227), beneficiary and addressee (229). In other words, it has acquired an abstract grammatical meaning 'goal of the action' with peripheral arguments.

(225) nu if-e=xa misafi gup=texé fédo-p
I this-LNK=MOD thing you=to give-1SG[INT]
'I want to give these things to you.' (Korowai, van Enk and de Vries 1997: 82)

(226) gu mbaxa=lexé wa-mol-mo?
you what=for that-do-do[NON1SG.RLS]
'Why do you do that?' (Korowai, van Enk and de Vries 1997: 82)

(227) noxup Lalop dad-u=ŋga lexé xai-mba-lé
we Lalop bath-VN=MOD reason go-DUR-1SG[RLS]
'We are on our way to bathe in the Lalop river.' (Korowai, van Enk and de Vries 1997: 82)

(228) . . .noxu- ŋgé abü=fexa olexi=lexén wai-mémo=xa
. . .our friend male=one faeces= because go.down-IMMP[NON1SG.RLS]=SUB
lu-mbo=bene?
enter- DUR[NON1SG.RLS]=Q
'. . .is one of our friends who went down to relieve himself, entering?'
(Korowai, van Enk and de Vries 1997: 82)

(229) nu ne-defo=texé dodépa-lé
I my-wife=to call-1SG[RLS]
'I called my wife.' (Korowai, van Enk and de Vries 1997: 88)

The element =texé (sometimes with final nasal as (228) shows) cliticizes to the preceding nominal constituent; only when this preceding constituent is a nominal infinitive is the =xa obligatory (227). In other contexts =xa is always absent (e.g. with personal pronouns, gup=texé 'to/for you').

4.4.3 Topic and focus postpositions

Greater Awyu languages have two pragmatic markers that adjust utterances to their informational contexts, topic markers and focus markers. Greater Awyu topic markers tend to derive from demonstratives, a process that always involves loss of deictic meaning and sometimes cliticization (see §3.5.2). These topic markers occur very often and this may have been the basis for their bleaching and phonological reduction from topic marker to syntactic connective in some Dumut languages, a further grammaticalization after the first development from demonstrative to non-deictic topic marker. Wester (2014: 151) notes that the Yonggom Wambon deictic *ep* 'that' has a shorter form =*e*. Digul Wambon also has an omnipresent clitic =*e*. This =*e* clitic in the Wambon dialects has been analyzed by Wester (2014: 151) and Jang (2008) as a topic marker. De Vries and de Vries-Wiersma (1992: 69) analyze =*e* as a syntactic vowel clitic, primarily because =*e* can be shown to have become part of a small closed set of syntactic vowel clitics that signal syntactic contrasts, see (230)–(231), repeated from (218a/b):

(230) *ev=o*   *lan*
       that=MOD   woman
       'that woman' (Digul Wambon, de Vries and Wiersma 1992: 43)

(231) *ev=e*   *lan*
       that=CONN woman
       'that is a woman' (Digul Wambon, de Vries and de Vries-Wiersma 1992: 43)

In some contexts a residual topic meaning of =*e* may linger but the extremely high frequency (often multiple occurrences in a single clause), bleached meaning and shortened form point to a contrast between the syntactic connective clitic =*e* and the topic clitic =*eve*. Note that the independent demonstrative *eve* 'that' (231) is in clear contrast to the topic clitic =*eve* (232)–(233), although the topic clitic =*eve* diachronically developed from the independent demonstrative *ev=e* (see §3.5.2): the topic clitic =*eve* must occur after the constituent that it marks as a topic, it cliticizes to the last word of the topic and it has no longer a deictic meaning (§3.5.2). The independent demonstrative is fully deictic, is phonologically an independent word and functions syntactically as an argument within clauses.

The topic markers occur with topical phrases (*nux=eve, nombon=eve* (232)) and with clauses (*ep=ka mba-l-eva-mbo-n=eve* (233)):

(232) *nux=eve nombo-n=eve, ndayo-nge kalepon=o*
I=TOP here- LNK=TOP paddle-be go.RLS.1SG. PAST-LNK=CNJ
'as far as I am concerned, I went by canoe and. . .' (Digul Wambon, de Vries 1995: 525)

The second word of (232), *nomboneve*, shows the loss of distal deictic meaning of the topic clitic *=eve*: it combines with the proximate deictic *nombo* 'here/this' into a new topic marker *nomboneve* that marks extra-clausal themes and has a meaning similar to English extra-clausal theme phrases 'as for X' or 'as far as X is concerned'.

(233) *Ep=ka mba-l-eva-mbo-n=eve, sanov=e ilo*
there=CIRC sit-RLS-1PL-PAST-LNK=TOP little.finger=CONN go.down
ka-l-eva-mbo
go-RLS-1PL-PAST
'After we had stayed there, we went downriver on Monday'.(Lit. 'given that we stayed there,. . .') (Digul Wambon, de Vries and de Vries-Wiersma 1992: 87)

Above we saw that focus markers in Dumut, Ndeiram and Becking-Dawi languages originate as affirmative copulas (§4.3.5). They mark arguments that present information which is the most salient in a given context, for example question words (e.g. Digul Wambon (235a)) and other contextually focal constituents (Korowai, (234), Digul Wambon, 235b):

(234) *Mül-alüp mbolo-mbolop mahüon uma-té=do*
former-time ancestor-ancestor story tell-[RLS]NON1PL=DS
xemilo-bo=xa mahüon uma-té=do, n-até
die[RLS.NON1SG]-COM=MOD story tell-[RLS]NON1PL=DS my-father
dai-bo=fexo n-até=lo nu umo.
hear[RLS.NON1SG]-COM=CNJ my-father=FOC 1SG tell[RLS.NON1SG]
'In former days it was the ancestors, the ancestors told a story, a story about a man who died they told and my father heard it and it was my father who told me.' (Korowai, van Enk and de Vries 1997: 156)

Focus markers occur with both focal phrases (235a/b) and focal clauses (236):

(235a) *ŋgup keno=nde heta=xe?*
you(SG) what=FOC see-RLS[NON1SG]
'What do you see?' (Digul Wambon, de Vries 1986: 16)

(235b) Oi=nde   heta-knde-p
         pig=FOC   see-RLS-1SG
         'I see a pig.' (Digul Wambon, de Vries 1986: 16)

(236) Malin   loxa-t-po;   ap=we   wesat-mo-ni=nde
        malin.bird sound-RLS[NON1SG]-PAST house=TOP sun-do[IRR.NON1SG]-INT=FOC
        'A *malin* bird had sung, it was at daybreak.' (Digul Wambon, Jang 2008: 127)

Aghu, of the Awyu subgroup, does not use its copula *de* as a focus marker. Instead, there is a focus marker *ke* that, according to van den Heuvel (2016: 284), is restricted to non-verbal clauses:

(237a) Xo   n-eto   de
         DST 1SG-father COP
         'that is my father' (Aghu, Drabbe 1957: 8)

(237b) Xo   ke   n-eto   de
         DST FOC 1SG-father COP
         'that one there is my father' (Aghu, Drabbe 1957: 8)

4.5 Clause combinations

4.5.1 Introduction

Clauses have four major combinatorial syntactic possibilities in Greater Awyu languages. They can function:
– as relative clauses, see §4.2.5;
– as adjuncts or peripheral arguments of other clauses, see §4.4.2;
– as extra-clausal themes, see §4.4.3;
– as chained clauses, see §4.5.2.

The first three types of clause combinations are forms of subordination, broadly defined. The last type, clause chaining, is a form of clause conjoining. Functionally, the opposition between subordination and clause chaining corresponds to the distinction between online and offline clauses.

The clauses in subordinate function are offline clauses, in the sense that they are off the event line and off the participant line expressed by the medial and final clauses of the clause chain: they do not monitor temporal or switch reference relations between clauses in the chain since they are not part of the chain. Speakers use them for a variety of tasks that necessitate them to break the event- and participant lines, e.g. to identify a referent with a relative clause, to introduce the setting or themes of another event, to correct or revise information and to give background information to events of the main event line in the clause chain.

Chaining linkage, on the other hand, creates series of online clauses that present the continuing event line, track the topical participants involved in those events and how the events of the chain relate to each other in terms of time. Topical participants are tracked by verbal morphology (switch reference, agreement). Temporal relations between events in the chain are encoded likewise by medial verb affixes of sequence and simultaneity and by temporal conjunctions that track the temporal relations (sequence, simultaneity). Clause chaining is the default mode of clause combining, it is by far the most frequent type of clause linkage in Greater Awyu texts.

Clauses cannot function as subjects or objects (core arguments) of other clauses. Speakers either use verbal nouns or infinitives (see §3.2.3) or use a clause chaining construction (see §5.5.3). Compare (238a) and (238b):

(238a) *Muxalé yu imo=tofexo y-afé élo-bo*
Muxalé he see[RLS.NON1SG]=DS his-brother sleep-be[RLS.NON1SG]
'Muxalé, he saw that his older brother was asleep.' (Lit. 'Muxale he saw and (DS) his brother was asleep') (Korowai, van Enk and de Vries 1997: 189)

(238b) *Naerop ju taep me etaga-t te amun mba-gen*
Naerop 3SG also come see-RLS[NON1SG] CNJ tree.kangaroo sit-RLS[NON1SG]
'Naerop he also came and saw that there was a tree kangaroo.' (Yonggom Wambon, Drabbe 1959: 147)

Verbal nouns and infinitival forms can be seen as "condensed" clauses that present events in such a way that they acquire enough nominal properties to be allowed as core arguments that require noun-headed phrases (see §3.2.3).

4.5.2 Clause chaining

In the Trans New Guinea context clause chaining is a type of clause linkage that chains multiple clauses, usually simply structured, into a clause chain with often paragraph-like discourse functions (Roberts 1997). In its canonical Trans New Guinea form the non-final (or medial) clauses of the chain contain dependent verbs with reduced or no TAM morphology that make the clause dependent for its TAM interpretation on the fully inflected verb of the final clause of the chain.

The dependent verbs in the medial clauses are more than just reduced forms of independent verbs because they tend to have two slots in the verb that final verbs lack, namely switch reference (Same Subject or Different Subject) and temporality (sequence and simultaneity) distinctions, often with complex subtypes. Speakers may deviate from the unmarked form of the canonical clause chain for special purposes in some Trans New Guinea languages, by placing a medial clause after the final clause (e.g. as a clarifying afterthought) or producing an utterance consisting of just a medial clause (e.g. as a form of commands), see Sarvasy (2015).

Unlike canonical clause chaining in mountain Trans New Guinea languages with fully developed switch reference and temporality categories and with a key distinction between medial and final clauses, Greater Awyu languages have a less elaborate clause chaining pattern. Consider the following opening paragraphs of a Yonggom Wambon text:

(239a) *Matirap-Koŋgorap   ja-net   i-r   ande-t,*
Matirap-Konggorap 3SG-older.brother kill-RLS[NON1SG] eat.II-RLS[NON1SG]
ja-n-ani   i-r   ande-t,
3SG-LNK-older.sister kill-RLS[NON1SG] eat.II-RLS[NON1SG]
ja-nan   ambae i-r   ande-t,
3SG-younger.brother one   kill-RLS[NON1SG] eat.II-RLS[NON1SG]
'Matirap-Konggorap kills and eats his older brother, kills and eats his older sister and kills and eats one of his younger brothers.' (Yonggom Wambon, Drabbe 1959: 153)

(239b) *Mir=e   ra-ko   tow   ambugut-ma-r-an*
bone=CONN take-go hole insert-do-RLS[NON1SG]-PAST
'He took the bones and threw them in a hole'.

(239c) *Ja   nan   ambae   i-r   ande-t.*
3SG younger.brother the.other kill-RLS[NON1SG] eat.II-RLS[NON1SG]
'The other younger brother he also killed and ate.'

(239d) *Mbaeop   pitip   ka-w-an   nde-ro me-me-j-op*
grandfather house go-1-PL[IRR] say-SS come-come-LNK-1SG[IRR]
'He used to say, 'Let us go to grandfather's house, let me come''

(239e) *Ndakmirop   page-t   te   sama-r=a*
Ndakmirop.bird sit-RLS[NON1SG] CNJ miss-RLS[NON1SG]=SEQ
Nguruŋgoron=ŋga raga-t   te
Nguruŋgoron=AGT say-RLS[NON1SG] CNJ
'There was a Ndakmirop bird and he missed it with his *ambot* arrow and Nguruŋgoron said (to him),

(239f) *ŋgo ŋgo nenŋgui=e   Matiram=ŋga ŋgotonde e-no*
2SG 2SG older.brother=CONN Matiram= AGT kill.I   eat.I-SS.SIM
mir=e   top   me   agumo mba-gen-op nde-t.
bone=CONN hole come insert sit-RLS[NON1SG]-HAB say-RLS[NON1SG]
'your younger brothers, your older brothers, Matiram killed and ate them and buried their bones in a hole", she said.' (Yonggom Wambon text, Drabbe 1959: 153–154, transcribed by R. Wester)

The less elaborate and emergent switch reference (see §3.6.1.5) and clause chaining systems of Greater Awyu languages were interpreted de Vries 2010 assuming that Greater Awyu languages were on their way to canonical clause chaining. However, given the scenario of migration described in chapter 7, with Greater Awyu origin placed in the mountains as Trans New Guinea language, it seems better not to assume just directionality *towards* canonical clause chaining but also *away* from it. When Greater Awyu ancestral groups moved out of the mountains and migrated away from canonical Trans New Guinea areas, they came in contact with languages in the southern plains completely lacking clause chaining such as Marindic languages, with high degrees of bilingualism favoring syntactic and discourse convergence (see chapters 6 and 7).

We find only clause chaining in the text (239a)–(239f), and none of the more marked types of clause combining discussed above. The chained clauses may contain either independent verbs conjoined by *te*, e.g. *Ndakmirop paget te ambot samara* in (239e), or non-finite SS clauses such as *eno* in (239f).

The chained clauses with semi-inflected or fully inflected verbs are in the vast majority of cases used in DS contexts, and are a signal that the next clause has a different subject referent. They are in opposition to the non-finite SS clauses that are used when there is no change in topical subject. The chained clauses with (semi-)inflected verbs cannot independently select their tense and/or mood. As chained clauses they are under the scope of the tense and mood specification of the verb in the final clause of the chain. Notice that Mandobo has a fusional medial suffix – *no* that encodes both switch reference and temporality distinctions. Fusion of switch reference and temporality occurs in quite a few Trans New Guinea languages (Roberts 1997).

Notice also that the conjunction *te* 'and' in Yonggom Wambon coordinates noun phrases (240a), conjoins chained clauses with semi-inflected or inflected verbs (239e) and it conjoins non-finite SS clauses to final independent clauses (240b). Medial SS clauses are also often linked asyndetically to the next clause.

(240a) *Kagup te raramun de munotit t[23] in-gin-in.*
 man COORD woman.PL COORD child.PL COORD eat-RLS-NON1PL
 'The men, women and children are eating.' (Yonggom Wambon, Drabbe 1959:145)

(240b) *Sumo te ko-gen.*
 lift.SS CNJ go-RLS[NON1SG]
 'He lifted (it) up and went.' (Yonggom Wambon, Drabbe 1959:134)

The clauses in (239a-f) are all linked by chaining and all clauses are on the event line. But there are exceptions to the rule that chained clauses are conjoined and on the event line. In at least some Greater Awyu languages there are intermediate constructions. Wester (2014: 162) observed that speakers of Yonggom Wambon may change the syntactic status of medial same subject clauses and give them a background function, by marking them with the circumstantial postposition =*ka*/=*ŋga* that normally marks time, place, instruments and other peripheral arguments, both phrasal and clausal (241).

(241) *Endom etogo-ro=ŋga raŋgandi-y-ip*
 Enemy see-SEQ=CIRC shout-LIG-FUT.1SG
 'When I see the enemy, I will shout.' (Yonggom Wambon, Drabbe 1959: 134)

The use of =*ŋga* with medial clauses is very marked and reduces the conjoined, online nature of medial same subject clauses, although the switch reference system is not switched off (Wester 2014: 162). Wester (2014: 162) regards this type of clauses as subordinate clauses. I view them as hybrids of chaining and subordinate linkage which allow speakers to continue the switch reference tracking of participants from one clause to the next, impossible in true subordinate linkage. In terms of the participant line, the speaker wants to stay online, in continuative fashion, but in terms of the event line, the speaker wants to go offline, presenting the event as background to the main event line, in subordinate fashion.

---

23 The schwa of *te* elides before the initial vowel of *inginin*.

The other exception (142), much more common in Greater Awyu languages and in mountain Trans New Guinea languages in general (Reesink 1983: 240, 242), is the opposite: in terms of the participant line, the speaker goes offline, by switching off the switch reference monitoring of participant continuity but in terms of the event line the speaker stays online. Here the participants are backgrounded. Consider (242):

(242) *Jaxov=e Woyo, ndun=e tembet nde-l-en=o*
3PL=CONN No, sago=CONN NEG.EXIST say-RLS-NON1PL=CNJ[DS]
et-mbel=o ep=ka nda-knd-ev=o sal=e inolapŋgelimo
leave-SEQ=CNJ there=CIRC come-RLS-1SG=CNJ sun=CONN set[SS]
ot numbum-ke-t-mbo
stomach empty-be[NON1SG]-RLS-PAST
'They said, No, there is no sago and I left them and came there and when the sun set, I was hungry.' (Digul Wambon, de Vries 1989: 63–64)

The clause *sale inolapŋgelimo* in (242) has a medial SS verb (a bare verb stem). This clause has a so-called 'false' SS marking because the next clause has a different subject referent, an experiential clause with the subject *ot* 'stomach'. But the switch reference system ignores different subjects such as *ot* that occur only once, are very low in the animacy/agentivity hierarchy and are in the background of the story. There are two participants in the foreground in (242), the narrator of this travelogue, referred to by the 1SG verb form *ndakndevo and* the people he met while travelling (*jaxove* 'they'). They are on the participant line and monitored by the switch reference system. The different subject *t*-form *ndeleno* signals the switch from the *jaxove* subject to the 'I' subject of the next clause. After *ndeleno* there are two switches of subject that are not signaled by DS marking, the switch to *sat* 'sun' and the switch to *ot* 'stomach'. The speaker indicates in this way that the 'I' remains the participant he is talking about (de Vries 1989: 64).

Weather clauses with inanimate subjects ('rain falls down'), experiential clauses, clauses with the sun as subject: they all have inanimate subject of low discourse topicality and by ignoring these subjects, the speaker leaves them in the background (Reesink 1983). Greater Awyu languages have two major ways of switching off the switch reference system, the use of "false" SS verb forms and the use of switch reference neutral conjoined independent verbs, for example *ndakdevo* in (242), before background clauses with non-topical subject of low topicality such as 'the sun set'.

4.5.3 Subordination

Subordination is the label under which we subsume three combinatorial possibilities of Greater Awyu clauses: their functions as relative clauses, as peripheral arguments of superordinate clauses (adverbial clauses) and as extra-clausal themes. The distinction between the last two types, adverbial and extra-clausal thematic clauses, is that adverbial clauses are syntactically and intonationally integrated in the main clause, as a constituent within that clause whereas extra-clausal theme clauses are not a syntactic constituent of the clause that they precede. They are furthermore separated from the main clause by a pause, and are not under the intonation contour of the main clause. Finally, they have the pragmatic function of theme, presenting the domain or theme with respect to which the following predication is relevant. This pragmatic function is encoded by topic clitics. The first clause of (244) is a good example of an extra-clausal thematic clause: it is marked by the topic marker =*eve*, it is intonationally separate from the following clause and it is not an argument of the verb of the the clause that follows, *kalevambo*. But the first clause of (243), *ndave-lepo-n=e* 'when I returned' is marked by the subordinator =*e*, and is intonationally under the contour of the main clause in which it functions as an adjunct with adverbial function:

(243) *ndavelepon=e*   *ev=o*   *sal=e*   *noxop*   *Mboma*
       come.1SG.PAST. LNK=SUB that=MOD day=CONN   we   Boma
       ndakndevan=o
       come.1PL.RLS. LNK=CNJ
       'when I returned that day we returned from Boma and...' (Digul Wambon, de Vries 1986: 47)

Subordination is marked and infrequent, compared to chaining linkage. Speakers go off the event line for specific reasons, to repair a mistake, to describe a referent to the addressee, to give background information relevant to the events on the event line, in short, conditions of discourse discontinuity. Clauses in subordinate linkage require an independent verb as head of the clause that selects its own tense and mood specification. They are not under the scope of the verb in the final clause. As Haiman (1985: 217) observed for Hua, it is the semantic independence given by independent verb forms in subordinate linkage that is characteristic for subordinate clauses in many Trans New Guinea languages, an independence that makes them suitable for offline tasks. And, conversely, it is the syntactic and semantic dependence of medial verbs (no independent TAM selection, for example) that makes them unsuitable for the offline tasks that speakers perform with clauses in subordinate linkage.

There are two contexts in Greater Awyu languages where we frequently find forms of subordination. First, in the initial paragraph(s) of narrative texts, where narrators introduce their topics, main characters, the time and place frames or setting of the story and other offline background material needed to get the story started. Consider the opening section of this Kombai text (see for the whole text de Vries 1993a: 106–108):

(244) [*Amaxalo xumolei=ro   mene*],   [*xe bo-xugi=ro*],
Amaxalo die.RLS[NON1SG=thing this(TOP)   he DUR-ill.RLS[NON1SG]=thing
[*dadagu   xe bo-xugi-n=o   ro   mofene*],   *xwai-migi*
first   he DUR-ill.RLS[NON1SG]=MOD thing TOP   demon-people
wa-luwano   wa-luwano]   *foro-moja-manone*
COM-say.RLS.NON1PL COM-say.RLS.NON1PL carry -descend-come.IMP.PL.
'As for the death of Amaxalo, when he was ill in the beginning, about his illness, the foreigners had said already, you have to bring him down.' (Kombai, de Vries 1993a: 106)

This text starts with three extra-clausal themes that contain relative clauses, headed by independent verbs, all offline. In Kombai, relative clauses used as extra-clausal themes have functions that correspond to adverbial clauses in English or Dutch (see §4.2.5.4). Demonstrative-based topic markers express the pragmatic function of the extra-clausal themes that present the topic of the story and its main participants.

The second context for subordinate linkage is in the initial zone of a clause chain, where speakers connect the new chain to the previous one. The default way to connect clause chains is to have a switch reference marked chained clause as the first clause of the new chain. But, occasionally and markedly, speakers use the chain-initial area to break the event line for specific purposes, e.g. provide background, carry out repairs or identify a referent that needs a lot of description for the addressee to identify it. In such cases, the chain is preceded by a subordinate clause with theme function.

The following Digul Wambon text provides an example of the use of subordinate linkage in discourse to reflect a break of the event line. Sentence (245b) is connected to (245a) by tail-head linkage (see §5.2.1). The first clause of (245b) does not have the default form of tail-head linkage, a chained recapitulative clause that marks switch rereference and is fully integrated in the syntax of the clause chain. But instead the repeated clause (245b) is placed in the extra-clausal theme slot, marked by the demonstrative-based topic marker =*eve*, in subordinate linkage, because the speaker breaks the event line (that continues in (245c)) to add a detail about the day that they travelled downriver to a spot in the (Digul) river where the water forms a whirlpool.

(245a) *Koiv=o   talom=o   mben=o   waxol=eve /*
        last=MOD year=MOD underarm=MOD[24] moon=TOP
        Mbonop-ŋgambun=ka   mbaxe-mbel=o / gerkaji   lavo-va
        Mbonop-whirlpool=CIRC sit[SS]SEQ=CNJ chainsaw take-1PL[IRR]
        ne-mbel=o[25]/   *ep=ka   mba-l-eva-mbo. #*
        say[SS]=SEQ=CNJ there=CIRC sit-RLS-1PL-PAST
        'Last year in July, we stayed at the Mbonop whirlpool to saw.'

(245b) *Ep=ka   mbalevambon=eve/   sanov=e*
        there=CIRC sit.RLS.1PL.PAST.LINK=TOP little.finger=CONN
        ilo-kalevembo#
        descend-go.RLS.1PL.PAST
        'Given that we stayed there, on Monday we went down (there).'

(245c) *Sanopkuniv=a/ jat-ke-lo   sanopkunvi=e*
        ringfinger=CONN light-be-SS ringfinger=CONN
        ilo- ŋgap-mo-knd-eva-n=o   ko   alip-ke-lo
        cut-do-PRES-1PL-LNK=CNJ go.down go[SS] afternoon-be-SS
        ndave-l-eva-mbo #
        return-RLS-1PL.PAST
        'On Tuesday we went down and cut (trees) until we returned in the late afternoon.' (Digul Wambon, de Vries and de Vries-Wiersma 1992: 86–87)

Demonstrative-based topic markers play a key role in marking subordinate linkage in Greater Awyu languages, both proximate and distal ones. For example, the Digul Wambon distal deictic =*eve* 'that' in (245b) marks the preceding clause as a topical, subordinate off-line clause. The Kombai proximate deictic *mene* 'this'/ 'here' marks subordinate thematic clauses that introduce the theme of the story (see (244)). Mandobo distal *mbo* 'that/there' marks off-line relative clauses (246) (=(27) from §9.2.2):

---

[24] The body parts in this section are used as numerals to denote days and months, e.g. underarm=seven, moon number seven, that is July. See §3.9.
[25] This is an example of quotative framing of purpose and intention, lit. saying 'let us take the chainsaw', see §5.3.

(246) ö   koujap reŋgi-ri itigio-gen   do   tagaŋ-gen,   mene
      dream   again   lie-SS   see-RLS[NON1SG]   CONN   say-RLS[NON1SG] now
      mb' orat ke-n   do,   tegep   mbo ri-gin
      TOP light do-[IRR]NON.SG CONN   nibung.palm   TOP stand-RLS[NON1SG]
      mbo oru-ko-non   ne-gen.
      TOP chop.down-put.in-IMP[SG]   say-RLS[NON1SG]
      'Again he had a dream in his sleep and someone said (in his dream):
      now when it will be light, chop down the *nibung* palm that stands there
      and put it in (the river)'

The relative clause modifier with the head noun *tegep* 'nibung palm' is bracketed
off from the main event line and marked as a subordinate off-line clause by the
double occurrence of *mbo* 'that' in (246). Drabbe (1959: 53) noticed that that there
is a pause after the head *tegep* and that *mbo rigin mbo* is spoken in one breath, in
other words the constituent is also intonationally bracketed off. This is also true
of other subordinate clauses: they are intonationally set apart from the main
event line.

Mandobo also uses the deictic-based topic marker to turn continuative
clauses with finite verb linked by the conjoining connective *do(ro)* into subordinate off-line clauses.

Tail-head linkage connects (247a) to (247b) and the recapitulated head clause
is turned off-line by *mbo* ('Given that it rained, . . . '.). The rain is a topical entity
in this story: it has multiple references and plays at least two key roles in the
story. The rain causes the small stream in the middle of the valley to become a
big river that blocks their return home but the heavy and persistent rain also
forms a cover for the crocodile to approach the house of Nggou undetected.

(247a) *Tarap togo-mba-gen   do   wemin ge-r-an   do*
       hut   enter-sit-RLS[NON1SG] CONN   night be-RLS[NON1SG]-PAST CONN
       raŋ-gen   do,   wemin ge-r-an   do
       lie-RLS[NON1SG] CONN   night be-RLS[NON1SG]-PAST CONN
       komöt   ŋgoŋgwan-gen,   murüp-ke-gen.
       thunderstorm break.out-RLS[NON1SG] rain be-RLS[NON1SG]
       'He went into the hut, it became night, they ate sago, slept, and in the
       night, there was a thunderstorm and it rained.'

(247b) *Ke-gen   do   mbo teet ke-gen.*
       be-RLS[NON1SG] CONN TOP day   be-RLS[NON1SG]
       'It kept raining until the next day.'

(247c) Matero itigiogen   do   mbügiarop mbo og   goneni
       get.up see.RLS[NON1SG] CONN valley   TOP river Big
       anema.gen
       block.off.RLS[NON1SG]
       'When he got up, the valley, a big river blocked it.'

Finally, *mbo* is used as topic marker with resumptive pronouns resuming extra-clausal themes:

(248) *Kiambot, ege mbo ndombakne-korü-gen.*
      crocodile 3SG TOP dive-go.down-RLS[NON1SG]
      'The crocodile, he submerged.'

Chapter 5
Discourse

5.1 Introduction

Greater Awyu texts show a number of characteristic patterns of language use that struck the earliest students of these languages as significant (Drabbe 1955, 1957, 1959; Healy 1964): recapitulative linking, quotative framing, distribution of arguments over series of clauses to reduce syntactic complexity, thematization, the preference to use verbs in mini clauses to carry out a wide range of grammatical functions and the tendency in verbal semantics to break down an action into its component actions. It is a heterogeneous set of patterns, with different functions in various domains. None of them are unique to New Guinea or to Papuan languages but they co-occur with striking frequency in this linguistic area (Heeschen 1998, de Vries 2005; 2006; Foley 1986; Foley 2000).

That high frequency in language use is also the basis for various conventionalization processes in individual Papuan languages which turned some of these discourse patterns into grammatical constructions, for example experiential (de Vries 2006) and comparative constructions (Schapper and de Vries 2018). These constructions also link Greater Awyu languages to other language families of New Guinea, that are genetically distinct but that have similar developments from frequent patterns in language use to grammatical constructions.

First, recapitulative linkage is discussed (§5.2), followed by quotative framing (§5.3). The representation of emotion is discussed in §5.4 and argument distribution in §5.5. §5.6 is about thematization and this includes adverbial, relative and experiential clauses. The topic of §5.7 is tracking of topical participants. §5.8 discusses the tendency in verbal semantics to break down actions into sequences of clauses denoting sub actions. §5.9 summarizes this chapter.

5.2 Recapitulative linkage

5.2.1 Tail-head linkage

Speakers of Greater Awyu languages prefer to link clause chains by repeating the final clause of the chain, the tail-clause, as the first clause of the next, the head clause (de Vries 2005). The repetition of the final clause may be done partially or completely. This strategy to create coherent discourse, especially in the area of referent and event continuity, is an areal phenomenon of New Guinea, areal not in the sense that tail-head linkage connections do not occur outside New Guinea but in terms of the high frequency and unmarked nature of this discourse device in New Guinea. Tail-head linkage has key discourse functions in referent continuity and event continuity, especially in narrative texts. It also has processing functions, especially in contexts of long narrative clause chains that consist of many mini clauses. The Mandobo text of §9.2.2 has numerous examples of tail-head linkage.

The recapitulative head clause has a characteristic intonation contour, with a rise towards the end and a slowed pronunciation, in both types of tail-head linkage. This intonation contour reflects the pause function of tail-head linkage: the speaker gets the time to process his next clause chain, while the addressees can process the information of the previous one. Often we find pauses or pause markers after the head clause in a tail-head linkage (de Vries 2005: 378).

There are two types of tail-head linkage in Papuan languages, continuative and discontinuative tail-head linkage and both occur in texts of Greater Awyu languages (de Vries 2005: 377). In continuative tail-head linkage (249a)–(249c), the repeated initial clause is a chained clause, syntactically integrated in the new chain as its first clause. When the repeated initial clause is a chained clause, with switch reference marking, switch reference monitoring of participants is continued across the boundary of the clause chain.

In discontinuative tail-head linkage (250b), the initial, repeated clause is an extra-clausal theme, not a syntactic part of the new clause chain, with an independent verb that does not express switch reference. Switch reference tracking of topical participants is disrupted across the boundary of the two clause chains.

Consider the following stretch of discourse from a Korowai text published by van Enk and de Vries (1997: 159–160), with three clause chains, linked by continuative tail-head linkage:

(249a) *Wof=è   gol   ül-ma-té=daxu   bando-lu   xaim=an*
there=CONN pig kill-do-[RLS]NON1PL=SS carry-enter treehouse=LOC
fe-nè   fu   bume-ma-té
get-SS put slaughter-HAB-NON1PL[RLS]
'After they have killed a pig there, they usually bring it and to the tree house and slaughter it.'

(249b) *Bume-ma-té=daxu   ol   di   fe-nè*
slaughter-HAB-[RLS]NON1PL=SS faeces get.out[SS] take-SS

> *fu-ma-té=do*   *ni-xü=to*   *bando-xe-nè*
> put-HAB-NON1PL[RLS]=DS mother-PL=FOC bring-go-SS
> *ao-ma-té*
> cleanse-HAB-NON1PL[RLS]
> 'They slaughter it and remove the faeces and put it down and the women take (the intestines) and cleanse it.'

(249c) *Ao-leful-mexo*   *xaim*   *gilfo-ma-té=do*
cleanse-end-do[SS] treehouse go.away-HAB-NON1PL[RLS]=DS
gol-e-xal   *di*   *fu-ma-té*
pig-LNK-meat cut put-HAB-NON1PL[RLS]
'When they have finished washing, they go away to the treehouse and (the males) cut the pig meat out and put it down.'
                                 (Korowai, van Enk and de Vries 1997: 159–160)

The final clause of the chain (249b) is recapitulated by tail-head linkage in the dependent verb SS clause *aolefulmexo* 'having cleansed' in (249c). In continuative linkage of (249b) to (249c) there is continuity of switch reference monitoring of participants, because the final verb of the tail clause in (249b), *ao-ma-té*, that has no switch reference, is repeated as a medial SS verb in the chained head clause of (249c) that does have a switch reference marking *ao-leful-mexo*.

The same type of continuative tail-head linkage created an unbroken event- and participant line in the transition from (249a) to (249b). We saw an example of discontinuative tail-head linkage at the end of the last chapter, where switch reference and event lines are broken (see (245a)–(245c) and discussion there), repeated here:

(250a) *Koiv=o*   *talom=o*   *mben=o*   *waxol=eve* /
last=MOD year=MOD underarm=MOD[26] moon=TOP
Mbonop-ŋgambun=ka   *mbaxe-mbel=o* / *gerkaji*   *lavo-va*
Mbonop-whirlpool=CIRC sit[SS]SEQ=CNJ chainsaw take-1PL[IRR]
ne-mbel=o[27] /   *ep=ka*   *mba-l-eva-mbo.* #
say[SS]=SEQ=CNJ there=CIRC sit-RLS-1PL-PAST
'Last year in July, we stayed at the Mbonop whirlpool to saw.'

---

26 The body parts in this section are used as numerals to denote days and months, e.g. underarm=seven, moon number seven, that is July. See §3.9.

27 This is an example of quotative framing of purpose and intention, lit. 'saying let us take the chainsaw', see §5.3.

(250b) Ep=ka   mbalevambon=eve/   sanov=e
      there=CIRC sit RLS.1PL.PAST.LINK=TOP little.finger=CONN
      ilo-kalevembo #
      descend-GO.RLS.1PL.PAST
      'Given that we stayed there, on Monday we went down (there).'

(250c) Sanopkuniv=a/   jat-ke-lo   sanopkunvi=e   Ilo
       ringfinger=CONN light-be-SS   ringfinger=CONN go.down
       ŋgap-mo-knd-eva-n=o   ko   alip-ke-lo   ndave-l-eva-mbo #
       cut-do-PRES-1PL-LNK=CNJ go[SS   afternoon-be-SS return-RLS-1PL.PAST
       'On Tuesday we went down and cut (trees) until we returned in the late afternoon.'   (Digul Wambon, de Vries and de Vries-Wiersma (1992: 86–87))

The speaker interrupts the event line in (250b) by the off line thematic recapitulative clause *epka mba-levambon=eve* that is marked by the topic marker *=eve* and syntactically nor intonationally a constituent of the following clause chain.

Tail-head linkage also connects imperative clause chains that are under the mood scope of their imperative final verbs and this is relatively uncommon in Papuan languages with tail-head linkage. For example in Korowai (251b) and Mandobo (e.g. (67)/(68) in §9.2.2):

(251a) wof-e=xa   mbolow=è   ge-mba-mbam-pexo   if-e=xa
       there-LNK=MOD   ancestor=VOC   your-child-child-COMIT this-LNK=CONN
       bando xe-nè lé-m=é
       carry go-SS eat-IMP.2SG=EXCL
       'Oh forefather over there, with your children, you should take this and eat it!'

(251b) lé-m=daxu   noxup   dél=o   füon=o
       eat-IMP.2SG=SS   1PL   bird=COORD   marsupial.species=COORD
       gol=o   fédo-m=do   le-fén=è
       pig-COORD   give-IMP.2SG=DS   eat-IMP.1PL=EXCL
       'Eat and give birds and marsupials and pigs for us to eat!'
                              (Korowai, van Enk and de Vries 1997: 159–162):

5.2.2 Generic verb linkage

Closely related to tail-head linkage is generic verb linkage (de Vries 2005: 376–377; de Vries 2019). But where tail-head linkage is a bridging construction that links two successive clause chains, by verbatim repetition, generic verb linkage links the clause chain to the preceding discourse in a more open way. The preceding discourse may be just the immediately preceding clause chain (as in (252b)) but also the preceding episode or even the story as a whole. Instead of verbatim recapitulation, generic verb linkage employs generic verbs of doing or being to link clause chains, often with deictic elements that have been verbalized with these generic verbs of doing or being.

For example, Yonggom Wambon has a deictic *e* 'that' which is verbalized with *mo* 'to do', resulting in the deictic verb *emo* 'to do that'. The medial SS form *emoro* is used in generic verb linkage in Yonggom Wambon, see (6c) in §3.1. By choosing a medial SS form of the deictic verb, the speaker indicates continuity of the subject referents and of the event line across the boundary between two clause chains. Consider this Digul Wambon example of generic verb linkage:

(252a) *Mituxup ali-knd-eva-n=o   kit-mbe=te /   maŋgo=te*
       all   wrap.in.leaves-RLS-1PL-LNK=CNJ finish-SEQ[SS]=CNJ jaw=FOC
       lava-l-ep-o. #
       take-RLS-1SG-PAST
       'I wrapped it all in leaves and then took the jaw.' (Lit. I wrapped it all in leaves until it was finished and then I took the jaw)

(252b) *Ja-mo-mbelo /   ketop   kenop   selem=ka /   ja-mo   jaxop*
       thus-do-SS.SEQ in.their.turn hindleg other.side=on thus-do[SS] them
       hala-l-ev=o /   ja-mo   ande-l-e-mbo. #
       put.down-RLS-1SG[DS]=CNJ   thus.do[SS] eat-RLS-NON1PL-PAST
       'Having done so, I gave them in their turn the other hindleg and they ate.'
                         (Digul Wambon, de Vries and de Vries-Wiersma 1992: 93–94)

Clause chain (252b) is connected to the preceding one by generic verb linkage with the verb *jamo-* 'to do thus/that'. The form used here is a medial form expressing switch reference (SS) and temporality (sequence) and this is a form of continuative linkage of clause chains. The generic linkage verbs are also often used as discourse conjunctions, for example *jamo* also occurs twice within (252b).

Generic verb linkage is a context in which generic verb forms may petrify into invariant discourse conjunctions that lose all or most of their verbal properties. Consider the next Kombai example, with a generic verb form *mana* 'he did' linking (253a) and (253b). Kombai is one of the Greater Awyu languages in which the use of independent verbs in conjoined sequences of clauses implies a switch of subject reference. If the linkage verb was still fully verbal, a plural form *manona* 'they did' would have been expected. The singular form *mana* has become an invariable discourse conjunction (de Vries 1993a: 73):

(253a) *Xumolei-n=a   ifama-no.*
　　　 die.NON1SG[RLS]-LNK=CNJ[DS] bury-[RLS]NON1PL
　　　 'He died and they buried him.'

(253b) *Man=a   xwai-migi   mene   waluwano:*
　　　 do[RLS.NON1SG]LNK=CNJ [DS] demon- PL   TOP   COM. say RLS.NON1PL[DS]
　　　 'Thus they did and the foreigners said:. . .'

(Kombai, de Vries 1993a: 108)

Just as in tail-head linkage, generic verb linkage creates a pause between the two clause chains, for the speaker to process his next string of mini-clauses and for the addressee to process the information.

5.3 Quotative framing

Greater Awyu speakers strongly prefer direct speech over indirect speech when they report what others said. This is not uncommon in Papuan language families, especially of Trans New Guinea. In fact, quite a few grammatical descriptions note the complete absence of indirect speech in their texts or even languages. Drabbe (1959: 23, 137) claims that Mandobo and Yonggom Wambon do not have indirect discourse. Similarly, de Vries (1993a) discusses the possible absence of indirect forms in Kombai. See also Wilson (1988: 46) for Yali, Murane (1974) for Daga, and Bromley (1981: 271) for Lower Grand Valley Dani. In Amele indirect speech is possible but rare (Reesink 1993: 218). Greater Awyu speakers not only have a strong preference to use direct speech in reporting the speech of others but also as a frame for a wide of range of meanings in the areas of intention, cognition, emotion, perception, indirect causation.

Early descriptions of Papuan languages (Healy, Drabbe) noticed the phenomenon of quotative framing. For example, Drabbe (1955: 133) wrote: "Notice how the thought, the motive is represented by direct speech"[28]. Drabbe (1957: 85) observes that in the Awyu language Aghu "*numo-gh,* to say thus, means here: to say

---

[28] Drabbe (1955: 133): "let erop hoe men de gedachte, het motief weergeeft in de directe rede".

thus to oneself, or: to think thus[29]". Healey (1964: 29) notices the use of quotative clauses in Telefol with 'to say, think, see, know, feel' and calls the use of direct speech forms for the expression of non-verbalized thought 'direct cerebration'.

The use of direct speech forms to represent thought, emotion and intention implies that first person subjects occur in the quoted "inner speech" (Reesink 1993), as the direct speech clause has its own deictic center (he said, I want to build a house=He wanted to build a house). Quotative framing is probably an universal phenomenon (Pascual 2014). However, in its highly conventionalized and grammaticalized forms, it has been reported to occur especially in Papuan languages, e.g. Telefol (Healy 1964), Amele, Usan (Reesink 1993), Mandobo (Drabbe 1959), Kombai (de Vries 1993a) and in the native languages of South-America (e.g. Aguaruna, Larson 1978; Kwaza, Van der Voort 2002; Quechua, Adelaar 1990).

By far the most frequent use of quotative framing in Greater Awyu languages (and more generally in Papuan languages with quotative framing) is to express intention, as in these examples (de Vries 1993a: 97):

(254a) *Ran   e-neti   ŋgou   a   gokmo mbendit kiambot teembo*
woman her-father Nggou belly be.hot bow   crocodile shoot
wo-gen   doro kiambot matere tima-gen
do-RLS[NON1SG] CONN crocodile rise   take-RLS[NON1SG]
'The woman's father Nggou stood up, was angry, took his bow and wanted to shoot the crocodile, but the crocodile forbade it.' (from Drabbe's Mandobo text, see (108) in §9.2.2)

(254b) *Yarimo xo   fera-f-e-ne*
garden go[SS] see-1SG. INT-CONN-QUOTE.SG
'He wants to see his garden.' (Lit. He goes saying "I want to see my garden")
(Kombai, de Vries 1993a: 97)

(255) *Koiv=o   talom=o   mben=o   waxol=eve /*
last=MOD year=MOD underarm=MOD[30] moon=TOP
Mbonop-ŋgambun=ka   mbaxe-mbel=o / gerkaji   lavo-va
Mbonop-whirlpool=CIRC sit[SS]-SEQ=CNJ   chainsaw take-[IRR].1PL

---

29 Drabbe (1957: 85): "*numo-gh aldus zeggen, betekent hier: aldus tot zichzelf zeggen, of: aldus denken*".
30 The body parts in this example are used as numerals to denote days and months, e.g. underarm=seven, moon number seven, that is July. See §3.7.

ne-mbel=o/   ep=ka   mba-l-eva-mbo. #
say-SS.SEQ=CNJ there=CIRC sit-RLS-1PL-PAST
'Last year in July, we stayed at the Mbonop whirlpool (with the intention) to saw.'   (Digul Wambon, de Vries and de Vries-Wiersma 1992: 86)

(256) *Nu ai   galemo-fo   ne-ra   wa-me-de*
      I   pig buy-1PL.IRR say-SS COM-come-1SG[RLS]
      'I have come to buy the pig.'   (Kombai, de Vries 1993a: 96)

When motion verbs are used in purposive contexts, Kombai must use quotative framing, as in (256) and this shows how such patterns of language use may conventionalize into obligatory grammatical patterns in certain contexts.

But Kombai, and Greater Awyu languages in general, also uses quotative framing to express thinking (257) and emotion (258).

(257) *Yafo-fina   wa-xumo-lei   neno*
      their-thought COM-die-lie[RLS.NON1SG] QUOTE.PL
      'They think that he has already died.' (Lit.: Their thought, 'he has already died' they said).   (Kombai, de Vries 1993a: 98)

(258) *Xarabuma-no   fene-mo-ra ma-xe-y-e-ne*[31]
      be.astonished-[RLS]NON1PL how-do-SS do-Q-LNK-CONN-QUOTE.SG
      'They were astonished because of the things he did.' (Lit.: They were astonished 'he does how and he does this?' they said)
                                            (Kombai, de Vries 1993a: 98)

This Mandobo example shows similar use of quotative framing triggered by emotion expressions:

(259) *Anema-gen   doro irupma-gen   kenemop kej'o*
      block.off-RLS[NON1SG] CNJ   be.amazed- RLS[NON1SG] what   Q
      ne-gen.
      say-RLS[NON1SG]

---

31 The second occurrence of the verb *mo* 'to do' shows the use of this verb as an independent verb, with the lexical meaning 'to do; to make'. The first occurrence shows one of the grammatical functions of *mo*: to turn words of other categories into verbs which can be used in mini clauses that enable speakers to distribute arguments over clauses (see §3.6.1 and §5.5). Here it is the question-word argument that receives its own mini clause.

'It was blocked and this amazed him.' (Lit. it (the valley) was blocked and so he was amazed, What is this, he said/thought.) (Mandobo, see (9) of §9.2.2)

The Kombai quote-markers *neno/nene/ne* are fossilized forms of a verb of speaking that is never used as an independent verb. But other Greater Awyu languages use their regular verb of speaking to mark direct speech, whether used to report direct speech or in contexts of reported intention, emotion and thought, e.g. the Korowai verb *de* 'to say' (260) or Yonggom Wambon *nde* (261).

(260) *Noxu Lalop   dade-fun-de=nè   xai-mba-lè.*
we Lalop.river swim-1PL. INT=say[SS] go-DUR-[RLS]1PL
'We are going to swim in the Lalop river.'
(Korowai, van Enk and de Vries 1997: 105)

(261) *Natew   ui   te   nde-gen-ep*
perhaps pig COP say-RLS-1SG
'I thought that it was perhaps a pig.'   (Yonggom Wambon, Drabbe 1959: 137)

To disambiguate between reported speech and reported thought (or "inner speech"), speakers may add references to the seat of emotion and cognition, when quotative framing is used to denote emotion, cognition or intention. For example, the reference to *fi-melon* 'guts' in Korowai (262), serves to indicate that inner states of others are described, not what someone said (de Vries 2013: 129):

(262) *Dajo-menél   ye-fi-melon   nu   if=è   Muxalé*
Dajo-young.girl her-belly-gall 1SG this=CONN Muxalé
duo=tofexo   él   y-afé-da-é   nu   Muxalé=lo
shoot[RLS.NON1SG]=DS yes his-older.brother-NEG-EXCL 1SG Muxalé=FOC
fo-p   xelüf=é   de
marry-1SG. INT desire=EXCL say[RLS.NON1SG]
'The Dajo girl thought 'I really don't want to marry the older brother, I badly want to marry Muxale.'   (Korowai, van Enk and de Vries 1997: 207)

5.4 Representation of emotion in discourse

To understand the background of the way emotions of others (as in (262)) are portrayed in Korowai discourse, it is important to know that Korowai speakers talk about emotions of others, such as anger or sadness, in two contrasting ways, from the inside perspective and from a performative, outside perspective.

When the emotion is manifested in visible and audible behavior, and performed following cultural scripts (e.g. feeling sad about the loss of a beloved person by smearing ash and dirt on the face and by singing laments), the emotion is a publicly known and observable fact and statements about such emotions are not seen as problematic (see for extensive examples and discussion, de Vries 2013: 117–122).

But when the emotions of others are invisible and inaudible and located in the "guts" of people, their inner center of emotion and thought, talking about these inner emotions of others is socially more risky. Korowai people have strong beliefs about the opacity of other minds (Stasch 2008b), not uncommon in Melanesian societies (see the opacity of mind discussion in Melanesian anthropology in Robbins and Rumsey 2008). The inner world of other people is uncertain and difficult to fathom (Stasch 2008b: 395). People may hide their true thoughts and emotions. Talking about what goes on in the "guts" of other people may be perceived as a threat to individual autonomy and dignity and may have all sorts of consequences for the relationships in the community.

This does not mean that Korowai speakers do not engage in such talk but when they do, they always use quotative framing means to signal that they talk about the emotions of others from the uncertain inside perspective, as in (262), with optional but frequent addition of expressions referring to internal organs of the belly (intestines, gall) (de Vries 2013: 121), for example *ye-fi-melon* in (262), her-intestines-gall. These references to the guts have two functions, first to reinforce the signal given by quotative framing that the speaker talks about the inner emotional movements of other people, not about externalized, performed emotions; and second, to disambiguate the two meanings of the verbs of saying that are used in quotative framing, viz. speaking (locutionary acts, uttering words) and thinking (inner speech). When the idioms are used that refer to the inner organs of the belly (intestines, gall), the verb of speaking means 'to think, to feel'. A frequent idiom to denote the inner emotional or thinking activity is the verb *duo-* 'to shoot' that takes nouns referring to organs in the belly as objects, for example in (262) Dajo 'shoots' her intestines-gall.

5.5 Argument distribution

Greater Awyu speakers prefer to have maximally one argument, whether peripheral or core, to be overtly expressed in a clause, as so many other Papuan speakers (Foley 1986: 170). It is a tendency not confined to New Guinea but has also been observed for Sacapultec Maya speakers (Du Bois 1987: 83–834) and for San languages (Wundt 1911). Heeschen (1998: 48–54), who showed the impact of this tendency on the grammar of Eipomek, described it as distribution because the tendency to have no more than one modifier per nominal phrase or clause leads to systematic distribution of nominals over series of clauses and of modifiers over serialized phrases. Foley (2000: 385) describes the effects of this tendency in Papuan languages as follows:

> (a) There is a relatively high ratio of verbs to nominals, at least compared to the literate styles of European languages [. . .](b) Given or presupposed information is normally omitted and independent pronouns which are rarely employed, have a contrastive force. (c) Only one piece of new information is introduced per clause. The net effect of these tendencies is to establish for the great majority of right-headed Papuan languages a structure like [(XP)V] as the normative clausal unit in wider stretches of text.

Notice that the mini clauses of the [(XP) V] type do not as a rule constitute intonation units in the sense of Chafe (1994) and the tendency to distribute arguments over a series of clauses seems to be primarily related to the avoidance of syntactic complexity rather than to information distribution within intonation units. Argument distribution is a discourse preference, not a grammatical constraint and clauses with two or three overt lexical arguments do occur in languages with a preference for argument distribution. Such clauses are marked and will be found in specific contexts. For example Heeschen (1998: 308) found Eipomek clauses with multiple lexical argument in summarizing and concluding sections of narratives.

Foley (2000) was not the first to suggest a link with oral speech and the incremental left-to-right processing constraints in the production of speech as opposed to writing. Heeschen (1998: 8) made the same connection, pointing to the work of Levelt (1989) on incremental production in speech, who in his turn refers to Wundt (1911) who already observed the possible link between processing constraints in speech and the form of clauses in San texts.

The overwhelming majority of clauses in Greater Awyu texts conforms to this preferred clause structure. Speakers use various strategies to keep their clauses in the preferred shape. Given participants are preferably tracked by verb agreements and switch reference rather than by anaphoric pronouns. Another strategy, discussed in this section, is argument distribution.

When a monoclausal construction would necessitate speakers to violate the [[XP] V] constraint, both core and peripheral or adjunct arguments are distributed over multiple clauses. Consider this Kombai example, where the speaker expresses the time setting in a separate mini clause:

(263) *Be-rei-xe-n=a*　　　　　　　　　*nu　meda*
　　　DUR-sun-become[NON1SG]-LNK=CNJ[DS]　1SG　come[IRR.1SG]
　　　'Tomorrow I will come.' (Lit. the sun rises and I will come)
　　　　　　　　　　　　　　　　　　　　　　(Kombai, de Vries 1993a: 16)

Perception verbs use chained biclausal constructions with the perceiver and the action of perceiving expressed in the first clause and the perceived event in the second clause. Again avoidance of syntactic complexity drives this strategy, avoiding the expression of the perceived event as a "heavy" clausal object of the verb *imo-* 'to see'.
　　Korowai:

(264) *Muxalé　yu　imo=tofexo　　　y-afé　　　élo-bo*
　　　Muxalé　he　see[RLS.NON1SG]=DS　his-brother　sleep-be[RLS.NON1SG]
　　　'Muxalé, he saw that his older brother was asleep.' (Lit. 'Muxale he saw and (DS) his brother was asleep')
　　　　　　　　　　　　　　　　　(Korowai, van Enk and de Vries 1997: 189)

(265) *Naerop　ju　taep　me　　etaga-t　　　　te　amun*
　　　Naerop　3SG　also　come[SS]　see-RLS[NON1SG]　CNJ　cuscus
　　　mba-gen
　　　sit-RLS[NON1SG]
　　　'Naerop he also came and saw that there was a cuscus.'
　　　　　　　　　　　　　　　　　　　(Yonggom Wambon, Drabbe 1959: 147)

Similar conjoining of clauses with the percept clause following the perception clause occur in several Papuan language families, in Mian, an Ok language (Wegener 2008: 278), Manambu of the Ndu family (Aikhenvald 2008: 556), Inanwatan of the South Bird's Head family (De Vries 2004: 58), Usan (Numugenan family, Reesink 2008: 883), Hua (Yagaria family; Haiman 1980; Reesink 2008: 883), Amele (Roberts 1987: 183) and Koromu (Reesink 2008: 88). In Moskona of the East Bird's Head family (Gravelle 2010: 339), Hatam (Reesink 2008: 880) and Maybrat (Dol 1999), both of the West Bird's Head family, serial verb constructions express the perception and percept events.

　　In line with the [(XP) V] constraint, Greater Awyu speakers also distribute the standard argument and comparee of comparative constructions over two clauses (267). But they can also choose to let their addressees contextually infer their comparative intentions, as in (266). Drabbe (1959: 119) observes about Yonggom Wambon: "Concerning the expression of comparative and superlative, for example *Juw e kamaeop te* may mean 'he is big', 'he is bigger' or 'he is the biggest' dependent on the context".³² Korowai uses intensifying adverbs that intensify adjectives with strong meanings to trigger superlative readings:

(266) *Juw=e   kamae-op*
     he=CONN big-ADJ
     'He is big (or: bigger, or biggest).'   (Korowai, van Enk and de Vries 1997: 71)

When comparee and standard arguments are both overtly expressed, they must be distributed over two juxtaposed clauses, as in the Korowai example (29), repeated from (35) in chapter 3:

(267) [*if-e=xa   abül=efè*] COMPAREE *xoŋgél=xayan* [*waf-e=xa*
     this-LNK=MOD man=TOP   big=very   that-LNK=MOD
     abül]STANDARD *be-xoŋgé-tebo-da*
     man   NEG-big-be[RLS.NON1SG]-NEG
     'This man is very big, that man is not big' (contextually derived reading: 'this man is bigger than that man.')   (Korowai, van Enk and de Vries 1997: 71).

The Korowai biclausal conjoined comparative construction is found in most, if not all Trans New Guinea subfamilies of central and south coast New Guinea (Schapper and de Vries 2018).

5.6 Thematization

Greater Awyu speakers prefer [theme, predication] expressions of the type 'that man, he is my father' (de Vries 2006). Heeschen (1998) used the term thematization for this tendency. Of course, many, if not all human languages use this strategy to separate a theme syntactically and intonationally from the sentence that follows but Papuan speakers really "overdo" it and this has led to the rise of families of constructions in grammars that are frozen thematizations, e.g. the well-known and very widespread Papuan thematic conflated adverbial/relative clause structure (Foley 1986: 201), or the "domain-creating constructions" of Reesink (1994).

    The high frequency and conventionalization of this pattern of language use also causes speakers in many cases to reduce the intonational separation of the

---

32 "Wat betreft het uitdrukken van comparatief en superlatief kan bv. *Juw e kamaeop te* naargelang de samenhang betekenen: hij is groot, hij is groter, of hij is de grootste".

extra-clausal theme and eventually also the syntactic separation and this creates a cline of clearly extra-clausal themes, intonationally and syntactically not part of the next clause (368), to intermediate cases where the intonational separation is reduced but syntactic integration in the next clauses seems not yet complete, for example in (264) and (265) *Muxalé* and *Naerop* and finally to fully integrated formerly extra-clausal themes, e.g. *nu* 'I' in (270).

In the case of Papuan "adverbial/relative" constructions, the thematization strategy is applied to a finite clause and the result can be paraphrased as 'Given this state of affairs x, I say (ask, command, etc.) y' (de Vries 2006: 815; Wester 2014: 152). Conditional constructions of Greater Awyu languages are examples of structures that have their origin in thematization processes, as in many other Papuan languages (Haiman 1978). Consider these Digul Wambon examples of extra-clausal theme clauses with a conditional (268) and a temporal reading (269).

(268) *Kixuv=e   nde-t   ke-xe-l=eve*[33]*/   eve*
    Digul=CONN   come-RLS[NON1SG]   be-be-RLS[NON1SG]=TOP   then
    Maŋgelum   ko-noksi-va
    Manggelum   go-NEG-[IRR]1PL
    'If the Digul rises, then we won't go to Manggelum.' (Lit. Given that the Digul comes, given that that is the case, then/in that case we will not go to Manggelum)
                              (Digul Wambon, de Vries and de Vries-Wiersma 1992: 31)

(269) *Simson=e   nde-t-mbo-n=eve   nexo-salip=e   wasi*
    Simson=CONN   come-RLS[NON1SG]-PAST=TOP   his-wife=CONN   already
    ande-t-mbo
    eat-RLS[NON1SG]-PAST
    'When Simson arrived, his wife had already eaten.'
                              (Digul Wambon, Jang 2008: 86; Wester 2014: 153)

Another construction that probably owes its existence to thematizing preferences of Greater Awyu speakers is the experiential construction, with the human experiencer as a clause-initial topic followed by a transitive or intransitive clause with a body-part as S or A and a verb that agrees with those third person

---

[33] Digul Wambon and Yonggom speakers use a form of the verb *ke* 'to be'/'to become' in thematic conditional constructions (Drabbe 1959: 142).

singular A or S body-part nouns, e.g. Kombai (270), Digul Wambon (271) and Yonggom Wambon (272):

(270) *Nu   rere   bo-mari*
      1SG   blood   DUR-go.down[RLS.NON1SG]
      'I am bleeding.'   (Lit. me blood is going down) (Kombai, de Vries 1993a: 16)

(271) *nuk   ot   wa-ghe-ghe*
      1SG   stomach   hot-be-RLS[NON1SG]
      'I am hungry.'   (Digul Wambon, Jang 2008: 23)

(272) *nu   enow   i-r-an*
      1SG   fever   hit-RLS[NON1SG]-PAST
      'I had fever.'   (Yonggom Wambon, Drabbe 1959: 143)

The human experiencer is most probably originally an extra-clausal theme that got integrated in the experiential clause as topic (de Vries 2006: 814–815). This would explain the similarity in structure between transitive (272) and intransitive experiential clauses (270) and (271). In (272) *nu* is not a direct object of the transitive verb (as shown by its position: objects do not precede subjects in Greater Awyu languages) and in (270) *nu* is not the subject of the intransitive verb (as shown by the lack of agreement) but in both cases *nu* is the topical human experiencer in an experiential construction where the topical experiencer is followed by an inanimate subject and a 3rd person verb which agrees with the non-topical subject (de Vries 2006: 814).

Finally, conventionalized thematization seems to have been the basis for the development of "double-headed" relative clauses in some Greater Awyu languages (see §4.2.5.4).

5.7 Tracking of topical participants

Greater Awyu narrators track topical discourse participants that are activated in the mind of the addressees (normally two at a time, rarely three) in the overwhelming majority of cases by verbal means subject person-number agreement and switch of subject reference. The grammatical subject is the topic of the clause. But the clausal topic is not always the discourse topic (that is, some clauses are about entities that occur only once in the story or are otherwise non-topical from a discourse perspective. Examples would be weather clauses ('rain came down' or time clauses ('darkness fell')).

5.7 Tracking of topical participants

Greater Awyu languages have a number of strategies to solve conflicts between discourse topicality and clausal topicality. Digul Wambon switch reference ignores such non-discourse topical subjects, that is: although grammatically there is a different subject, it is a non-topical or background subject and switches to such subjects do not count as different subjects. Another strategy is the use of switch reference neutral forms in such cases (see §3.6.1.4 for these strategies). Yet, other Greater Awyu languages seem to be more oriented towards switches of all syntactic subjects in their switch reference operation, irrespective of their discourse topicality. Mandobo for example uses finite verbs (=DS signaling verbs) also before clauses with non-topical subjects, e.g. *wemin* 'darkness', *komöt* 'thunderstorm' and *murüp* 'rain' in (273):

(273) *Tarap togo mba-gen do, wemin ge-r-an do,*
hut go.in stay-RLS[NON1SG] CNJ night e-RLS[NON1SG]-PAST CONN
ndu ane raŋ-gen do wemin ge-r-an do
sago eat lie-RLS[NON1SG] CNJ Night be-RLS[NON1SG]-PAST CNJ
komöt ŋgoŋwan-gen, murüp ke-gen.
thunderstorm break.out-RLS[NON1SG] rain be-RLS[NON1SG]
'He went into the hut, it became night, they ate sago, slept, and in the night, there was a thunderstorm and it rained.'
(Mandobo, §9.2.2 (6), from Drabbe (1959: 50–60)).

Personal pronouns are avoided to track given, topical participants, especially in chaining paragraphs connected by tail-head linkage. Generally, the use of personal pronouns occurs in discontinuative contexts: e.g. to resume extra-clausal themes, to mark a topical participant as contrastive with other participants. Consider this example from the Mandobo text in §9.2.2. Nggou is the main character of the story cycle but in this passage his wife and daughter travel with him and form minor characters. They are referred to as a topical collective in (274a) by the 2nd /3rd person plural suffix – *on* of the verbs. In (274b), Nggou is the only topical participant and the addressees are given two clues, a grammatical one combined with one from the cultural context assumed to be known by the audience. The verbal agreement switches from plural to singular in (274b) and it is the task of the men to construct a shelter for the night when people have not reached their destination after nightfall. Nggou is continued as topical participant by tail-head linkage in (274c) but then in (274d) Nggou is contrasted to wife and daughter by the use of the 3SG personal pronoun and the topic marker *mbo*. There is no tail-head linkage because the wife and daughter are discontinued as active participants at this crucial point in the story: it is

Nggou and only he who goes off to cleanse the pig stomach, wife and daughter stay behind. The story is now about Nggou and the stomach of the pig. By mentioning the cleaning, addressees know that Nggou goes off searching for a stream or pool.

(274a) *Orumop me-gen-on   wüop   me-gen-on   do, wemin*
       back   come-RLS-NON1PL middle come-RLS-NON1PL CNJ night
       ge-gen.
       be-RLS[NON1SG]
       'They (=Nggou, his second wife and their daughter) came back, they came halfway and the night fell.' (=In the middle of their return journey home, the night fell (and this forced Nggou to make a shelter for the night.))

(274b) *Rogo   rüo   mbügiarop tarap ti-gen.*
       go.downhill go.down valley   hut   build-RLS[NON1SG]
       'He went down to a valley and built a hut.'

(274c) *Tarap Ti   amboto e-metip   e-aŋgen   In*
       Hut   Build Finish 3SG.POSS-daughter 3SG.POSS-wife Firewood
       küomo-ro- me-ro   In   mbo köŋ-gen-on.
       break-take- come-ss Fire TOP build-RLS-NON1PL
       'When he finished building a shelter, his daughter and his wife collected firewood, brought it and built a fire.'

(274d) *Ege mbo u-j-ogömö   tiri   korö   mbügiarop wüop*
       he TOP pig-LNK-stomach   clean   go.down   valley   middle
       ro   kaoma-gen.
       put.down   divide.in.two-RLS[NON1SG]
       'But he went to rinse the pig stomach, went down to the middle of the valley, put it (stomach) down and divided it in half.'

(Mandobo, from Drabbe 1959: 50–60)

When (only) two topical participants are active, and the story continues in an unbroken event-line, it is only by looking at the verb forms that we know who of the two is the referent of the subject and therefore the clausal topic. For example in (275a)–(275b) Nggou and the crocodile are the two active topical participants and it is only because of the Mandobo switch reference system (finite verb in conjoined clause sequence implies switch of subject, non-finite form implies same subject) and the continuative type of tail-head linkage that we know in (275b) that the crocodile is the subject of the first *negen* 'he said' and *Nggou* the subject of the second *negen* 'he said':

(275a) Ro   ndogo   eiga   ro-p   to,
       take go.across other.side   put.down-[IRR]1SG   CJN,
       undo-nog-a   ne-gen.
       go.across-IMP[SG]-CONN   say-RLS[NON1SG]
       'I will take you to the other side and put you down, you must go across, he (crocodile) said.'

(275b) Ne-gen   doro jok ne-gen
       say-RLS[NON1SG]   CONN yes say-RLS[NON1SG]
       'He (the crocodile) said and he (Nggou) agreed.'
       (Mandobo, from Drabbe 1959: 50–60)

5.8 Verbal semantics: actions and their components

Foley (1986: 113) described the tendency in the verbal semantics of Papuan languages to break down an action into its component acts and express each one of these acts by a separate verb. These component actions or events are then narrated in chronological order, with each sub action or subevent expressed in its own mini clause in the chain or in a serial verb construction. In the latter case a series of verb roots combine to form a single verbal head of the clause denoting one concept, under one intonation contour and without allowing conjunctions or switch reference marking. In other words, semantic, phonological and syntactic integration but with the subevents specified in chronological order, see §3.6.1.2.

For example, Greater Awyu speakers strongly prefer to express the notion of killing with two mini clauses where the subevent of dying is expressed in a separate mini clause that must come after the clause denoting the subevent of the violent act that results in this dying:

(276) i-r-ip   (te)   kima-r-an
      hit-RLS-1SG   (CNJ) die-RLS[NON1SG]-PAST
      'I killed him.' (lit. I hit and he died)
      (Yonggom Wambon, Drabbe 1959: 133)

Example (276) shows the subevents expressed with chained mini clauses, with the possibility of the insertion of the conjunction *te* and a semi-finite verb form in the first clause. But the same integrated concept of killing is expressed as a serial verb construction *ü-ro* in Drabbe's Mandobo texts (Drabbe 1959: 58–59):

(277) *Ruŋ-gun   do wegi   timo wombut*
   bind-RLS[NON1SG] CNJ bamboo.knife take tail
   teengwamo-ü-ro-gen.
   put.down-RLS[NON1SG]
   'He bound (the crocodile's jaw) and he (Nggou) took a bamboo knife and cut off the crocodile's tail and killed him.' (Mandobo, Drabbe 1959: 58–59)

Drabbe (1959: 59) was aware of the tendency in Greater Awyu verbal semantics to break down events in subevents ordered chronologically, either as a sequence of conjoined clauses or as a sequence of verb roots in a serial verb construction. For example, he annotates his text in (277) this clause as follows: "*Ruŋ-gun domba-gen* hij bindt en het zit: hij bindt het vast" [He binds and it sits: he fastened it]. And he annotates *ü-ro-gen* at the end of (277) as follows: "The verb *ü* has the very generic and vague meaning of impacting someone violently with a harmful intention, and is used for hitting, kicking, stumping, hurting and killing; there is no single word for the last meaning, but *ü ro* 'hit put down' almost always means to kill".

More generally, results of actions tend to be expressed in this sequential and componential fashion

(278) *difiŋ-ge-ne   doto-de*
   wake.up-NON1 RLS[SG]- DS get.up-1. RLS[SG]
   'he woke me up (and I got up)'   (Aghu, Drabbe 1957: 39)

Drabbe (1957: 39) observed that these combinations should be described in a dictionary of Aghu and he mentions as examples the combinations *üfü(ox)* 'hit' and *kü* 'die', *taku-* 'hang (transitive)' and *i(g)* 'hang (intransitive) and the verb *peme-* 'to cast' and the verb *oto(x)* 'to go away' that should be given in a dictionary as Aghu equivalents of 'to kill', 'to hang something' and 'to cast away'.

(279) *Pem-oxo-n   oto-xe*
   cast-RLS.NON1[SG]-DS.SEQ go.away-RLS.NON1[SG]
   'He cast it away.'   (Aghu, Drabbe 1957: 39)

Actions such as blowing into a smoldering fireplace to get flames (used as light here) have the result expressed in the second clause, following the clause with the cause or reason:

(280) *Ömböma-gen   do   Urut   doro   itigio-gen   do,   kaoro*
blow-RLS[NON1SG] CNJ flame CNJ   see-RLS[NON1SG] CNJ flight
go-gen.
go-RLS[NON1SG]
'He blew into the fire and the flame came, and he looked, but he (the crocodile) has fled (from the women's section of the house).'
(Mandobo, from Drabbe (1959: 50–60), see Appendix §9.2.2 (105))

5.9 Concluding remarks

Thematization, recapitulative linkage and argument distribution tendencies are not randomly distributed over texts (de Vries 2005; de Vries 2006). In narrative texts we find thematization most often in discourse-initial paragraphs, where speakers introduce the theme of their story, the main participants and the setting of the events (time, place). The number of complex noun phrases is relatively high in these passages and the text does not revolve around the event line. Tail-head linkage tends to be absent or minimal. Once the story is underway, speakers change their style and focus on the progression of the event line, with a high amount of mini clauses, argument distribution and tail-head linkage connecting the clause chains. Thematization does occur once the story is underway in conditions of thematic re-orientation when the speaker interrupts the event line.

This division of labor between "nouny" thematising opening sections and "event" line paragraphs has been found all over New Guinea (Heeschen 1998, Farr 1999). Farr (1999) uses the terms thematic paragraphs and chaining paragraphs for this division of labor. In thematic paragraphs, we find discontinuative types of clause linkage, within clause chains and between clause chains. In chaining paragraphs, continuative forms of linkage are found both within the clause chains and between them (e.g. continuative types of tail-head linkage).

These patterns of text cohesion will now be illustrated by a Korowai text on the origin of the Xomei clan and about its totemic ancestor, a *bembüol* lizard, who determined where the various sub clans of the Xomei would live (for the whole text, see van Enk and de Vries 1997: 170–173).

The text (281a)–(281b) form the initial paragraph, where the narrator introduces the topic of his story *noxup laibo=xa=fefè* (281c), the time setting (*mül-xuf-efè* in (281a)) and the participants (*Noxuf-efè, bembüo-lo* (281a)). It is a typical example of a thematic paragraph: with multiple extra-clausal themes marked with a demonstrative-based topic marker, no tail-head linkage to connect the clause chains within the paragraph, except a discontinuative clause linkage (*wa-mo-bo =xa=fefè* in (281a)), with many nouns and with personal pronouns.

The transition into the main event line commences in (281c) and all the clause chains that follow are connected by continuative tail-head linkages, with the exception of (281d) which adds details to the information given in (281c). These continuative tail-head linkages carry the switch reference monitoring of the main participants across sentence boundaries. For example, *wai lai*, the tail clause of (281f), is repeated as *wai le-nè*, the head clause of (281g), thus continuing the event and participant line (by an SS medial clause *le-nè*) from (281f) to (281g).

The section after (281c) is a typical chaining or conjoining paragraph in the terms of Farr (1999), with simply structured and verb dominated mini clauses that have no more than one overt argument which itself is simply structured. Personal pronouns are avoided to track given participants, instead switch reference and subject agreement on the verbs take care of that. The text also contains an example of generic verb linkage discussed in §5.2.2., in (281b) *amo=do* 'he did so and (DS)'. The difference between tail-head linkage and generic verb linkage is the scope of the anaphoric reference. Generic verb linkage gives speakers the opportunity to point back to the preceding discourse in an open, vague way, leaving it up to the addressee to contextually derive what the intended scope of the anaphoric reference is. This can be the immediately preceding clause chain, just as tail-head linkage does, or it could be a much larger unit, say an episode or even the whole preceding story (see de Vries 2019 for a detailed treatment of tail-head linkage and generic verb linkage in Korowai).

(281a) *Noxuf=efè,   mül-xuf=efè,   buom   buom,*
       we=TOP   former-time=TOP   lizard.species lizard.species
       buom-da=é   Apa   ye-ŋgé   bembüo=lo
       lizard.species-NEG=EXCL Only   his-friend lizard.species=FOC
       lai=daxu=fexo   lai-bando-xe-nè   lefu=fefè   wolaxip
       come[RLS.NON1PL]=SS=CNJ   come-bring-go-SS   some=TOP   higher.place
       gil-bolüp   fu=daxu   lefu=fefè   bando-xe-nè   noxu
       festival-place   put[RLS.NON1SG]   some=TOP   bring-go-SS   out
       dif-e=xa=la   fu-daxu
       this-LNK=CONN=LOC   put[RLS.NON1SG]=SS

>
> wa-mo-bo=xa=fefè   wo=fè noxup
> that-do-COM[RLS.NON1SG]=SUB=TOP that=TOP us
> laibo=xa=fefè
> be.born=[RLS.NON1SG]=SUB=TOP
> 'As for us, in former times, the *buom* lizard, the *buom* lizard, no, not the *buom* lizard, just its friend, the *bembüo* lizard, came and brought some to high ground, the festival place, others he took to where we are now and given that he did so, as for us, that is (the story of) origin.'

(281b) *Amo=do   mül-xuf=efè af=efè du-lalé*
> do[RLS.NON1SG]=DS former-time=TOP there=TOP tree-big
> *yaxuo-talé alo-bo=dompexo   wap=ta=sü*
> yaxuo.tree-big stand-COM [RLS.NON1SG]=DS here=LOC=at
> *Xiŋgo-imban=tompexo mumeŋga fuai-mémo=tofexo*
> Xinggo-member=FOC dog   hunt-IMM [RLS.NON1SG]=DS
> *sé Xomei noxu laibo=xa   abül*
> next Xomei our be.born[RLS.NON1SG]=MOD man
> *xol-mémo*
> walk-IMM [RLS.NON1SG]
> 'He did so and in former times there the big tree, the big *yaxuol* tree stood there and a member of the Xinggo clan just hunted, when Xomei, the man who brought us forth, walked there.'

(281c) *Xol-mémo=do   fulo=daxu=fexo*
> walk-IMM [RLS.NON1SG]=DS meet[RLS.NON1SG]=SS=CNJ
> *mumeŋga=lompexo sé ye-mumeŋga lena ülmo*
> dog=FOC   next his-dog little kill[RLS.NON1SG]
> 'He just walked and met (the other man) and it was the dog that killed his little dog.'

(281d) *Xailfüoalop=tena fu-ai-mémo=do*
> Xailfüoalop= DIM put-go.out- IMM[RLS.NON1SG]=DS
> *fu-ai-mémo=dompexo   sé xeyop xa-lulo=xa*
> put-go.out- IMM[RLS.NON1SG]=DS next house go-NEAR[RLS.NON1SG]=SUB
> *ye xai=tofexo   é y ai   xa-lulo=fexo*
> he go[RLS.NON1SG]=DS EXCL he move.down[SS] go-NEAR[NON1SG]= CNJ
> *xenè xeyop Lu   é-felulo   sé*
> next house move.up[SS] sleep- NEAR[RLS.NON1SG] next

xai=tofexo   amomeŋga   ü-felulo=xa   abül
go[RLS.NON1SG]=DS this.way   kill- NEAR[RLS.NON1SG]=MOD man
'He had just hunted with the little (dog) Xailfüoalop, he just had put it down and he went the way he had gone home the day before, yes, he had gone out and then he walked and having entered the house he slept, then he went that way to the place of the man who had killed (his dog) and where the big *yaxuol* tree had broken down the day before.'

(281e) *xolüx-mo-lulo=do*   *xenè imo=tofexo*
        break.down-do- NEAR[RLS.NON1SG]=DS next look[RLS.NON1SG]=DS
        xa-ŋgo=fexo   daüm=ta=fexo bau   siop=ta=fexo
        top-there=CIRC end=LOC=CIRC be[RLS.NON1SG] lower.end=LOC=CIRC
        bau   mexe-té=dompexo   walüpinè gun-telo-bo
        be[RLS.NON1SG] do-[RLS.NON1SG]=DS   half.way group-be-stay[RLS.NON1SG]
        'It broke down and he looked and in the top was a man and in the lower end was a man and half way there were lots of people.'

(281f) *gun-telo-bo=dompexo*   *Aful*   *a-mo=dompexo*
        group-be-stay[RLS.NON1SG]=DS   think[RLS.NON1SG]   that-do[RLS.NON1SG]=DS
        xeyop   gelü-nè xenè mbayap   fo=daxu   *Séx*
        house   run-SS   Next penisgourd get[RLS.NON1SG]=SS   skirt
        fo=daxu   *wai-lai.*
        get[RLS.NON1SG]=SS   move.down-come[RLS.NON1SG]
        'Lots of people there were and he worried and ran home and took penis gourds and took skirts and came out again and arrived.'

(281g) *Wai-le-nè*   *Mbayap*   *mbala-mo=daxu*
        move.down-come-SS   penisgourd   distribute-do[RLS.NON1SG]=SS
        séx   mbala-mo=daxu. . . .
        skirt   distribute-do[RLS.NON1SG]=SS
        'He came out and arrived and dispensed the penis gourds and he dispensed the skirts and . . .'   (Korowai, van Enk and de Vries 1997: 170–173)

Chapter 6
Language in Greater Awyu society

6.1 Introduction

This chapter describes how language functions in the social and cultural worlds of Greater Awyu speakers.[34] Those worlds can be described in terms of the opposition and interaction between the ancestral clan lands and the settlements. We look at language from the perspective of the clan lands, discussing language names, language and identity, linguistic ideology, forms of linguistic exogamy, lexical substitution registers, person reference practices, kinship systems and multilingualism. But the chapter also looks at language from the perspective of the settlements and from the perspective of the interaction between settlement and clan, with the relationship between Papuan Malay and Greater Awyu languages as the central theme. Since little research has been done on these issues for the Awyu subgroup, our observations are mainly valid for the Becking-Dawi, Ndeiram and Dumut languages.

Most speakers of Greater Awyu languages live in two locations, going back and forth between these locations: the ancestral clan lands and the settlements or villages (Indonesian: *kampung*) that were created under the influence of missions and local governments when Greater Awyu communities gradually were integrated in larger nation-state contexts. This process of *kampung* formation started in the 1940s in the coastal zone and slowly moved upriver toward the northern foothills. When I did my fieldwork in the Korowai and Kombai areas in the early 1980s, *kampung* formation started to reach these northern groups but most northern Kombai and Korowai clans still lived in tree houses on clan territories (see Figure 3). The process of *kampung* formation in the Korowai area is described by van Enk and de Vries (1997: 4–6) and de Vries (2007).

The *kampung* is the place where schools, churches, mosques, shops and health clinics were built, where local forms of Indonesian (Papuan Malay) function as interethnic lingua franca and where people of different clans and often of different languages, live together (see Figure 2). The houses in the *kampungs* are built on poles of around 1 meter high, while the houses on the clan territories were mostly tree houses in the Greater Awyu area, around

---

34 This chapter is a revised and expanded version of de Vries (2012a). The expansions on kinship and clan names are based on de Vries (1987) and van Enk and de Vries (1997). The work on the linguistic anthropology of Korowai of Stasch (2001, 2007, 2008a, 2008b, 2009) formed the other major source of expansions vis-à-vis de Vries 2012a.

https://doi.org/10.1515/9781501506956-006

Figure 2: Kampung Wanggemalo (Kombai), courtesy Dineke Groen.

12–20 meters high on average (Figure 3). There still are tree houses today in the northernmost parts.

People have only rights to harvest sago, to fish, to hunt and gather food on their clan lands. Since many speakers subsist on what their clan lands offer them, the clan lands still are crucial for survival for most speakers. Clan lands are much more than a source of food: they give people a sense of belonging, of place, origin and continuity (Stasch 2009: 28).

It is misleading to present the settlements as the present, as modernity, and the clan lands as the past. Clan lands and clan structures are still vital to life and language. Actually, many villages are almost empty most of the time because people live on their clan lands. The relationship between the world of the clan lands and the world of the *kampung* changes over time and varies from place to place but everywhere the dynamics of the interaction of the two worlds determines the place of language in these communities, as well as in the lives of individual speakers.

The chapter starts with a section on clans (§6.2), followed by a section on language and identity in Greater Awyu clan communities (§6.3). Section 6.4 discusses

Figure 3: Tree house of the Bilambanen clan (Korowai), courtesy Johannes Veldhuizen 1986.

language names, both exonyms and designations for languages which are used by Greater Awyu speakers themselves. The clashing linguistic ideologies of outsiders and Greater Awyu speakers are the topic of §6.5. Lexical substitution registers (that reflect several aspects of Greater Awyu perspectives on language) are discussed in §6.6. Section 6.7 is about linguistic and cultural practices of personhood and person reference of Greater Awyu communities. Section 6.8 discusses the relationship between Greater Awyu languages and Papuan Malay from the perspective of the *kampung* and clan land opposition. Section 6.9 describes language attitudes, language naming and the way Greater Awyu speakers talk about Papuan Malay and their own languages.

6.2 Clans

Small, named patriclans, with often no more than around 20 or 30 people, each with their own clan land, are the basis of life and social organization for the majority of speakers of Greater Awyu languages. Clan lands give people a place and the noun denoting clan land has 'place' as its primary meaning, for example Kombai *mbürü* 'place; clan land' and its Korowai cognate *bolüp* 'place; clan place'. Clan territories are the central element of clan based conceptualizations of social life (see Boelaars 1970: 16 for Mandobo; Stasch 2009: 26–36 for Korowai). Rights to live on a clan land are based on patrilineal descent (or marriage: wives move to the clan lands of their husbands and derive their right from their husband). However, co-residence on a clan land "tends to make people owners and co-residence tends to make people clan mates, as non-agnates over time become identified with a homeland, grow comfortable residing there". (Stasch 2001: 308). Stasch (2009: 28) writes:

> Landownership tightly joins three categories: "place", "clan," and "owner". A place (*bolüp*) is usually a contiguous, irregularly shaped segment of land, typically about a square mile in expanse. A place is by definition the territory of a particular named clan and all clans have places. Korowai ubiquitously speak of different parts of the landscape by combining clan names with the term *bolüp*. For example, *dambol-bolüp* is "place of Dambol". The term *clan* (*gun*) itself also means "species, type", an indication of the strong sense that a clan identity is a *type* of human.

Stasch (2009: 9) emphasizes that Korowai clans are not to be thought of as collectivistic groups, tightly integrated and homogeneous. On the contrary, Korowai people highly value their individual autonomy. Residential choices, choices of marriage partners and choice of networks of relations are all individual to a high degree. Apart from the organization of a sago grub feast that implies decisions at clan level, life is mostly led in small families, a man, his wives and children, perhaps one or more unmarried brothers and one or two of his mother's brothers' sisters' sons, with a certain preference to live somewhat apart from others on the clan land, in two or three tree houses.

The strong tendency toward political autonomy and egalitarianism favors dispersion: people like to be left alone and do not want to intrude upon the autonomy of others. Residential mobility at the individual and family level is very high, especially of young bachelors, but also more generally. People move often for shorter or longer periods to their mother's brother's clan lands, couples may live for a while with the clan people of the wife. Families move regularly from one tree house to another on the clan land. Rupert Stasch writes about the Korowai: "This situation of extreme residential mobility and residential dispersion is one of the most striking aspects of Korowai social life". (Stasch (2001: 70)). Boelaars (1970: 64) noticed similar patterns of dispersion and fragmentation in Mandobo communities. I saw the same patterns of egalitarianism, individualism, dispersion and political fragmentation in the Kombai and Digul Wambon areas.

Sociolinguistic studies of small communities living far away from urban centers in deserts or jungles tend to assume that such communities are tight-knit "societies of intimates" in terms of Trudgill (2011: 147). Characteristics ascribed to such communities are for example that the members of such communities share a large amount of information that is presupposed in their verbal communication, are collectivistic rather than individualistic, that they form dense, socially stable networks. The study of Stasch (2009) paints a rather different picture of Greater Awyu social life: an emphasis on the autonomy of individuals, high residential mobility, the importance of individual social networks, and social dynamism rather than stability.

6.2.1 Korowai clan names

Van Enk and de Vries (1997: xiv, Map 4) published a map of fifty Korowai clans and they note that throughout Korowai land there are stretches of land not specifically claimed by clans, called *laléo-bolüp* 'demon territory/place' (van Enk and de Vries 1997: 18) (see §6.7.1 for the *laléo* concept). Clans may have sub clans, with adjacent territories. For example, the Xomei have three sub clans called the Xomei Xayaxatun, the Xomei Walofexatun and the Xomei Walüfexatun (van Enk and de Vries 1997: 18). The noun *xatun* means offspring and occurs in Korowai in compounds with proper names of females with the meaning 'children/offspring of mother X', for example *Ŋgaiŋgatun* (*Ŋgain-xatun* 'offspring of Ŋgain').

Sometimes clans have the same name and a distant kinship relation but the territories are not adjacent and they have a more distant kinship relation than in the case of sub clans. The naming practice is different in such cases (van Enk and de Vries 1997: 18) and based on the names of rivers and streams where the different groups live, e.g. *Afiüm Lemaxa* 'Afiüm river Lemaxa' versus *Bafé Lemaxa* 'Eilanden River Lemaxa' or on terms for upstream and downstream, without mentioning of the name of the river, e.g. *Xosübolexa Dajo* 'Downstream Dajo' versus *Xülolexa Dajo* 'Upstream Dajo'. People of these clans of the same name but different locations address each other with sibling terms. On the other hand two clans with different names may share one territory and then names of the clans are combined (van Enk and de Vries 1997: 19), e.g. *Aremél-Dondon*, *Xenei-Saxén*, *Xaul-Nandup*, *Yawol-Sayax*.

6.2.2 Marriage and bilateral clan links

Greater Awyu patriclans are exogamous and women will leave their clan lands and live with their husbands in the clan territories. Although clan membership is inherited from the father, this patrilineality is balanced by strong links that a woman's children have with her brothers and with the clan lands of her brothers, her clan of origin. This link is institutionalized in the avunculate, the dyadic relation of mother's brother and sister's son, found in many variations in New Guinea, usually in the context of Omaha-type kinship systems (see below), for example Manambu, Aikhenvald (2008: 17). Boys will often stay with their uncles (mother's brothers), demand indemnity payments upon their uncles' deaths, protect their uncles (and they protect their sisters' sons) in case of accusations of witchcraft and other conflicts. Mother's brothers, who gave mother as a bride to ego's patriclan, are also often helping to find brides for their sister's sons, among their own classificatory sisters or among the women of their own mother's brothers' clan (de Vries 2012a: 8).

Men have to find brides outside their own clan and will often marry women with a (very) different language, especially in border areas. These women do not drop the language of their original clan when they go to live on the clan territory of their husbands. They do learn their husband's language but it is vital for a child to establish and maintain links with both father's people and mother's people and therefore a woman will pass on at least something of her language. Children will often spend a lot of time on their maternal uncles' clan lands and learn their language. One regularly meets speakers who grew up with two or three languages or dialects, for example Korowai-Kombai-local Malay and Korowai-Citak-local Malay speakers in Yaniruma. The sociolinguistic survey of Susanto (2004: 16) observes about Jair (Awyu) speakers in the village of Boma: "People in Boma II understand Kombai, also, since there is a lot of intermarriage in this village between Jair and Kombai".

6.3 Language and identity

Clan membership is the key element in a person's identity and clan names constantly surface in conversations of Greater Awyu speakers when a person is identified (Stasch 2001: 304). Clan lands are the most focal element in the clan notion as clan territories are literally and figuratively your place in life. The father's clan is the most important in identity construction but a person is not only a son of his father but also a husband and a cross-cousin and this brings the other clans into the identity equation.

Since people of many different clan lands may share a single language, language does not stand for a clan or for any other group identity (de Vries 2012a: 9–19). Language, being a clan transcending entity, therefore has a modest place in the construction of Greater Awyu identities. This does not mean that language is irrelevant in identity construction.

That relevance concerns lexical items that are linked to the origin of clans and to the origin of individuals, mostly names of ancestors and ancestral places. Greater Awyu clans commonly have oral traditions that describe a plant or animal as the totemic ancestor of the clan. (See e.g. the origin story of the Korowai-speaking Xomei clan, published by van Enk and de Vries (1997: 170–173), that tells how their ancestor, a lizard, determined where his offspring should live and how some of the offspring of the lizard became Kombai and others Citak-speaking clans). Totemic clan names are taboo names, called *xondum fi* 'hidden names' by the Korowai (Stasch 2001: 310), they form secret knowledge. In myths of origin of Greater Awyu speakers we encounter many 'hidden names'.

For example, Drabbe (1959: 10) describes how Mandobo origin myths contain two kinds of names, names that may be known by everyone and names that are *ketpon* 'taboo/secret'. Women and children cannot know these 'hidden names'. The creator ancestor *Tomorüp* has a *ketpon* or taboo name *Ngoü* (see the Mandobo text of §9.2.2). The secret part of the myth of origin of people and animals starts when this name is used after an introduction in which he is called *Tomorüp* (Drabbe 1959: 14). The *ketpon* name of the bird *Aceros plicatus* (Papuan hornbill), Indonesian *burung tahun*, is *Tüot-Kejenip* (Drabbe 1959: 70). These 'hidden names', the part of vocabulary linked to clan origins, clan identities and oral traditions of the clan, reflect and express clan identity in language (de Vries 2012a: 11).

The second way in which language plays a role in expressing identity in Greater Awyu communities is linked to relational concepts of personhood, the person as a cluster of dyadic relations. Each relationship contributes to who you are, is an element of your identity. Foley (1997: 266) speaks in this context of a sociocentric construction of identity. Exchange of wealth items, compensation/indemnity payments and other forms of exchange are used to express and maintain these dyadic relationships. Foley observes that:

> New Guinean conceptualizations of personhood are radically different: a partitive amalgamation of various substances from the different exchange interactions that one is ultimately built up from. From such a vantage point, the understanding of a speaker, the articulation of personhood through language is also radically different. This has fundamental implications for how New Guineans think about language and questions of language varieties and language purism (the latter notion in fact unintelligible in such a scheme). (Foley 2005a: 163)

By borrowing linguistic elements from these relations and by learning and using their languages, these sociocentric conceptions of identity are expressed in language. For example, by learning the language or speech variety of its mother's people, in addition to the language of its father's people, a child expresses its bilateral identity that is grounded in the links with father's and mother's clan. In other words, not only a person or a clan but also language itself is "a partitive amalgamation of various substances from the different exchange interactions" (Foley 2005a: 163). Since each language in the Greater Awyu area has just around 2000–3000 speakers, there are many languages in a relatively small area and this makes marriages across language boundaries a frequent phenomenon.

6.4 Language names

All names of Greater Awyu languages as found in government reports, missionary writings and linguistic publications (Korowai, Kombai, Aghu and so on) were created by missionaries, government people or linguists for arbitrary sections of Greater Awyu dialect chains that happened to be spoken around government or mission posts. These languages are arbitrary constructs that do not reflect linguistic realities and certainly do not reflect emic distinctions of the speakers themselves. In fact, Greater Awyu speakers did not have names for their languages. They did refer to their own speech as 'our talk' or 'people's talk' or 'talk of clan X', 'talk around this river/stream' and so on, depending on the context. 'Person talk' was perhaps the most used designation and the term 'person' in that expression refers to boundaries of social personhood, to which we will return below. Languages of outsiders (e.g. Papuan Malay) are called demon language (Stasch 2007) because outsiders are outside the boundaries of personhood (see below). These indigenous self-designations do not correspond at all to the exonyms of linguists, missionaries and other outsiders, in sense nor reference. For example, the normal Korowai self-designation is *bolü-anop* 'place/clan territory- person' (Stasch 2009: 41), i.e. 'people that belong to this place/ clan land' and "The terms *bolü-aup* 'homeland language' and *bolü-an-aup* 'homeland-LOC-language' are Korowai speakers' main nominations for their own language . . . . being somewhat more frequent than *kolufo-aup*" (Stasch 2001: 60). The latter name *kolufo-aup* is in fact an exonym that means 'upstream language' (Stasch 2009: 43) and is an example of a stream-based name given by outsiders who Indonesianized the term *kolufo* 'upstream' into the exonym Korowai.

Nouns glossed as 'language' or 'talk' are grounded in Greater Awyu perceptions of language as sound and action. For example, the noun *lu* in the Kombai expression *xombaye-lu* 'person's speech' may mean sound (of humans and animals), promise, message, quarrel, question, talk, utterance. *Xombaye lu* as self-designation means '(how we) people sound'. Birds and humans all have their own *lu* 'sound'. When people pronounce a speech variety differently, even with mutual intelligibility, they sound differently; they have a different *lu* 'speech' although the speech varieties may be mutually intelligible.

Outsiders used these 'person/people' based self-designations which they often did not understand and mispronounced, to name the "languages" or "ethnolinguistic groups" that they encountered. These "languages", however, were constructs that reflected arbitrary parts of dialect chains spoken around newly established settlements. For example, the language name Kombai is based on an Indonesian version of the expression *xombaye lu* 'people's speech' (de Vries 1993a: 1) and the language name Kaeti stems from the ethnic self-designation *küap kaeti* 'true/real person' (Drabbe 1959: 4). Aghu comes from *aghu* 'person' (Drabbe 1957: 1).

Another source for exonyms of Greater Awyu languages are the names of rivers and streams, not surprising in the swamps and rainforests of southern New Guinea where rivers dominate cultural geography and spatial orientation (see §6.10). Kaeti (or Mandobo) is also known as Ndumut, the name of a river along which they live. Mandobo speakers told Boelaars (1970: 27) that civil servants who started the Tanahmerah government post called them Mandobo. This exonym might be a combination of Mandup and Wambon, terms Mandobo speakers use for people on the right and left banks of the Kao River (Boelaars (1970: 27)). The language names Shiagha and Jenimu are also stream-based names given by the Catholic missionary linguist Drabbe (1950: 93) to the speech varieties of clans living close to those streams. Drabbe (1959: 4) was very aware of the nature of self-designations and the differences between the exonyms that he invented and the way Kaeti (=Mandobo) people talked about their language: "Thus people say *areg gaeti* 'real language' and they mean their mother tongue and that is why we also, in the absence of a better, or rather in the absence of a real name, speak of Kaeti language, or Kaeti".[35]

The name Awyu is used for a subgroup of the Greater Awyu family (Healey 1970) but also occurs in the label Greater Awyu family (de Vries, Wester and

---

[35] "Zo zegt men ook *areg gaeti* echte taal, en men bedoelt daarmee zijn moedertaal, en daarom spreken ook wij, bij gebrek aan beter, of liever bij gebrek aan een werkelijke naam, van Kaeti-taal of van het Kaeti".

van den Heuvel 2012). The term Awyu is an exonym. Drabbe used the term as a collective term for all the Awyu-Dumut languages that were known to him and that he suspected to be members of the same language family. He took the term from the Jaqaj, the southern Marindic neighbors of the Greater Awyu family. The term refers to fibre skirts to cover the genital area. The Jaqaj themselves went naked but their Awyu neighbors covered their genitals (Drabbe 1950: 93) and that is why they called them Awyu.

6.5 Linguistic ideologies

Missionaries, linguists and government people that first entered the Greater Awyu area tended to have linguistic ideologies born in nation-states with national languages, ideologies that correlate languages, cultures and political entities and that tend to construct languages and cultures as homogeneous, discrete, bounded entities. The language labels they invented for Greater Awyu speech varieties such as Kombai or Aghu they associated with 'cultures' and with ethnic identities based on these language-culture units: if there was a Kombai language, there had to be a "Kombai culture" that reflected and expressed that language. If there was a language-culture complex called Kombai, then that Kombai language had to be an essential part of their identity as a group.

Government workers and missionaries forced or strongly pressured people to leave their clan lands and live in the villages that they made them build, often around airstrips. The linguistic ideologies of these civil servants informed the way they structured the villages and the way they set up an administrative structure for these egalitarian communities which had no formal political structure and did not recognize authorities beyond the informal leaders of their own clans. The multilingual villages created by outsiders were divided into sections, each section with its own "language" and its own "tribal head". In this way, Kombai speaking clans would be settled together in one part of the village, as a political unit under a head appointed by the government. Thus village formation expressed the linguistic ideologies of the outside agents. From the perspective of Greater Awyu clan communities, their own clan is the only relevant political unit, corresponding with the clan lands, and the group of persons speaking one language is certainly not a political unit, or a socially relevant unit, for that matter.

Greater Awyu people who lived in those settlements and spoke Papuan Malay there to communicate with people from other languages (who were settled in the same village), soon adopted the terms such as *suku Korowai* 'Kombai tribe' and *bahasa Kombai* 'the Kombai language' which the foreigners had introduced to talk about them and to organize the settlements. When in *kampung* contexts, Greater Awyu speakers learned to talk and think about themselves in Indonesian as *orang Kombai* 'Kombai people' or *orang Mandobo* 'Mandobo people'.

From the point of view of the clan world of Greater Awyu speakers linguistic, cultural and political units are not perceived as correlated. This is because small patriclans are the highest political units. Patriclans control a territory, their clan lands, core and basis of their identity and existence. Language, however, transcends clan boundaries. Many clans share one Greater Awyu variety and some of these clans may be mortal enemies, whereas other clans, speaking different languages, may be your own people, for example the clans of your maternal uncles.

Every clan has its own network of relations with other clans, for example Korowai clans in areas adjacent to Citak speaking clans (Citak is an Asmat language) have relations with Citak clans, through marriage and otherwise. It is this network of relations which influences linguistic and cultural practices. Therefore linguistic and cultural units do not correlate in a clan world. For example, Greater Awyu clans of the Awyu subgroup that settled in downriver and coastal areas between Marind and Asmat speaking clans adopted cultural practices from these clans, for example their counting practices and numerals (see chapter 3) and their headhunting practices (Drabbe 1957: 55).

6.6 Lexical substitution

So far, we mentioned elements that do not occur in Greater Awyu linguistic ideologies such as purism, ideas of language as expressing group identity and the absence of language in clan identity construction (with the important exception of names tied to clan places, clan ancestors). More positively, elements that do have a prominent place in Greater Awyu linguistic ideologies are notions of iconicity, power, origin, secret knowledge and avoidance (Stasch 2008a). The Korowai lexical substitution register called *xoxulop* as described by Stasch (2008a) illustrates some of the core elements in the Greater Awyu perspective on language.

From the Korowai perspective, language is not just an instrument to refer to things and words are not arbitrary labels for things. Rather, in certain contexts, words are perceived as elements intrinsically, causally and iconically linked with the origin, essence and hidden nature of things (Stasch 2008a: 9–11) and with the spiritual power and presence of the things or persons referred to by the words. That is why pronouncing words in certain contexts is a dangerous and undesired act because it may have all sorts of consequences, such as evoking the presence and power of persons or things; diminishing the spiritual power of these things and persons; weakening the clan; diseases; earthquakes and other disruptions of the natural order of things. That is also why avoiding certain words or using substitutes for them is part and parcel of everyday language use, a constant and central part of linguistic behaviour. This leads to institutionalized links between word pairs in the lexicons of clan languages called lexical substitution registers.

Lexical substitution registers with various forms and functions occur all over New Guinea (and Australia). Registers of vocabulary substitutions may have poetic, artistic functions, ritual functions, function in kinship contexts (e.g. affinal avoidance and respect) or may have pragmatic functions of indirection, humour, persuasion, or function to express anger and frustration with things and persons (Stasch 2008a: 7). These registers often reveal key aspects of linguistic ideologies of New Guinea clans.

The Korowai *xoxulop* register described by Stasch (2008a) exemplifies some of these aspects of linguistic ideologies emerging in Greater Awyu clan contexts. Stasch compares the lexical substitution register that the Korowai call *xoxulop* with the substitution practices of the neighbouring Asmat (Stasch 2008a: 7). According to Stasch (2008a: 8), *xoxulop* is a compound noun consisting of *xoxu* 'root, rhizome, pelvis, butt, origin, cause, meaning' and *-lop* 'location, site' which means something like 'underlying identity'. Both the Asmat and Korowai substitutive pairings are based on iconicity (Stasch 2008a: 10): Asmat and Korowai speakers perceive resemblances between the paired items. Certain pairs, e.g. 'moon' as the substitute for 'sun' and certain marsupial species names for dogs, are shared by Korowai and Asmat (Stasch 2008a: 10) but whereas Asmat lexical substitution functions in song composition in an affirmative relation between poetic substitution term and referent (Voorhoeve 1977), Korowai *xoxulop* is negative and transgressive, implying a relation of danger and physical damage between substitute vocabulary and referent, for example saying aloud a *xoxulop* word in the presence of its paired referent may cause damage to the referent (Stasch 2008a: 7). Stasch (2008a: 6) gives this example of the word for snake that is the *xoxulop* of the word vine: "Vines originally *were* snakes and saying 'snake' around vines causes them to break". According to Stasch (2008a: 7), Korowai *xoxulop* overlaps with abusive speech forms including obscenities, slurs and misfortune-causing curses.

Korowai speakers often talk about the *xoxulop* register of which they have a high metalinguistic awareness (Stasch 2008a: 6) and say things like 'A, its *xoxulop* is B'. Table 11 gives some examples of *xoxulop* substitutions.

According to Stasch (2008a: 16) the force of these pairings goes beyond metaphorical correspondence or iconic resemblance and is ultimately based "on ontological, causal closeness that is felt to be behind that manifest iconic

Table 11: Korowai word with their xoxulop substitutions (from Stasch (2008a: 10–13)).

Normal designation	Xoxulop subsitution
dul 'penis'	wafol 'earthworm'
yanop-xabian 'human head'	nggonngon-loxul 'round parasitic growth on trees'
nan 'rattan'	yanop-xul 'human intestines'
laun 'pandanus sauce'	xi-ol-ax 'dysentery'
melil 'fire'	bun-xa 'blood'
ati 'bow'	beka 'snap, sound, crack, cry, burst'

similarity". Stasch (2008a: 6) writes: "Speech is not only *about* the phenomenal world but *of* it. Language is analogous to touch and other sensory channels and analogous to forms of interaction in those physical channels such as bodily harm". In the *xoxulop* pairs, the sameness goes hand in hand with otherness, alterity and strangeness. The *xoxulop* "portrays as strange and alarming what is close at hand" (Stasch 2008a: 24).

Persons also have *xoxulop* names and "personal *xoxulop* correspondences underscore the force of sound alone, or a speaker's form-fetishizing sense of the transparency and directness of the relation between a *xoxulop*'s term's phonological shape and its meaningful force. An individual does not need to know his or her *xoxulop* in order to be damaged by hearing it uttered [. . .] Even accidental utterance of a homophone or near-homophone of a person's hidden name is enough" (Stasch 2008a: 20). This leads to elaborate linguistic avoidance behaviour, so extensive in fact that Stasch concludes that the *xoxulop* register exists in three ways, as transgressive, performative speech act, metalinguistically as a register often talked about but especially in linguistic avoidance behaviour. People constantly try to talk around *xoxulop* nouns. Thus, paradoxically, the *xoxulop* register is perhaps most intensely present when it is absent because people's effort to talk around *xoxulop* words (Stasch 2008a: 5).

6.7 Linguistic and cultural practices of personhood and person reference

In the politically fragmented world of Greater Awyu small communities, clan affiliation and kinship give a person a place in life. Therefore, clan names and kinship terms dominate the way people refer to each other, address each other and greet each other. However, clan affiliation and kinship give only "persons" a place in life and not everyone is a "person". Greater Awyu communities make a distinction between normal persons and people who are outside the cultural boundaries of social personhood. Unfortunately, our knowledge of cultural practices of most Greater Awyu communities is very limited. We only have information of boundaries of social personhood in Korowai and Kombai communities, where the term for person, human being is contrasted with two other terms to refer to people: male witches and demons/zombies. First, we will discuss Korowai social personhood (§6.7.1), then turn to clan and kinship terms as cornerstones of person reference and address systems (§6.7.2). § 6.7.3 discusses joking avoidance forms of person reference.

6.7.1 Social personhood: humans, witches and demons

Korowai and Kombai distinguish between persons (Korowai *yanop*, Kombai *xo*) and non-persons, people outside boundaries of social personhood (Stasch 2009). The term for (normal) person contrasts with two terms for categories of people that fall outside the boundaries of social personhood: 'demons' or 'zombies' and '(male, cannibalistic) witches'. Following Stasch (2001, 2009), the relationship between the terms for 'person', 'demon' and 'witch' can be described as follows: 'witches' are the *cause* of death of 'persons' and 'persons' turn into 'after death demons' or 'zombies' as the *result* of their death.

For example, in Korowai perceptions every death of a *yanop* 'person' is caused by a *xaxua* 'male cannibalistic witch' and all *yanop* become *laléo* 'after-death demon' once they are dead. In the words of Stasch: "Thus, Korowai experience of death is dominated not by one monstrous figure but by two. Death's outcome is personified in the figure of the *laléo* 'demon', while death's source is personified in the figure of the *xaxua* 'witch'. In between stands *yanop* 'human'. It is difficult to exaggerate the scale and intensity of people's daily preoccupations with these two monsters". (Stasch 2001: 444).

The Korowai noun *laléo* 'after-death demon, zombie' has at least five senses. The basic, literal sense is 'after death zombie/demon'. According to Stasch (2001: 324) "demons are the principal thing humans become after death. People describe these demons with vivid horror and worry daily about the possibility of these monsters interfering with their lives". Glosses like zombie or demon are inadequate to render the meaning of the demon terms. 'Demons' are corporeal, with rotting, disfigured, stinking bodies, with skin and flesh sliding down from their bodies, their bodies are decaying corpses (Stasch 2001: 327).

These features of putridity and processes of decay and disintegration are also reflected in a Kombai story about the journey of the dead to the clan territory of the dead published by de Vries (1993a: 110–127). The story describes how a person after death turns into a *xwai* 'after death-demon' during the journey to the place or clan territory of the dead. The dead person, having arrived at the long house in the clan land of the dead, must eat worms that cause him to vomit. His beloved ones meanwhile observe his dead body at their wake and see that his belly swells and that corpse fluids come out (the result of the zombie being forced to eat worms). Dead people are only temporarily zombies, in the transition period between death, when they have just left the world of the living but have not yet arrived in the clan lands of the ancestors, where they will be fully restored to personhood. That transition period makes them dangerous: they are decaying and rotting but are still around and try to contact, to communicate with the living, to intrude in the lives of the living. Contact with zombies is dangerous and to be avoided at all costs.

The other meanings of the zombie terms are metaphorical extensions that focus on the intrusiveness and repulsiveness aspects of zombiehood, repulsive and intrusive otherness. Newborn babies and foreigners are not (yet) persons, socially and that is why they were (and partly still are) routinely called *laléo* 'demon' in Korowai and *xwai* 'demon; zombie' in Kombai.

As for newborn babies, "the substances of childbirth: placenta, blood, slimy baby and their odors, bear all of the same negative medical associations as menstrual blood but even more strongly" (Stasch 2001: 248). Newborn Korowai babies begin their lives as *laléo* 'demon' rather than *yanop* 'person'. They can be gradually and ritually turned into *yanop* in the course of the first weeks and months of their lives, if the mother decides to keep the newborn baby, as infanticide of newborn babies occurred quite frequently (Stasch 2001: 249).

The third meaning of the nouns denoting zombies are foreigners. Just like zombies, they are weird non-persons, with abnormal skins and unpredictable, strange behavior, who dangerously interfere with the lives of normal people on their clan lands and who claim clan land for airstrips and settlements. All these things contribute to the idea that foreigners are not *yanop* '(normal) person' but *laléo* 'zombie'. Foreigners are not within the boundaries of social personhood and this makes the metaphorical extension of the term *xwai* (Kombai) or *laléo* (Korowai) to foreigners understandable. Many things brought by foreigners, including the Indonesian language, are referred to by compound nouns with the zombie noun as modifier as can be seen in Table 12.

Two other uses of demon terms concern their use as swear words and in teasing. When something goes wrong unexpectedly or when someone hurts himself, Korowai frequently use *laléo* as a swear word. I also often heard Kombai kids call

Table 12: Noun compounds formed with the word for 'demon' (from de Vries 2012a: 22).

Kombai	Demon compund
doü 'sago'	*xwai-doü* 'rice' (demon-sago)
riya 'torch'	*xwai-riya* 'flash light' (demon-torch)
lu 'sound; voice; language'	*xwai-lu* 'Indonesian' (demon-language)
Korowai	
aup 'word, language'	*laléo-aup* 'Indonesian language' (demon-language)
ndaü 'sago'	*laléo-ndaü* 'bread' (demon-sago)
xal 'skin'	*laléo-xal* 'clothing' (demon-skin)
menil 'fire(wood)'	*laléo-menil* 'matches' (demon-fire)

each other *xwai* 'demon' playfully; the 'demon' terms are further useful as pejorative terms in conflicts and quarrels.

Younger speakers, those who live in *kampungs* and have gone to school and with aspirations to go to cities such as Merauke or Jayapura, use the demon terms *laléo* and *xwai* in a more neutral sense, meaning probably just 'foreigner' (Stasch 2007: 105).

Stasch (2007: 105) even observed that Korowai speakers experiment with compounds such as *amerika-anop* 'Americans', *Indonesia-anop* 'Indonesians', *turis-anop* 'tourists' to talk about categories of foreigners. This implies that these foreigners are no longer denied personhood, at least for these speakers. However, as Stasch (2007: 105) points out, "nonetheless, it is important to acknowledge the severe intellectual and emotional shocks that the Korowai have experienced in their involvement with the new foreigners. Some Korowai who have not interacted much with foreigners continue to posit a relation of literal identity between foreigners and the demonic dead".

6.7.2 Clan and kinship in person reference

It is clan affiliation and kinship relations that determine who someone is and it is clan names and kinship terms that dominate the way Greater Awyu speakers talk about people and address them. The use of personal names is avoided, both in reference and address, especially the personal names of adults in their presence. Names of children are less taboo (with the exception of their 'hidden' birth names) and speakers very often use the names of children in matronyms and patronyms in referring to and addressing adults (Stasch 2001: 122–123). For example, one of my daughters' name is Charlotte and I was very often addressed as 'father of Sarlota' and my wife as 'mother of Sarlota'. The default way to identify a person is by clan name (Stasch 2001: 304). Since clan membership is so crucial for a person's place in life, clan names are also prominent in person reference practices. Stasch (2001) writes about the role of clan names in Korowai person reference practices:

> Clan membership is a common noted attribute of persons. Speakers routinely say, for example, that such-and-such person is a "member" (*imban*) of such-and-such named clan. Clan names are never directly collocated with personal names or other person-reference forms to make binomials, as in the manner of given-name-plus-surname formulae now common in the English language community and ones akin to it. Nonetheless, it is quite common for speakers to refer to a particular person by such designations as "Dayo guy", "Dayo girl", "Dayo member", and the like in place of other person reference forms. In many contexts (and especially among older speakers), the clan name and the person are the same thing. (Stasch 2001: 304).

Kinship terms distinguish categories of people within clan communities, and clan members refer to each other and address each other almost always with kinship terms. This makes them very frequent in daily life on the clan territories. Greater Awyu kinship presents itself as dyadic in nature, in the sense that paired kinship terms such as mother's brother-sister's son, wife's mother-daughter's husband, husband-wife are prominent in discourse and such dyadic pairs refer to culturally prominent relations that imply very specific norms, obligations and behavior (Stasch 2001, 2009). Exocentric compounds such as Korowai *yum-defol* 'couple' (literally: husband-wife), *lalum-bandaxol* 'daughter's husband-wife's mother', Kombai *momo-laŋge* (mother's brother-sister's son) are very frequently used to refer to such dyadic relations. The English gloss 'couple' for *yum-defol* is one of the few glosses for these compounds that succeeds in conveying the relational, dyadic nature of these notions in which the paired items have no existence independent of the dyadic relation that defines them (Stasch 2009). Whereas other Greater Awyu languages use exocentric noun compounds to refer to dyadic relations (see §3.2.4), Aghu has a special construction for dyadic noun phrase coordination that contrasts with the default coordination construction for non-dyadic nouns (see §4.2.7).

We have information on kinship systems of four Greater Awyu languages, Korowai, Tsaukambo, Kombai and Mandobo, representing all subgroups, with the unfortunate exception of the Awyu subgroup. The kinship terminologies of which we have more or less complete descriptions (Mandobo, Boelaars (1970:

95–112); Korowai, Van Enk and de Vries (1997: 139–153); Kombai, de Vries 1987) are all Omaha type systems. To illustrate Omaha kinship as they operate in the cultural contexts of Greater Awyu communities, I will discuss some aspects of Kombai kinship terms, based on de Vries (1987).

Just like most other nouns, kinship nouns are polysemic. For example, the term *are* in Kombai means father but is also used for the husband of parent's sister, two clearly distinct senses (and a wide range of other senses, see below). What defines kinship nouns as a semantic field is the specific set of rules, patterns and distinctions that connects the multiple senses of kinship terms, for example generational extension, the cross-parallel distinction and the Omaha rule mother's brother=mother's brother's son (Lounsbury 1964). Kinship nouns also stand out morphologically among Greater Awyu nouns because they have plural forms and because they almost always take possessive prefixes and this reflects that kinship nouns denote dyadic relations.

At the same time, the patterns and distinctions that set kinship nouns apart within Greater Awyu languages as a semantically distinct class of nouns connect Greater Awyu languages to many other languages of the world, in the sense that the extension patterns, equivalence rules and basic semantic distinctions belong to a limited set of such patterns found in different combinations in many languages around the globe (Foley 1997).

Of course, these extension patterns do not exhaustively describe what the kinship nouns mean to specific communities in their own cultural contexts, nor do they imply that speakers have to know precise genealogical links to use these terms. In a small clan community of around 20 people, a child will easily learn how its siblings call the few people on the clan lands and on those of their uncles.

The Greater Awyu kinship nouns that we have enough data on all exhibit the cross-linguistic very common extension rule, aptly termed generational extension by Merrifield (1983a: 182) that extends the range of reference of a kinship noun collaterally to include all other kinsmen of the same generation and of the same sex. Other cross-linguistically common extension patterns and distinctions found in Greater Awyu kinship nouns are the distinction parallel and cross, the Omaha equivalence of mother's brother and mother's brother's son (which leads to skewing of biological and terminological generations), self-reciprocal extension, affinal extension and bidirectional extension, as defined in Merrifield (1983a: 182–186). We will illustrate some of these extensions with Kombai kinship nouns that denote members of the parent generation. For the other Kombai kinship nouns, de Vries (1987) and for Korowai kinship nouns, van Enk and de Vries (1997: 139–151).

Kombai like the other Greater Awyu kinship systems distinguishes in the parent generation fathers (male parallel parent), mothers (female parallel parent), father's sisters (cross female parent) and mother's brothers (cross male parent). The distinction between cross and parallel kinsmen is fundamental to the Greater Awyu kinship systems that we have data on, as in various other kinship systems of New Guinea (Merrifield 1983b: 295). Following Merrifield (1983b: 295) the opposition may be defined as follows:

> Parallel (Seneca): Within the genealogical chain that links ego to alter, the two kinsmen of the first generation above that of the junior member of the ego-alter dyad are of the same sex. Cross (Seneca): Within the genealogical chain that links ego to alter, the two kinsmen of the first generation above that of the junior member of the ego-alter dyad are of the opposite sex.

The cross and parallel distinction is morphologically expressed in the Becking-Dawi branch, e.g. in Korowai by the prefix *sa-* 'cross', e.g. in *lal* 'daughter' (ego's daughter/female ego's sister's daughter/male ego's brother's daughter') and *sa-lal* 'niece' ('male ego's sister's daughter'/female ego's brother's daughter') (van Enk and de Vries 1997: 143)) and in Tsaukambo with *ha-* 'cross relative' *na-la* 'my daughter (my parallel female child)' and *na-ha-la* 'my cross female child' (de Vries 2012b: 170). The parallel term is the unmarked one in this opposition.

Within the set of cross terms, the mother's brother term in Kombai (and other Greater Awyu languages) is interesting for two reasons. First, because of the Omaha type of equivalence of mother's brother and mother's brother's son (and his son and so on, in vertical extension down the generations), there is a skewing of terminological and biological generations. For example, if ego's father calls someone *momo* 'maternal uncle' who is his mother's brother's son's son, or even his mother's brother's son's son's son and therefore often an infant or small child, then ego calls this child or baby, persons of biological generations below ego, 'my grandfather'.

The cross term *momo* 'maternal uncle' is also interesting because of the local cultural practices and institutional contexts within which it functions and which give the term its local cultural meaning. The dyad mother's brother-sister's children, especially mother's brother-sister's son is a key kinship relation in many New Guinea communities. Van Baal (1982: 83) wrote about the avuncular dyad:

> The marriage of a girl into another group establishes an alliance between the groups concerned. The factuality of this alliance is reflected in the widely spread custom known as the avunculate, the institutionalized relationship between a mother's brother and his sister's children which obliges the uncle to act as the children's protector, helper or mentor, all as the case may be.

This observation is certainly true for the relationship between Kombai maternal uncles and their sister's children, especially sister's son, his cross male child, *langge* (de Vries 1987: 112). When a boy grows up, he will often spend a lot of time on the clan territory from which his mother came, the clan territory of his uncle(s). His uncle will give him ceremonially his first penis gourd along with sexual instruction when he comes of age. Finding a bride is complicated and requires bridal payments and the maternal uncle is often the one who finds a bride for his sister's son and assists with the bridal payments. When uncle dies, the people in his household have to pay compensation money to the sister's son for the loss of his uncle. When either uncle or sister's son is accused of *xaxua* witchcraft (an accusation that often leads execution of the accused), they will flee to the territory of the other and protect each other.

The avunculate is a hereditary institution: when your mother's brothers have all died, it is their sons (and their sons), all of whom you call *momo* 'maternal uncle', who take up the obligations and prerogatives of this key kinship dyad. The vertical extension down the generations is only valid for the maternal uncle, not for the cross female parent, *moro* 'father's sister'. The term *moro* is only extended to father's classificatory sisters, his sisters by generational extension.

The cultural and linguistic equivalence of MB and MBS is the key to a whole range of other avunculate-related extensions of meanings of kinship nouns (Kombai, de Vries 1987: 113); Korowai, van Enk and de Vries(1997: 142–143). For example, a Kombai person calls the wife of mother's brother *yeni* 'mother'. By generational extension this includes the sisters of mother's brother's wife. By Omaha equivalence of MB to MBS (and MBSS etc.), the wives of these MBS and their sisters are also *yeni* 'mother'. Likewise, because of the avuncular MB=MBS equivalence, ego treats the sisters of MBS as the sisters of MB, i.e. as ego's mother and her sisters and accordingly calls his mother's brother's daughters *yeni* 'mother'.

By treating MBD as his mother and her sisters, as members of the parent generation, the children of MBD are treated as ego's siblings, thus MBDS=B and MBDD=Z(sister). Another avuncular extension, based on the MB=MBS equivalence concerns ego's father's sister's children. They call ego *momo* 'maternal uncle' because he is their MBS (=MB). The male reciprocal to *momo* (MB) is *langge* (male ego's sister's son), so ego calls his father's sister's children terminologically as members of the child generation, although they are his own biological generation.

The Kombai the noun *are* 'father' (male parallel parent) denotes ego's father (F), ego's father's brothers (FB), father's father's brother's sons (FFBS) and so on in generational extension (FFFBSS) (de Vries 1987: 107). By affinal extension *are* 'father' is applied to the husbands of mother's sisters and of father's sister, thus neutralizing the cross and parallel contrast in these affinal relations. Finally, *are* is also used for mother's brother's daughter's husband. The last extension is avunculate-related and was discussed above.

The Kombai term *yeni* 'mother' (female parallel parent) is generationally extended to mother's sisters and her classificatory sisters by generational extension. Affinally, *yeni* extends to the wives of ego's parents' brothers and classificatory brothers (FBW, MBW). Above we saw two avunculate-related extensions of *yeni* to MBD and MBSW.

The affinal terms in the parent generation are self-reciprocal, with one significant exception, the term *xuni* 'male ego's mother-in-law'. The relationship between a man and his mother-in-law (*xuni*) is a taboo relationship, not just in Kombai but generally in Greater Awyu communities, in some form or another. A man must avoid all forms of sensory contact (including sight avoidance) with his mother-in-law, avoid her name, and if he needs to refer to her or address her, he will use various forms of indirection, very vague, plural expressions, and so will she, reciprocally. Stasch (2001: 154) writes:

"Rather, each addresses and refers to the other using plural pronouns, plural verb inflections, and other plurality-expressing grammatical elements." He observed the following cases of indirection by pluralization: ". . . one woman refers to her daughter's husband as *Eli-ate-xül* "fathers of Eli, that father of Eli bunch", one woman refers to her daughter's husband as *Xawan-um-xül* "Xawan's husbands," and another woman uses a joking avoidance relation with her grandson to refer to the daughter's husband as *ne'-walol-ate-xül* "fathers of my lizard." (Stasch 2001: 154).

There is a self-reciprocal kinship noun for a man and his male parent-in-law in Kombai, *nemo* 'wife's father/daughter's husband'. The term neutralizes the cross and parallel distinction and is extended to wife's mother's brother. Self-reciprocally, the term extends to both male ego's daughter's husband and male ego's sister's daughter's husband (de Vries 1987: 114). But the term that a man uses for his wife's mother (and by generational extension for his wife's mother's sisters), *xuni* 'wife's mother', is not self-reciprocal. Wife's mother (and wife's mother's sisters) call their daughter's husband *nemo*.

Whereas a man must use different terms for his wife's male (*nemo*) and female parents (*xuni*), a woman uses one self-reciprocal noun *nuno* 'husband's parent/son's wife' for all (classificatory) members of the parent generation of her husband: her husband's mother, father, father's brother, mother's sister, mother's brother and father's sister, thus neutralizing both the gender and the cross-parallel distinction (de Vries 1987: 115). The term also extends to husband's father's brother's wife (and to HMBW, HMZH, HFZH). The special taboo place of the dyad wife's mother and female ego's daughter's husband is clearly reflected in the affinal terminology of Kombai and other Greater Awyu languages.

6.7.3 Korowai joking avoidance

Stasch (2001: 102–141) describes Korowai joking avoidance in great detail. Korowai speakers form pairs or dyads on the basis of an extraordinary event that affected them both and formed the start of the joking avoidance dyadic relation (Stasch 2001: 10--141). Stasch gives many examples such as: "Two women call each other *ne-mbux* "my pitfall", based on their having fallen simultaneously into a concealed hole that a man had dug to catch game". (Stasch 2001: 103). The women have to avoid each other's personal names and call each other with the joking term. Although indeed in many cases the founding event has a humorous aspect to it, the joking avoidance term that occurs most is *ainap* 'compassion'. Stasch (2001: 118–119) writes:

> Until recently, many children were recruited into avoidance partnerships on the very day they were born. The most frequent among all avoidance terms is *ainap* "compassion" (145 attestations), based on a senior, non-parental partner's open expression of compassion for the other on the immediate scene of the junior partner's birth, preventing the infant from being killed.[36]

Here are some examples of reciprocal joking avoidance forms of person reference and address (from Stasch 2001: 111–113):

(282)

Term	Gloss	Founding event
nen	rotten	shared rotten fish
ol-man-ax	turd water	drank from pool thought to contain feces
xosol	unripe	shared unripe fruit
xoto-xal	earlobe of pig	shared earlobe of pig
xembaxi	ant	bitten together
xoxu	ass	slept buttocks adjoined
xabian	head	banged heads
lambul	calf	banged calves dancing at a feast
ol-ax	diarrhea	suffered cramps and runs, defecated from same log
ainap	compassion	infanticide prevented because of compassion
sanip-ol	cassowary-turd	stepped in cassowary-turd together
bokox	cough	coughed at same time

(Korowai, Stasch 2001: 111–113)

---

36 See §6.7.1 for the infanticide practices Stasch refers to.

Joking avoidance terms are "a historicizing or commemorative mode" (Stasch 2001: 124) to refer to persons and this reflects a more general tendency among Greater Awyu speakers in person reference practices, for example the strong tendency to give names to babies that reflect special circumstances or events surrounding the birth (Stasch 2001: 124).

6.8 Language in *kampung* and clan lands

Kampung formation brought regional forms of the Indonesian language to Greater Awyu speech communities, mostly Papuan Malay with strong Moluccan Malay influences. When south coast New Guinea was under Dutch control, speakers of Moluccan Malay played a crucial role as policemen, evangelists, school teachers and so on.

Whereas evangelical missions (e.g. United Fields Mission, Christian and Missionary Alliance, Asia Pacific Christian Mission) with headquarters in the United States or Australia used local languages from the start, the Catholic missionaries and the protestant missionaries of the mission of the Dutch Reformed Churches used local Papuan Malay varieties of Indonesian in their school, health and church activities, under both Dutch and Indonesian rule. Since the majority of Greater Awyu speakers lived in areas with Dutch Catholic or protestant missionaries, Papuan Malay soon became an important language in their lives. Missionaries tended to be the first foreigners who settled in Greater Awyu lands, followed by government people, usually very few and confined to main stations in the interior and by petty traders, often Buginese or Maccassarese, who opened shops in the main stations.

These outsiders were strongly associated with *kampung* settlements, not with clan lands where they seldom showed up. When they travelled, they would travel either by boat or by plane, from one *kampung* to another. Missionaries and civil servants expected Greater Awyu speakers to come to the *kampungs* and live there so that they could go to the schools, clinics and churches.

Outsiders tended to remain in (main) stations or mission posts, in *kampungs*, rather than live on clan lands. Most outsiders, including policemen and military rarely left the stations except for short, sporadic trips to clan lands, hardly ever sleeping there. Greater Awyu communities tend to appreciate this, because the clan lands are autonomous and outsiders pose a threat to that autonomy. A clear separation of clan lands and *kampungs*, with outsiders sticking to the *kampungs*, also made it possible to continue cultural practices on clan lands that missionaries and civil servants did not want in the *kampungs*, varying from witchcraft trials and cannibalism to polygamous marriage and elaborate pig or sago grub festivals that took months of preparation and disrupted the programs of missions and government. This separation of clan lands and *kampungs* set up a system with two parallel worlds, the world of the *kampung* and its institutions and the world of the clan lands in what outsiders in the villages called *hutan* 'the jungle'. These two worlds are connected of course and co-evolve over the course of time (de Vries 2012a).

Greater Awyu speakers are aware of these two parallel worlds, each with its own linguistic and cultural practices and they express that opposition in various ways. For example, in the late 1980s when I lived in the Kombai *kampung* of Wanggemalo and the Korowai-Kombai *kampung* Yaniruma, some people had begun to adopt two personal names that they called in Indonesian *nama gelap* 'dark name' and *name terang* 'light name' (de Vries 2012a: 17–18). The *nama terang* was an Indonesian name, often taken from the Bible or from objects associated with foreigners, for example Petrus or Pilot or Maik (after a pilot's name). They used these Indonesian names when they were in the *kampung*. While on the clan lands, they used indigenous personal names. For example, one of my Kombai language consultants was called Petrus in the *kampung* Wanggemalo but his folk on the clan land called him *Mbürüfare* (incidentally the name means 'clan land person'). There are strong restrictions on the uses of these names, both the 'dark names' and the 'light names', see below. In the initial phase of kampong formation, people would use only wear Indonesian style clothing while in the *kampung* and change into grass skirt/penis gourd while on the clan lands.

Other cultural practices also expressed the dichotomy clan lands versus *kampung*, for example witch executions as a rule took place on clan lands, not in *kampungs* where the Indonesian justice system was supposed to be in force. Sago grub feasts were (and are) always celebrated on clan lands, never in the *kampung*. Church services, on the other hand were never on clan lands, always in *kampungs*. On clan lands people performed rituals related to their ancestors. For sickness people used western medicine while in the settlements and traditional cures and plant medicine while on the clan lands (de Vries 2012a: 18). Of course, over time the dynamics of the opposition clan lands versus *kampungs* changes (de Vries: 2007) but the opposition itself remains crucial to the linguistic and cultural practices of Greater Awyu speakers.

The dichotomy of clan lands and *kampung* settlements strongly influences the use of local Papuan Malay and Greater Awyu speech varieties. Papuan Malay is mostly used in *kampung* contexts as interethnic lingua franca and as language of certain institutions, such as school and church. Interaction in school, shops and government offices in the villages is exclusively in varieties of Indonesian, ranging from basolects of Papuan Malay to acrolects that approach standard Indonesian. Greater Awyu languages are used both in *kampung* contexts between speakers of the same language and of course on clan lands. Although Greater Awyu languages are the preferred languages of the clan lands, during sago grub or pig feasts when hundreds of people from a wide area come together, Papuan Malay may be used as lingua franca when people cannot understand each other.

The closer to the coast, the more Papuan Malay is used in clan land contexts, if people still have their lands (because land is constantly being taken for economic activities in urban coastal zones). In coastal cities of West Papua landless Papuan people (Merauke, Sorong, Sentani and so on) tend to live together according to area of origin but increasingly use Papuan Malay there.

Roughly speaking, age, gender and distance to the coast determine the extent to which people know Papuan Malay. Most interior villages have elementary schools where children learn Indonesian but both the teachers and the pupils tend to be away from the villages many months a year. The pupils often go to the clan lands of their fathers or mother's brothers for a long time and the teachers stay in Merauke, the capital city of the regency. Men generally speak Papuan Malay better than women and younger people speak it better than older ones. Because brides bring the languages of their clan of origin with them to the clans of their husbands and also learn the languages of their husbands, women are "sometimes particularly associated with multilingualism in languages *other* than Indonesian" (Stasch 2007: 101).

Towards the foothills of the central mountain ranges where *kampungs* opened either very recently (the last decade) or where people still live exclusively on clan lands in tree houses (e.g. some parts of North Korowai), people know very little Papuan Malay, if at all. Papuan Malay slowly advanced from the coast to the foothills of the central mountain ranges. To give an idea of the advance of Papuan Malay in relation to the start of village formation: the missionary Johannes Veldhuizen started the Kombai-Korowai village Yaniruma in 1979–1981, when hardly anyone of the Korowai around the mission station spoke Indonesian (van Enk and de Vries 1997: 4) and "as of 2002, about 5 percent of Korowai spoke Indonesian well enough that they would do so regularly in the presence of more than just one person and the number of Indonesian speakers was growing quickly" (Stasch 2007: 100). Greater Awyu languages are not endangered, at least not in the short or medium term. In the long term Indonesian and local forms of Malay will form a threat to Greater Awyu languages, starting in coastal areas.

6.9 Language of humans and demons

Stasch (2007: 98) characterized Korowai attitudes towards Papuan Malay as fundamentally ambivalent. Papuan Malay is strongly associated with the *kampungs*. And many Greater Awyu speakers have an ambivalent relationship with the *kampungs*. *Kampung* settlements bring goods (iron axe heads, nylon, fishhooks) and services (clinics, schools, shops) from the wider world and most speakers deeply appreciate this. But at the same time, *kampungs* bring that same wider world threateningly close to the clan worlds and form a direct threat to clan autonomy and to their cherished clan lands. This ambivalence is a general attitude among Greater Awyu speakers.

The positive aspect of the attitude towards Papuan Malay is based on the usefulness of having a common language, an interethnic lingua franca amidst so many local languages and language families, each with a small number of speakers. Therefore, Greater Awyu speakers when they speak varieties of Indonesian, they always use the phrase *bahasa umum* 'general language' to refer to Indonesian and hardly ever use the term *Bahasa Indonesia*, 'Indonesian language' (Stasch 2007: 99). The preference for the term *bahasa umum* and the avoidance of the term *Bahasa Indonesia*, a term many Greater Awyu speakers learned in elementary school, is not a reflection of anti-Indonesian political sentiments (Stasch 2007: 98), rather it simply reflects is basic function as a lingua franca. The other reason why the association of Papuan Malay with the Indonesian Republic is not so strong is that all successive powers that controlled (parts of) western New Guinea in the past (Sultanate Tidore, the Dutch, the Japanese and the Indonesian Republic) used local Malay varieties in their dealings with locals (Stasch 2007: 98).

Young men, who want to buy things sold by Buginese or Chinese itinerant traders and who want salaried jobs, are highly motivated to learn the *bahasa umum*. It is a requirement to get access to jobs and money and to the wider world. Young Greater Awyu bachelors seem to be constantly on the move, residing on paternal and maternal clan lands and in the *kampungs* where they are overrepresented, just as elderly men and especially elderly women are overrepresented in the clan lands. The young Greater Awyu speakers generally have a pragmatic attitude towards the *bahasa umum* as a tool to improve their life. Given the sociocentric practices of identity expression, discussed above, it is natural for (usually younger and male) Greater Awyu speakers who have valued ties with foreigners in *kampung* contexts, to reflect these personal relationships in their language use. They do this both by speaking *bahasa umum* when in the *kampung* (also when no foreigner is around) and by mixing in many lexical and grammatical elements from Indonesian when speaking Greater Awyu languages, even when they are on their clan lands. By doing so, they signal their valued relationships with these *bahasa umum* speaking people, relationships that are part of their personal identity, alongside clan and other relationships.

However, there is also a strong negative attitude towards Papuan Malay. It is not only seen as the *bahasa umum*, a language for interethnic communication, it is also strongly associated with the world of the foreigners in the settlements. And these foreigners are a threat to the autonomy of the clan lands. They bring laws that oppose certain cultural practices (cannibalism, infanticide, witchcraft trials) and they need clan lands for airstrips, village formation, and modern economic activities (mining, logging, forestry).

These threats to clan lands and clan autonomy are the basis for the ambivalent attitude of most Greater Awyu towards Papuan Malay. That is why they use very negative terms to refer to varieties of Indonesian when speaking Greater Awyu languages, terms that reflect the aspects of 'otherness' (Stasch 2007). For example, the name for the Indonesian language in Korowai is *laléo-aup* (demon-language; van Enk and de Vries 1997: 103) and in Kombai *xwaye-lu* (demon-language; de Vries 1993a: 2). The background of these Greater Awyu 'demon language' terms found in Korowai (Becking-Dawi) and Kombai (Ndeiram subgroup), the unmarked and normal way to refer to Indonesian, lies in notions of personhood discussed in the previous section. To refer to their own languages they use terms that contain the notion of (normal) person, for example Kombai use *xwaye-lu* 'demon language' to refer to Standard Indonesian (and to local varieties of Papuan Malay) but they use *xombaye lu* 'person language' to refer to their ancestral language.

6.10 Cultural geography and spatial orientation

Rivers and streams, and features of rivers such as whirlpools, inlets, high banks and low banks carved out in the landscape by meandering processes form the frame of reference for spatial orientation in all Greater Awyu languages (van Kessel 2011). Rivers and streams are usually the only features of the landscape that are systematically named (Stasch 2001: 34; Stasch 2009: 26) and these names constantly surface in everyday life and in oral traditions. In dense rainforests that are frequently flooded, where small, fordable streams, sometimes with improvised bridges made of trees felled for that purpose, can turn overnight into powerful rivers, travel on foot is often problematic. Rivers and streams are therefore essential for travel, transport of food, connecting with other people, trade and many other things. Stasch (2001: 36) writes: "All Korowai speech is saturated with the words for these stream-based directional categories, whether people are describing travel across the landscape, the motion of the sun or any other atmospheric entity, the position of an object in a house or in someone's bodily vicinity, or an endless variety of further kinds of spatial relationships of diverse scales". The following figure 4 from Stasch (2001: 37) represents the core of Korowai riverine terminology.

Korowai also understand the landscape and the trajectory of the sun as a stream (Stasch 2001: 38). The point where the sun sets on the horizon is the sun's *maxol* 'downstream end' and the location of the sunrise is its *gun* 'upstream end' (Stasch 2001: 59). The upstream-downstream opposition sets up an kind of absolute east-west orientation (Stasch 2001: 38).

Not only the sun and the landscape but also other domains are spatially understood in stream-based categories. Stream-based terminology for example saturates talk of domains such as social relations (Stasch 2001: 38). In tree houses, the side of the tree house which faces the rising sun, is the 'upstream' side, the men's quarter, and the opposite side the 'downstream' side, where women and their dependent children live. A central wall separates the two halves. People motivate the division in terms of the necessity to separate mothers from their daughters' husband (affinal avoidance relations) and in terms of gendered pollution taboos, the fear among men that menstrual smells or blood would make them ill if the women lived in the 'upstream' or east side and the men in the 'downstream' section. (Stasch 2001: 152). The sun is thought to push such smells 'downriver' (Stasch 2001: 152).

Korowai marks elevational distinctions in a closed class of elevational adverbs that express five riverine distinctions, in two subsets, one based on the direction of the river flow and the other based on the river banks (see fig. 4). The elevational adverbs occur mostly as modifiers of verbs in verb phrases but may also function adnominally as postnominal elevational demonstratives in noun phrases.

Xülol 'upstream' versus *sübop* 'downstream' form the first subset that locates referents relative to the deictic center (by default the speaker, sometimes a narrative participant) as downstream from the speaker or upstream from where the speaker is, along the axis of the river.

The second subset expresses three distinctions based on the land axis perpendicular to the axis of the river: *aüp* 'downland/downbank towards the river' versus *lax* 'upland away from river' versus *mén* 'across the river'/on the other bank/side of the river'. The riverine elevationals are geophysical systems of elevationals in the typology of Burenhult (2008): they are tied to rivers and streams and have not developed into what Burenhult (2008) calls global elevationals such as *up* and *down* in English that are tied to specific features of the landscape.

These elevational roots occasionally occur with demonstrative function in noun phrases, (283), or highly frequently as adverbs modifying verbs of motion, (284):

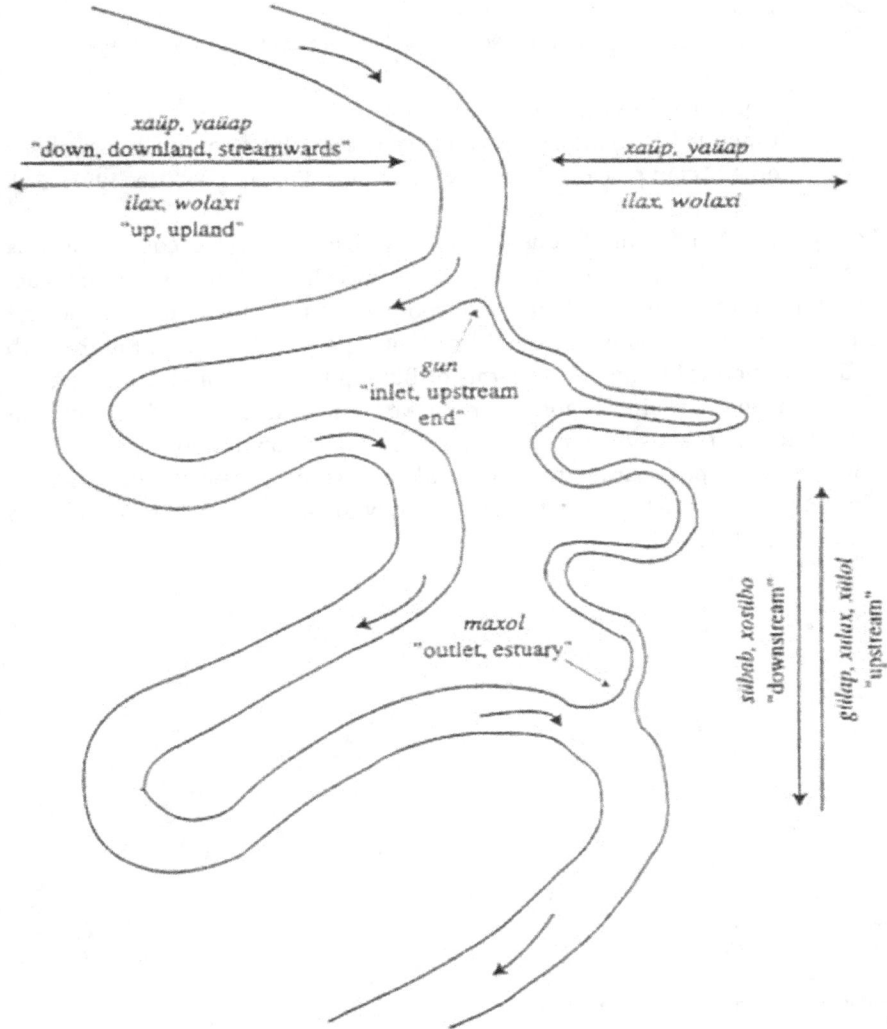

Figure 4: Stream-based spatial deictics.

(283) *balüm-tax-telo   ndemop   ip-ta-da   dé*
mud- LOC -be[RLS.NON-1SG] swamp   here-LOC-NEG say[RLS.NON-1SG]
gülaf-exa   fiu-ma-la-xolo   dé
upstream-MOD land-also-LOC-Q   say[RLS.NON-1SG]
'it is mud here, a swamp, not here, he said, but perhaps on the upstream land?'   (Korowai, van Enk and de Vries 1997: 196)

(284) aomekho   ye   xülo   ye-mom-él   bolüp
      plant[SS] 3SG   Upstream   3SG-mother's.brother-PL   clan.territory
      ye   loxté
      3SG   go.away[RLS.NON1SG]
      'He planted (banana sprigs) and went away upstream to his mother's brothers' clan place.'   (Korowai, van Enk and de Vries 1997: 174).

Korowai has four highly frequent motion verbs: *le/la/lai* 'to come' (towards speech act location), *xa/xo* 'to go' (away from speech act location), *wai/ai* 'to descend (river, tree house, hill) and *lu* 'to climb up' (a tree or tree house). The first three very often combine with the riverine elevationals of Figure 5. But the verb *lu* denotes verticality proper, in terms of Burenhult (2008), and cannot be applied to moving up a hill or going upriver. Korowai lacks the specific directional verbs found in the Awyu-Dumut branch that denote motion upriver, downriver, towards river, upland away from riverbank, across river. Instead, Korowai combines its elaborate sets of directional adverbs with more general verbs of motion (van Kessel 2011: 33).

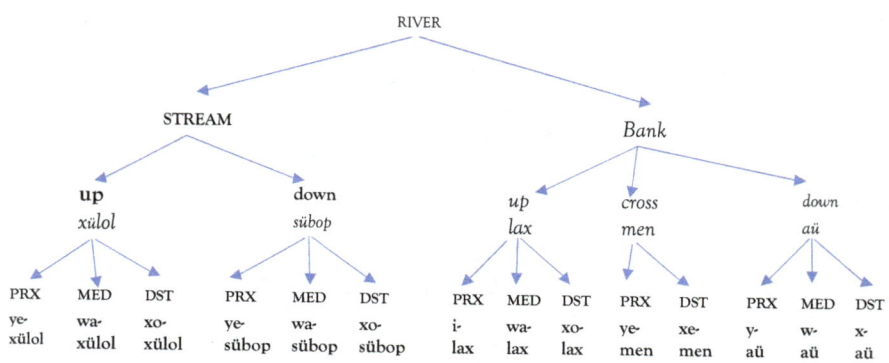

Figure 5: Korowai riverine elevationals.

The five basic riverine elevationals may also form compounds with three non-riverine place deictic roots that locate referents with respect to the speech act participants in terms of three degrees of proximity: *ip* 'here/ proximate', *wap* 'there'/medial and *xop* 'there'/distal 'over there'. This leads to a closed set of 13 compound elevational adverbs/demonstratives besides the 5 simplex riverine elevationals,[37] for example (285):

(285) ye alè-debüf Lai   alè-debüf Banam Banam=tom=pekho
      he canoe-way come[RLS.NON-1SG] canoe-way Asmat Asmat=FOC=EMPH
      alèf alimexe-té=do   ye-gülol   la-la-ma-té
      canoe row-[NON1PL.RLS]=DS PRX-upstream come-come-HAB-NON1PL
      'The Citak Asmat, it was the Citak Asmat who used to come here upstream by canoes.'   (Korowai, van Enk and de Vries 1997: 194)

6.11 Conclusion

This chapter dealt with the cultural context of Greater Awyu clan communities and the historical contexts of *kampung* formation and of the processes of gradual integration into the successive nation-states that claimed West Papua as their territory. These cultural and historical contexts have crucial linguistic consequences, for example in the areas of linguistic ideologies, patterns of language contact, language attitudes, multilingualism, language names and metalanguage, speech registers (e.g. linguistic avoidance and lexical substitution) and lexical domains (e.g. kinship).

There are two parallel worlds that Greater Awyu languages function in, the clan worlds and the world of the *kampungs*. Processes of *kampung* formation that started in the coastal zone in the 1940s and are now reaching the northernmost parts of the Greater Awyu area, brought varieties of Indonesian to the area. Greater Awyu speakers have an ambivalent attitude towards that language. It is seen as a positive thing because it is a useful lingua franca, not strongly associated with the Indonesian Republic, since regional varieties of Malay were already a trade and contact language long before the Republic gained control of West Papua. But it is also seen as negative, because it is associated with foreigners who form a threat to individual and clan autonomy and to the clan lands. Kombai and Korowai express the negative perception of Indonesian by using the demon term for Indonesian.

---

37 All elevationals of Figure 5 have been confirmed by occurrences in transcribed texts apart from *wa-xülo*. Note also that the compound forms occasionally occur with the stream-based root first: *xülo-xo*. The elevationals have quite a few synonyms and variants, for example *xülol* has *gülol, gülap* and *xulax* as synonyms, all meaning 'upstream' (Stasch 2001: 36–37).

The world of the *kampungs* interacts with the world of the clan lands, a world fundamentally structured by clan notions that also determine the way language functions and is talked about. Language, as a clan transcending entity, is not central to group identity and Greater Awyu speakers had no names for their languages other than 'person talk', 'talk of clan X' or 'talk around river Y'. The language names of Greater Awyu languages are exonyms that reflect linguistic ideologies of foreigners that needed labels for the arbitrary chosen parts of dialect chains around government or mission stations.

Certain words (mostly names) related to the origin of clans, to clan ancestors and clan totems are exceptional, because they do indeed express a group identity, that of the patriclan. Otherwise, Greater Awyu languages do not represent group identities, as language is a clan transcending entity and clan membership is the core of Greater Awyu group identity. The combination of clan exogamy and the presence of many different languages, each with around 2000–3000 speakers, resulted in many children growing up with two languages, of the father and the mother. Because of the importance of the avunculate, the institutionalized mother's brother-sister's son dyad that reflects the strong bilateralism of these communities, the language of mother's people is also crucial for children, especially the boys who depend on their mother's brothers for protection against witchcraft accusations and for acquiring a bride. More generally, multilingualism, borrowing and code switching are linguistic expressions of a relational, sociocentric concept of the person as an amalgam of relations.

Chapter 7
Greater Awyu languages in context

7.1 Introduction

This chapter aims to place the findings of the previous chapters into various contexts, both linguistic and non-linguistic. Teasing apart the various historical, cultural, genetic, typological and areal factors that shaped Greater Awyu languages is very difficult. Because of the complicated interaction of these different factors (some of which are not well-understood at present), this chapter cannot be more than tentative and preliminary.

First, the genetic context is discussed (§7.2), followed by the areal context (§7.3) and the typological context (§7.4). The cultural and historical contexts of Greater Awyu languages were discussed in chapter 6. Section 7.5 presents a migration scenario for the Greater Awyu language family. The chapter ends with a summary (§7.6).

7.2 Genetic context

7.2.1 The Awyu-Dumut language family

Wester (2014) revised and completed the proto Awyu-Dumut phonologies of Healey (1970) and Voorhoeve (2001). She also reconstructed major parts of proto Awyu-Dumut morphology and described the internal structure of the family, with two well-established subgroups (Awyu and Dumut) and a third, the Ndeiram subgroup, that needs further research, both in terms of the languages that are considered to be Ndeiram languages and to determine the position of Ndeiram languages within the Awyu-Dumut group.

The only relatively well-documented Ndeiram language is Kombai. Wester (2014) convincingly argued that Kombai is an Awyu-Dumut language. But in terms of its relation to the other Awyu-Dumut languages, she finds that the evidence is conflicting (Wester 2014: 197). Statistical methods applied to lexical data led Wester (2014: 41–48) to group Kombai with Dumut languages. On the other hand, Kombai participated in morphological innovations of the Awyu subgroup, namely the presence of two alternating realis markers –*d* and –*k* (Wester 2014: 197). The phonological evidence is also inconclusive according to Wester (2014: 16). Kombai has a range of unique morphological innovations not found in any Awyu or Dumut languages: in its 3PL pronoun, the absence of Past tense(s), the marking of Realis and its negated verb forms (de Vries, Wester and van den Heuvel 2012: 289).

Evidence from shared (bound) morphology plays a key role in Wester (2014: 18), in line with the emphasis placed by Foley (2000: 359) on the use of bound morphology in establishing genetic relations in the New Guinea context:

> However, for non-Austronesian languages, the vast majority of which have no documentation older than 50 years, it is problematic to sift what is true, genetically inherited material from what is borrowed from other languages, especially the borrowings from related contiguous languages or from languages now defunct. Consequently, comparative linguistics in Papuan languages must proceed with care and the utmost rigor. It would appear that bound morphological forms are the most resistant to borrowing [again, however, not entirely immune (see Donohue 1999, Foley 1991)], so that bound morphological forms that appear cognate are the most reliable guide to genetic relationships between Papuan languages.

The use of (bound) morphology as one of the diagnostic tool for genetic relations, as proposed by Foley (2000: 359), is only reliable, if these conditions are all met: morphological correspondences must be shown to correlate in form *and* grammatical meaning, extend over paradigms and must be systematic, i.e. found in multiple, independent parts of languages under comparison.[38]

If correspondences in (bound) morphology receives relatively the most weight, it makes most sense to place Kombai in the Awyu group. Not only did Kombai participate in morphological innovations of the Awyu subgroup in the realis paradigm, namely the presence of two alternating realis markers *–d* and *–k* (Wester 2014: 197), but there are also other indications. For example Proto Awyu-Dumut did mark the distinction realis and irrealis in verb stems, with a short stem for realis forms and a longer stem for irrealis forms. The Awyu languages plus Kombai continued this distinction but the Dumut group did not (Wester 2014: 90). Kombai also continued the double negation **fe-verbstem-do* of proto Awyu-Dumut just like the Awyu subgroup did, and with a close reflex of proto Awyu **fa-/fe-verbstem-de* namely Kombai *fe-verbstem-do* (Wester 2014: 139–140).

Kombai is lexically closer to the Dumut than to the Awyu subgroup but this is hardly surprising given their intensive interaction, intermarriage and often co-residence with Mandobo, Yonggom Wambon and Digul Wambon speakers along the upper reaches of the Digul river.

---

38 Wester (2014: 18) calls these constraints the paradigmaticity constraint (referring to Ross 2005: 50), the form-function correlation constraint (referring to Foley 2005b: 110) and the systematicity constraint (referring to Foley 2005b: 141). When all these constraints are applied, the chance that morphological correspondences are the result of borrowing is significantly reduced.

7.2.2 The Greater Awyu language family

Wester's work on the proto phonology and proto morphology of the Awyu-Dumut family made it possible to understand the Awyu-Dumut family as a branch of the Greater Awyu family, with two branches, the Awyu-Dumut branch and the Becking-Dawi branch (Korowai, Tsaukambo, Komyandaret) (de Vries, Wester and van den Heuvel 2012).

Besides systematic sound correspondences (de Vries, Wester and van den Heuvel 2012: 294), Becking-Dawi and Awyu-Dumut languages share morphological patterns and matter in systematic and paradigmatic ways, with good form-function correlations: a verb paradigm with adhortative and intentional meanings, including subject person-number suffixes (§3.6.3.3), personal pronouns (§3.4.1), possessive prefixes (§3.2.1), negation circumfix (§3.6.3.5), interrogative sentence clitic (de Vries, Wester and van den Heuvel 2012: 298) and the focus clitic (=tV/=lV in Becking-Dawi (de Vries 2012b: 185), =te/nde in Dumut languages).

None of these morphological correspondences between Becking-Dawi and Awyu-Dumut are found in the neighboring language families, with the exception of correspondences in the pronominal paradigms, attributed to shared Trans New Guinea descent by van den Heuvel and Fedden (2014). But Becking-Dawi and Awyu-Dumut pronominal paradigms share innovations vis-à-vis Trans New Guinea pronouns (Ross 2005: 29) which do not occur in the neighboring families: the vowel quality /u/ and the final /p/ of the personal pronouns (de Vries, Wester and van den Heuvel 2012: 298). Given the challenges of establishing subfamilies of Trans New Guinea in convincing ways, these Greater Awyu innovations with respect to Trans New Guinea are a significant finding that deserves further research into other distinctive innovations of the Greater Awyu subfamily of the Trans New Guinea family.

7.2.3 Genetic links between Greater Awyu, Greater Ok and Asmat-Kamoro

Placing the Greater Awyu language family in a genetic (sub)group with one or more of its neighboring families is difficult, at least with conservative standards of evidence. Voorhoeve (2005) compared wordlists of Awyu-Dumut, Asmat-Kamoro and Ok families and his results give some idea of the lexical relations between the groups. Whatever the nature of the lookalikes (borrowed or inherited), the number of good lookalikes is low. Voorhoeve (2005: 164) finds only 25 cognates between Asmat-Kamoro and Awyu-Dumut (out of 500 items) and between Awyu-Dumut and Ok 65 cognate forms (out of 500 items). The Mountain Ok-Asmat-Kamoro comparison yields 67 cognates, a lexical similarity Voorhoeve (2005: 164) attributes to ancient contact in the mountains (Van den Heuvel and Fedden 2014: 8–9).[39]

Van den Heuvel and Fedden (2014) review the evidence for a Trans New Guinea subgroup consisting of Greater Awyu and Greater Ok. They conclude that there is insufficient evidence for such a subgroup. Voorhoeve (2005) had already dismissed a subgrouping of Asmat-Kamoro and Awyu-Dumut languages, because he found just 25 cognate forms and insufficient evidence for regular sound correspondences that would set them apart as a subgroup within Trans New Guinea and also because Voorhoeve found the morphologies of both families to be very different, in pattern and matter (Voorhoeve 2005: 164).

There are indeed very few similarities in morphology, in pattern and matter, between the language families on the southern plains. There are similarities in free pronouns, to be sure and these are ascribed to shared inheritance from proto Trans New Guinea by Ross (2005), Pawley (2005) and van den Heuvel and Fedden (2014). But it is very hard to find other similarities in morphology beyond pronouns. Voorhoeve (2005: 165) writes that a number of Awyu-Dumut and Ok languages share infinitival forms ending in a *–Vn* suffix. Indeed, proto Ok-Oksapmin has a verbal noun suffix *-Vn* (Loughnane and Fedden 2011: 27) and so do Korowai, Aghu and Sawuy (van den Heuvel and Fedden 2014: 9–10). Given the distribution of this infinitival suffix over two branches of the Greater Awyu family, this is certainly a promising piece of evidence from bound verb morphology. But on the other hand verbal nouns of Greater Awyu languages are members of the open noun class and the verbal noun suffix may have spread by diffusion of (verbal) nouns (van den Heuvel and Fedden 2014: 9–10).

Van den Heuvel and Fedden (2014: 11–12) observe that the proto Ok kinship plural suffix *–Vl* occurs also in two Greater Awyu languages, Digul Wambon and Korowai. However, both these languages border on Ok languages and the kinship plural morpheme may have been borrowed along with

---

[39] Van den Heuvel and Fedden (2014: 8) observe: "Given that Voorhoeve also used nonreconstructed forms in his search for cognates, it is important to take note of the total number of lexical items available to him. For Awyu-Dumut, Voorhoeve had (in addition to the list of 108 reconstructed forms) a lexical inventory at his disposal of maximally 500 words.[. . . .] Finally, for Asmat-Kamoro (AsK), he had far more data available: a comparative wordlist of 500 words plus 418 reconstructed forms (Voorhoeve 1980), Drabbe's (1937) 160-page dictionary of Kamoro and his own 400-page dictionary of Central Asmat (Voorhoeve 1999)".

the kinship term in the context of cross-language marriages. Proto Awyu-Dumut has a plural suffix *-gi, with reflexes in all Awyu-Dumut languages, including Digul Wambon (Wester 2014: 8).[40]

7.2.4 Greater Awyu and Trans New Guinea

Although there is at present not enough convincing evidence to reach scholarly consensus on subgroups of the Greater Awyu family with one or more of the neighboring families on the coastal plains, there is a certain consensus that the Greater Awyu family is part of the Trans New Guinea family (in its latest version, Pawley and Hammarström 2018). But it is important to remember that the Trans New Guinea hypothesis is based on a top-down comparison of hundreds of languages and that for many of these languages there are no dictionaries, just short wordlists and/or sketchy descriptions. Pawley (2012: 103) describes the situation as follows: "The top-down method, applied to the Trans New Guinea family, has major limitations. It yields reconstructions that are approximate, broad brush, leaving some details indeterminate. For another thing, the pool of widely distributed cognate sets and therefore the pool of reconstructions that can safely be attributed to pTNG, is small". The implication of Pawley's assessment is that the term family when applied to Trans New Guinea means something different from when it is applied to families that were established by bottom-up reconstruction, based on systematic sound correspondences and shared bound morphology (in patterns and matter).

Van den Heuvel and Fedden (2014: 6) give the following evidence for a genetic link of the Greater Awyu (and Greater Ok) language families to Trans New Guinea: "Proto–Awyu-Dumut *na 1SG and *ŋga 2SG can be traced back to PTNG *na 1SG and *<ng>ga 2SG (for the PTNG forms see Ross 2005:29). The same is true for Proto Ok *na-1SG, *ka-b 2SG. Likewise, Proto Ok *ya 3SG.M, *yu 3SG.F can be traced back to PTNG *[y]a, *ua 3SG, while Proto Ok *nu[b] and *ni[b] reflect PTNG *ni, *nu 1PL".

---

[40] In unpublished work that is still being worked on and that can be accessed through the website *NewGuineaWorld* (https://sites.google.com/site/newguineaworld/families/trans-new-guinea/central-west-newguinea/digul-river-ok), Usher (2018) presents systematic sound correspondences between a steadily increasing number of cognates of Greater Awyu and Ok languages and this leads him to suggest that Greater Awyu languages form a subgroup of Trans-New Guinea languages (contra Van den Heuvel and Fedden 2014). This debate is the familiar splitter-lumper debate that is difficult to resolve with the limited datasets that are available at present. Usher (2018) recognizes that there is very little in the way of shared bound inflectional morphology to link Greater Awyu languages to Ok languages.

In addition to this morphological evidence, they point to seven lexical items from Proto Mountain Ok and five forms from proto Awyu-Dumut that can be "taken as reflexes of PTNG forms as reconstructed in Pawley (2005b: 85–88)". (Van den Heuvel and Fedden 2014: 6).[41] These forms are listed in Table 13, with the bold forms considered reflexes of proto Trans New Guinea by Van den Heuvel and Fedden (2014: 6):

Table 13: Reflexes of proto Trans New Guinea forms (from Van den Heuvel and Fedden (2014: 6)).

1)	PAD *kat 'skin'	PMO *kaal	proto TNG *(ŋg,k)a(nd,t)apu
2)	PAD *ŋgom 'blood'	PMO *keim;*kaim	proto TNG *ke(ñj,s)a
3)	PAD *bege; *mit 'bone'	PMO *kun;*kuun	proto TNG *kondaC
4)	PD *si(n) 'nose'	PMO *mutuum;	proto TNG *mundu
5)	PAD *paŋgat 'tongue'	PMO *fooŋ; *fIlaŋ; *fAlaŋ	proto TNG *mbilaŋ; *me(l,n)
6)	PAD *mbe(ndo) 'hand'	PMO *siKiiL; *saKaaL;	proto TNG *sikal; *sakil
7)	PAD *om; *am 'breast'	PMO *muuk	proto TNG *amu
8)	PAD *kum; kym 'to die'	PMO *Caan-; *cwaan	proto TNG *kumV-
9)	PAD *ok 'water'	PMO *ook *ok	proto TNG *ok[V]; *nok
10)	PAD me 'to come'	PMO *tele	proto TNG *me
11)	PA *maga 'mouth'	PMO *niŋ; *niiŋ;	proto TNG *maŋkat *maŋgata;

Van den Heuvel and Fedden (2014) conclude that the evidence for the link of the Greater Awyu family to the Trans New Guinea grouping needs strengthening (van den Heuvel and Fedden 2014: 6). They point out that beyond reconstruction of proto- or early Trans New Guinea pronoun sets,[42] the only other

---

[41] Regarding the evidence presented by Voorhoeve (2005), van den Heuvel and Fedden (2014: 6) write: "Voorhoeve sums up a number of cognates between Proto Ok and Proto Awyu-Dumut which exhibit more or less regular sound correspondences. In this respect one might say that another of Pawley's criteria is met, viz. that there should be a sizeable body of cognates exhibiting regular sound correspondences with cognates of another Trans New Guinea language. There is the danger of circularity here, however, in the sense that one first has to prove independently that one of the two language groups (Awyu-Dumut or Ok) is Trans New Guinea, before the regular sound correspondences can count as evidence for TNG membership of the other language groups".

[42] It is important to point out that Ross (2005) describes his top down reconstruction of Trans New Guinea pronouns as a *preliminary* diagnostic for Trans New Guinea membership.

morphological paradigm reconstructed for proto Trans New Guinea is "a partial and very tentative reconstruction of bound pronominal suffixes on the verb (Pawley 2005: 91)" (van den Heuvel and Fedden 2014: 7). The subject person-number suffixes of the Greater Awyu family do not correspond to any forms of this tentative, partial proto Trans New Guinea paradigm. This means that the systematicity constraint of the comparative method (see note 1) which requires paradigmatic correspondences in multiple, independent parts of the grammar, cannot be applied.

Palmer (2018: 16) observed that "Membership of Trans New Guinea is an area of particular uncertainty". Different criteria can be used to establish membership, and different weight can be given to various criteria. Foley (2018: 199) gives a key methodological role to evidence from bound morphology. When membership is based on just a handful of (often disputable) reflexes of (equally) putative proto Trans New Guinea words, without reliable sound correspondences, in combination with some reflexes in free pronoun paradigms, the claim to membership is a working hypothesis that needs to be backed up with evidence from bound morphology (Foley 2018: 199–200). This chapter follows this prudent approach of Foley (2018) and van den Heuvel and Fedden (2014) to view the Trans New Guinea membership of the Greater Awyu family as a working hypothesis in need of further evidence.

7.3 Areal context

The area where Greater Awyu speech communities live, with the exception of the foothill area south of the central ranges where the northernmost Greater Awyu groups dwell, was slowly formed in the course of the last 6,000 years when the southern plains of New Guinea gradually emerged after sea levels fell and rivers originating in the mountains brought sediments (Chappell 2005: 531). This means that the ancestors of Greater Awyu speakers and their neighbors, the Ok, the Asmat-Kamoro, the Marindic-Jaqajic, to mention just the three major groups, must have moved relatively recently into their coastal home lands.

Rivers, streams, swamps and estuaries dominate the geography and ecology of the southern lowlands. Deictic verbs that mean 'come/go down river/up river/ across the river' and complex systems of secondary demonstratives derived from

---

Hammarström (2013) did a statistic analysis of the role of chance in Ross's pairwise mass comparison of short, often monosyllabic pronouns and concluded that when very many language pairs are compared, chance matchings in (a number) of these language pairs cannot be ruled out (van den Heuvel and Fedden 2014: 12).

those verbs (§3.5.3) are very frequently used in Greater Awyu texts (see e.g. the Mandobo text in §9.2.2). This is because river based terminology is not only used in spatial orientation but also to talk about many other domains (see chapter 6).

The southern plain that emerged consists of two parts and to understand the history of Greater Awyu communities, it is important to distinguish the two: the upper part, the Upper Fly-Digul plain and the lower part, the South Coastal plain. Ecologically and culturally, the Upper Fly-Digul plain is different from the South Coastal plain (see Knauft 1993 for historical and cultural characteristics of the South Coastal plain and Welsch 1994 for those of the Upper Fly-Digul plain).

The Upper Fly-Digul plain does not have the rhythm of dry and wet seasons of the South Coastal plain, has much less protein-rich food available and can only support a small and dispersed population. In contrast, the abundance of protein-rich food from the sea and from the estuaries, in combination with massive supplies of sago, made population numbers grow on the South Coastal plain. Big villages of 1, 000 to 2,000 persons were not uncommon on the South Coastal plain, among for example Asmat or Marindic-Jaqajic speaking communities (Knauft 1993: 66).

This contrasts strongly with the small clan communities of the Upper Fly-Digul plain, with for example Kombai or Korowai clans often numbering no more than 20 persons (Stasch 2009). I regularly saw people with serious food deficiencies, protein-starved, in the upriver and foothill parts in the early 1980s and vast stretches of jungle were uninhabited. Although the South Coastal plain has more inhabitants than the Upper Fly-Digul plain, both plains are home to billions of mosquitos. Malnutrition, tuberculosis, malaria, elephantiasis, anemia and venereal diseases kept population density very low, in the past as today.

The South Coastal Plain has a long history of headhunting. Knauft (1993) describes the pre-colonial South Coastal region in terms of cultural emphasis on the creation of life-power through ritual sexuality and on the acquiring of life-power by bringing back enemy heads from raids. Throughout the South Coastal plain, cosmological links between fertility, ritual sexuality and headhunting practices were found (Knauft 1993). The large scale and seasonal military operations by Marindic-Jaqajic groups which found their cultural basis in this headhunting–fertility complex, required a firm ecological basis and the abundance of storable and transportable sago made these raids possible: the sago was taken aboard the large war canoes (Knauft 1993).

The inhabitants of the Upper Fly-Digul plain were victims of these raids well into the 1960s and their cultural practices were not centered around ritual sexuality, fertility and headhunting. Instead, we find an emphasis on regular, large-scale pig feasts and sago grub feasts that created socio-economic, marriage and cultural ties throughout the Upper Fly-Digul plain (Welsch 1994), feasts with guests from a wide area, based on systems of chain-invitations (van Enk and de Vries 1997: 32–33). We also find high levels of internal aggression among Upper Fly-Digul groups (mostly in the form of witchcraft-related executions and cannibalism, van Enk and de Vries 1997: 47–48) rather than external aggression in the form of headhunting or other raiding traditions of their neighbors on the South Coastal plain. The integrative feast cycles of the Upper Fly-Digul plain were (and are) a counterforce against the fundamental tendency towards individualism, dispersion, high individual mobility and socio-political fragmentation that characterize people of the Upper Fly-Digul plain (e.g. Boelaars 1970 for Mandobo; Stasch 2009 for Korowai).

We do not claim that the South Coastal plain and the Upper Fly-Digul plain had two contrasting "cultures" but rather that a recurrent number of cultural practices, in different permutations and configurations, distinguish both plains culturally and historically, two plains that also differ ecologically, although there is no sharp boundary between them.

Languages of the Greater Awyu family are spoken on both plains, along the Digul river but also between the Digul and the Mappi River and from close to the Fly River in the east to the south-west of the Wildeman River. Speakers of the Greater Awyu languages on the South Coastal plain participated in the cultural practices of that area, e.g. headhunting (for example Aghu, Drabbe 1957: 55). Speakers of Greater Awyu languages on the Upper Fly-Digul plain were (and are) culturally fully part of that area, with their pig- and sago grub feast cycles, social personhood defined in terms of 'witches, humans and demons' (see chapter 6), no headhunting and no ritual sexuality, very high levels of internal capital punishment and internal cannibalism.

The relatively poor ecological conditions, the internal aggression related to witchcraft accusations and the external aggression by the headhunting groups from the South Coast plain kept Greater Awyu clans on the Upper Fly-Digul plain small and dispersed. It formed the basis for the socially and politically fragmented way of life, with very small clans, a strong emphasis on both clan and individual autonomy and a high level of residential mobility. In this context language, as a clan transcending entity, never became associated with culturally significant units or with social or political group identities. Within clans individuals have different repertoires of multilingualism, dependent on their individual residential history and maternal clan bonds (see chapter 6).

How did and how do speakers of the various language families on the southern plains interact with each other and how did those contacts shape their languages? Given our limited knowledge of the history of the southern plains and with limited lexical data, there is only a few things we can say with any certainty.

7.3.1 Headhunting

Let us first have a closer look at the history of Marind groups and the patterns of interaction they developed with their northern neighbors (de Vries 2004: 14–15). The intense interaction of the Marind with other groups in the coastal areas of south New Guinea is relatively well-documented (Van Baal 1966). Marind headhunting practices involved expansionist tendencies where headhunting groups turned neighbors and former victims into allies that functioned as support and bridge to more remote groups. This led to Marindinisation of non-Marind groups in the interior of south New Guinea (van Baal 1966, 1984). Van Baal (1984: 129) writes: "Marind-Anim culture was an expanding culture, spreading from the coast to the interior and along the coast from east to west". Marind groups organized annual headhunting raids, with large war parties that travelled hundreds of kilometers. We have credible eyewitness reports from the last decades of the 19th century. Van Baal (1966: 713) mentions reports of colonial civil servants from 1884 (Captain Strachan, encounter with 1200 Marind in 35 war canoes across the international border, 300 kilometers east of their Marind villages, see also Knauft 1993:156) and in a report from 1896 (Lieutenant William MacGregor, 75 manned Marind war canoes, with over 500 headhunters and lots of sago, 250 kilometers away from their Marind villages).

The Digul river was strongly associated in Marind mythology with headhunting (Knauft 1993: 157): it was via the Digul river that they reached the Greater Awyu and Greater Ok groups on the Upper Fly-Digul plain. The numbers of Marind headhunters involved in these raids (500, 1200) is enormous in the context of the Upper Fly-Digul plain with dispersed and politically fragmented small clans of around 20 people and with whole linguistic groups numbering between 500 (Tsaukambo) and 3000 (Kombai). The Marind groups were not the only headhunters, the Yéi-Nan (Van Baal 1982: 57) and Asmat-Kamoro groups such as the Citak (Baas 1990: 3ff, 8) were very active as well. Citak headhunting raids on the Korowai and the Kombai stopped in 1966 (van Enk and de Vries 1997: 14) but when I lived in the Korowai and Kombai areas in the early 1980s the fear of the Citak was still very strong among the Kombai along the Ndeiram Hitam River and the Korowai along the Becking River.

One should not imagine this Anim expansion as a kind of systematic ethnocide, or even as aiming at ethnocide or at replacing the cultures of the conquered groups by "Anim culture " or "Anim" languages. Although Anim clans were generally much bigger than the small clans of Upper Fly-Digul groups, and could strike alliances with other clans, it was not an Anim "nation-state" with a nationalistic linguistic ideology based on clan-transcending notions of "Anim" language and culture. Rather, clan ancestors, clan totems and clan fertility rituals (rather than a language or a clan-transcending "pan-Anim" culture) informed their identity construction. If anything, Marindinization or Animisation will have meant grand scale multilingualism, co-residence, linguistic exogamy with its concomitant convergence effects. Clearly, the Marind expansion went hand in hand with the absorption of many linguistic and cultural practices of non-Trans New Guinea groups by Marind warrior groups. So much so, in fact, that the Marind language lost its Trans New Guinea profile and was typologically integrated in non-Trans New Guinea South New Guinea (Evans and Klamer 2012: 6).

The highly developed canoe technology with very big sea-going war canoes is very useful in South New Guinea coastal zones but much less so on the Upper Fly-Digul plain where the thousands of smaller tributaries of the major rivers such as the Digul are often largely dry, with huge stone banks and with frequent, very sudden and dangerous flash floods. The upper reaches of the Digul itself are often unnavigable. Therefore, small Greater Awyu clans tended to build their tree houses away from big rivers that could carry headhunting war canoes. Even if Marind war parties managed to reach the dispersed clan territories, the high tree houses could be well-defended: the very hard ironwood trees are impossible to set on fire and extremely difficult to cut, the tree house staircase (see fig. 3 in chapter 6) is designed to be easily and quickly pulled upward (e.g. not tied to anything on the ground) and the tree house can easily store enough food and water for a long time, not to mention the arrows that would be aimed at attackers from from 15 to around 30 meters above them. This explains that linguistic and cultural processes of 'Animisation' as described by van Baal (1966) and by colonial sources will have been less intensive on the Upper Fly-Digul plain where the raids will have had the character of hit-and-run actions affecting people that happened to be along the banks of the navigable stretches of very major rivers, for example people working in gardens on the banks. However, warning yells will have announced the war parties coming upriver, as I witnessed myself in the early 1980s when a couple of Citak-Asmat canoes came up the Becking river (with peaceful intentions) and yells announced their arrival long before they became visible. Local Korowai people became very scared and ran for cover, taking my daughter with them to safety. Korowai and Kombai clans that did not appreciate contact with outsiders still withdrew to areas far away from major rivers in the time I lived there (1982–1992).

7.3.2 Linguistic effects of Marindinisation

De Vries (2004: 15) points to the presence of a two-gender distinction in Lower Ok languages such as Southern Kati, both in nouns and 3SG pronouns, based on back vowel (feminine) versus front vowel (masculine) ablaut, just as in Marindic-Jaqajic, as possible linguistic effects of Marindinisation. But if Marindinisation left traces anywhere in Greater Awyu languages or cultural practices, it must be in the Awyu subgroup, the Greater Awyu group that settled amidst Marindic-Jaqajic groups. The Awyu subgroup does indeed show some cultural and linguistic impact from Marindic-Jaqajic. The Awyu subgroup has a different numeral system than all the other Greater Awyu subgroups that have body-part tally systems, using the hands, arms and head (see §3.9). The Awyu languages have the same numeral system as their Marindic-Jaqajic neighbors, a hand-and-feet system with 5 and 20 as base numbers (§3.9). Awyu speakers also adopted headhunting practices (for example Aghu, Drabbe 1957: 55), whereas the other Awyu-Dumut and Becking-Dawi subgroups in the foothills and upper parts of the river systems were victims of such practices.

What about lexical influence from the Marindic-Jaqajic languages? Drabbe (1955: 149–150) published a list of 97 basic vocabulary items (including personal nouns) for five Marindic-Jaqajic dialects and for Boazi and Jaqaj. I looked for credible lookalikes for each lexical item in Drabbe's list in the list of 430 basic vocabulary items of 9 Greater Awyu languages presented in Wester (2014, Appendix A). There is only a total of 9 lookalikes and 6 of them have to do with things exclusively associated with lowland ecology, with key aspect of lowland life that are unknown in the mountains. None of these six lowland life items correspond to etyma in the proto Trans New Guinea list of Pawley (2005: 86).[43]

Two palms that grow in the coastal lowlands but not in the mountains of New Guinea, coconut palms and sago palms, are of supreme importance in the past and present of lowland dwellers: staple food, material for clothing, houses, core elements in rituals.

---

[43] The three other lookalikes, apart from the six lowland items, are *ma(n)* 'to come' in Marind and *me* 'to come' in Mandobo, Yonggom Wambon and Kombai, the word for star, Jaqaj *mind*, Digul Wambon *mindui* and the word for teeth, Marindic-Jaqajic *maŋgat* 'teeth', *maga* in Yenimu, Pisa and Aghu. Wurm (1982: 103, 107) regarded Marindic-Jaqajic *maŋgat/maga* 'teeth', *maga* (proto Oceanic *maŋa(t)* and *mind/mindui* 'star') as Austronesian loans. But Pawley (2005: 86) lists *maŋgat[a]* 'teeth/mouth' among his proto Trans New Guinea etyma. Usher and Suter (2015: 130) propose to include Marindic-Jaqajic in a broader Anim family and they reconstruct proto Anim *mano* 'to come' and *maŋga(o)t(o)* 'mouth/teeth'.

The word for coconut in the Awyu languages Shiagha, Yenimu and Aghu is *peyo* (the letters *y* and *j* reflect the same sound). It is *biyo* in Kombai, *mbiyon* in Korowai and *mbian* in Mandobo and Digul Wambon. The word for coconut in the Marindic-Jaqajic language Jaqaj is *pajo*. How do we know that the Greater Awyu languages borrowed the term for coconut rather than giving it to Jaqaj? If we assume that Greater Awyu speakers entered the southern plains from the central New Guinea mountains rather than at the coast, it is more likely that they borrowed the noun for coconut from Jaqaj, their immediate Marindic-Jaqajic neighbors, since coconut palms do not grow in the mountains. This is confirmed by independent observations of Healey (1970: 1000) and Wester (2014: 25) that the initial /p/ in words of the Awyu subgroup reflects a history of borrowing since proto Awyu-Dumut initial *p is reflected by initial /f/ in the Awyu subgroup and the Awyu words that begin with /p/ cannot be reconstructed to a proto Awyu-Dumut form with an initial *p.

The general word for sago[44] is *da* in the Marindic-Jaqajic varieties of Drabbe and Boazi has *dow* and this corresponds to do in Shiagha, *du* in Yenimu and Pisa, *dü* in Aghu, *ndu* in Mandobo, *ndun* in Yonggom-Wambon, *ndu* in Digul Wambon, *doü* in Kombai and *ndaü* in Korowai. The Ok language Mian has *mifim* for sago (Fedden 2007: 216) and Muyu, also Ok, has *om* (Drabbe 1959: 171).

Rivers, streams and swamps (with billions of mosquitos) are another key feature of lowland rainforest ecology. The word for mosquito in all Marindic-Jaqajic dialects as described by Drabbe is *naŋgit* (*naŋgir* in modern Jaqaj, Bruno Olsson p.c.). Mbian has *ningat* and Boazi that has *nangat*. Usher and Suter (2015: 130) reconstruct proto-Anim *nag(a,i)t(i) 'mosquito'. Aghu has *nigi* and Yenimu *negi*, both members of the Awyu subgroup. The Awyu subgroup is characterized by final consonant deletion and denasalization of prenasalized plosives (Wester 2014: 35). Shiagha has another word: *syimpere* (Wester 2014: 208).

---

44 Greater Awyu languages have many specific terms for sago palm subspecies, for sago flour, sago in the form of big lumps or balls ready to be grilled in the fireplace, sago ready for consumption and so on. For example, Korowai has at least three nouns for thorny subspecies: *balép, bayol, xum* and *lé*; four terms for subspecies without thorns: *amo, bandüp, lahial, milon*. And a number of terms for subspecies of which we do not know whether it concerns a thorny subspecies or not, e.g. *ganim* and *mayum* sago palms (van Enk and de Vries 1997: 276). Korowai uses *xo* for sago flour. Big chunks of sago ready for grilling called *ndaü-lax* 'sago lump'. The normal, daily way to prepare sago is to place a small lump of sago in the fire until the outer layer is done. That outer layer (*abéax*) is peeled off with the fingers and eaten. Then the remaining lump is placed back in the fire and the procedure is repeated with the next layers (*gaul*) until the last layer or piece (*mup*) is done. Sago must be shared with everyone in the house (van Enk and de Vries 1997: 30–32).

Since the Awyu subgroup had Marindic-Jaqajic neighbors (on both sides), unlike the other Greater Awyu subgroups, it is to be expected that we find some loans exclusively or predominantly in the Awyu subgroup, as loans from their direct neighbors. Other Greater Awyu languages have these words for mosquito (Wester 2014: 208): *sowen* (Yonggom Wambon), *taenop* (Mandobo), *etenop* (Digul Wambon), *gegemo* (Kombai), *letün* (Korowai).

The noun for paddle is *kavi* in Boazi and *kavia* in the Eastern dialect of Coastal Marindand that corresponds to Shiagha *kafe*, Yenimu *kefi*, Pisa *kafi* and Aghu *kefi* as counterparts. The other Greater Awyu languages use a range of words for paddle or oar (Wester 2014: Appendix A): Mandobo *igio*, Yonggom Wambon *suguyŋ* and Digul Wambon *ndayoŋ*, a loan from Indonesian. Usher and Suter (2015: 130) reconstruct proto Anim *kawea. Bruno Olsson (in p.c.) proposes the reconstruction *ka-ewea for proto Anim, as a polymorphemic word, with *ka- as a derivational prefix that derived the instrument noun from the verb *ewea 'to paddle', observing that the polymorphemic nature of the Anim term proves that the direction of the borrowing was from Anim into Greater Awyu.

The word for canoe is *javun* in three Marindic-Jaqajic varieties according to Drabbe (Easter dialect, Kumb-dialect, Mbian) and *jahun* in the Western and Atih dialects. According to Bruno Olsson (in p.c.) in Jaqaj it is *yun* (or *jun* as Drabbe would have spelled it) and he adds that medial -v- is regularly lost in Jaqaj, making Jaqaj or perhaps rather proto Jaqaj-Marind *yawun the source for this borrowing. In Pisa and Aghu we find *yefü* and *yofü*, in Mandobo *yoün* and in Kombai *yafu*. (The letters *y* and *j* reflect the same sound). The other Greater Awyu languages use a wide variety of words for canoe. Shiagha and Yenimu have *xaya* and *xeya*, Wambon and Korowai have *alep* and Yonggom-Wambon has *konoi*. It stands to reason that ancestors of Greater Awyu speakers borrowed terms for canoe when they descended from the mountains in cultural and ecological lowland conditions where waterways, fishing and warfare all require canoe technology.

The word for the southern crowned pigeon (*Goura scheepmakeri*), a bird only found in the southern lowlands of New Guinea, is *mahuk (maghuk)* in Marindic-Jaqajic and corresponds to Yenimu *moxow* and Shiagha *moxosy*. (The spelling letters *x* and *gh* both reflect a velar fricative). Proto Marind *mahuk 'crowned pigeon' (Bruno Olsson in p.c.) would have been adapted in the Awyu subgroup to a word ending in a vowel (because of final C deletion in that group) and [h]/[x] alternation is not uncommon phenomenon in Greater Awyu languages. The other Greater Awyu languages have a range of words for the southern crowned pigeon: *kute* (Pisa), *üküte* (Aghu), *kutea* (Mandobo), *kotim* (Yonggom Wambon), *yawoe* (Digul Wambon), *feruwo* (Kombai) and *aülem* (Korowai). The Ok language

Muyu has *kutim*, corresponding to Yonggom Wambon and probably also to Pisa, Aghu and Mandobo. (Drabbe 1959: 173; Wester 2014: 203).

Finally, there is a credible Marindic-Jaqajic lookalike *makan* 'below' that has counterparts in Shiagha and Yenimu *moka* and Aghu *maka*. Again, the lookalikes are restricted to the Awyu subgroup, the only subgroup neighboring Marindic-Jaqajic languages. The word glossed as 'below' by Drabbe may be a noun meaning the ground or soil under a tree house, a culturally very significant place because it was one of places where dead relatives could be buried and also the place where the notched pole that gives access to a tree house touched the ground. Tree houses were unknown to mountain Trans New Guinea groups whereas they were the basic type of house on the southern plains. But it is uncertain whether the *makan/moka/maka* item indeed refers to the place under the tree house. Korowai shows the plausibility of this conjecture because it uses the noun *belüp* that primarily means 'the place under the tree house' as a relator noun with the generic meaning 'below' (van Enk and de Vries 1997: 84).

These lexical data are consistent with a migration scenario that has the ancestors of Greater Awyu speakers descending from the mountains, borrowing terms from Marindic and/or other Anim speakers for key items of lowland swamp and rainforest life unknown in the mountains.

7.3.3 Patterns of peaceful contacts between Greater Awyu speakers and their neighbors

Two patterns of significant peaceful contact need to be mentioned, marriage and regional pig- and sago grub festivals. These patterns date back from pre-colonial times and survived when Greater Awyu groups became slowly integrated in first the Dutch and later the Indonesian nation-state.

Welsch (1994) described the key role of pig feasts on the Upper Fly-Digul plain in forming and maintaining extensive regional networks of trade and exchange, emphasizing the socio-economic relations. Greater Awyu groups such as Korowai and Kombai have sago grub feasts with socio-economic functions but also ritual functions related to fertility of crops and clans (van Enk and de Vries 1997: 34–35). These sago grub feasts are held so frequently that they form the most important reason for the fact that most settlements are often empty, or with just a handful of people: everybody else is off to sago grub or pig feasts, or is preparing for one on their clan lands. The system of chain invitations (A invites B, B invites C, C invites D) plays an important role in bringing together hundreds of people from a wide area to these feasts, where things are traded and marriages are arranged between people from very different clans and different linguistic backgrounds. Papuan Malay is appreciated as lingua franca in these multilingual encounters during feasts, although Malay varieties are also associated with loss of clan lands and intruders in other contexts (see §6.9).

The small, independent clans, dispersed over a wide, sparsely populated area, with a lot of residential mobility and individual autonomy in matters of choice of marriage partner or place of residence needed systems to counter-act the extreme political and social fragmentation and the regional feast cycles provided a framework for peaceful relations and for exchange of goods and women.

The other peaceful pattern of contact is marriage. The pattern that husbands stay on their native clan lands and women travel from a wide area to the clan lands of their husbands is widespread in New Guinea and the practice has had similar linguistic and genetic consequences all over the island. Linguistically, the consequence is multilingualism on the clan lands because the women bring their languages or dialects to the clan lands of their husbands; the women learn the languages of their husbands but teach their own languages to their children, in order for them to maintain relations with her brothers (see for the meanings and functions of the mother's brother-sister's son dyad, §6.7.2). Since brothers may marry women from different clans, brothers often have wives from different linguistic backgrounds. Marriage across language and language family boundaries was and is a frequent phenomenon among Greater Awyu speakers. It is not preferred nor avoided: language is simply not an issue in relations between clans, nor in marriage or in any other area.

In terms of population genetics, the consequences of these cultural practices of marriage have been formulated clearly by Harley et al. (2005: 169). In their genetic research of 6 populations in Papua New Guinea they found that "with few and mostly population-specific haplotypes, the Y-chromosome is very contained, implying a tendency of men to stay closely bound to their region of birth". But for women the picture is dramatically different: "Virilocality . . . has been observed throughout mainland New Guinea [. . .] it is proposed that the migration rate of women is substantially higher than for men due to this phenomenon and that virilocality results in the dispersal of maternal haplotypes over time while paternal haplotypes remain stationary". These findings imply a "significant movement of women from their village/region of birth" (Harley et al. 2005: 169).

Let us have a closer look at the cultural and linguistic interaction of a Greater Awyu language, Mandobo and its Greater Ok neighbor, Muyu. Van den Heuvel and Fedden (2014) could study Mandobo-Muyu interaction in some detail, because we have language descriptions, word lists, information on cultural practices and patterns of contact, trade and marriage for both Mandobo and Muyu. The findings of van den Heuvel and Fedden (2014) are summarized in the next section.

7.3.4 Mandobo (Greater Awyu) and Muyu (Greater Ok)

The Mandobo and Muyu are neighbors on the Upper Fly-Digul plain (see Map 3) and they had intense contact and interaction, reflected in all major sources since the 1950s, our earliest significant sources. Van den Heuvel and Fedden (2014: 16–17) summarize these sources as follows:

> As the first contacts of Mandobo and Muyu speakers with the outside world date from the first part of the twentieth century, very little is known about the history of these speaker groups before this period. From sources of the 1950s and later, however, we know that contact between the two groups has been quite intensive, at least since then. Schoorl (1988), who describes the situation of the late 1950s, speaks about intensive contacts through marriage, co-residence and trade between Mandobo and Muyu speakers. Boelaars, who wrote an ethnography of the Mandobo, describes Mandobo culture as a kind of hybrid: "We are inclined to say that the Mandobo live according to Muyu customs in an Awyu setting" (1970: 16–17).[45] The Muyu have a relatively strong tradition of migration, trade and building cross-linguistic and cross-cultural networks by marrying off their women to other people in their region, including the Mandobo (Schoorl 1988: 543–45). A very valuable source, finally, is Robert Welsch (1994), who describes the role of pig feasts for establishing extensive socio-economic relations as a regional phenomenon all over the Upper Fly-Digul Plain. Welsch (1994: 90–94) argues that the great number of cultural traits shared over the plain (and not outside of it) can only have spread through contact.

The Mandobo-Muyu patterns of interaction are not exceptional in the Greater Awyu area. When I lived there between 1982 and 1992, I saw the same intensive contacts across language boundaries and across boundaries of language families in the northern and western parts of the Upper Fly-Digul plain, e.g. Korowai-Citak interaction and contact and Korowai-Kombai contact. Most major settlements (e.g. Boma, Kouh) housed speakers of three or four languages. It is important to emphasize that patterns of contact, borrowing, diffusion and exchange cannot be understood at the level of languages as defined by linguists (Kombai,

---

[45] In Dutch: "Wij zijn geneigd te zeggen, dat de Mandobo een Muju-adat beleeft in een Awju-setting".

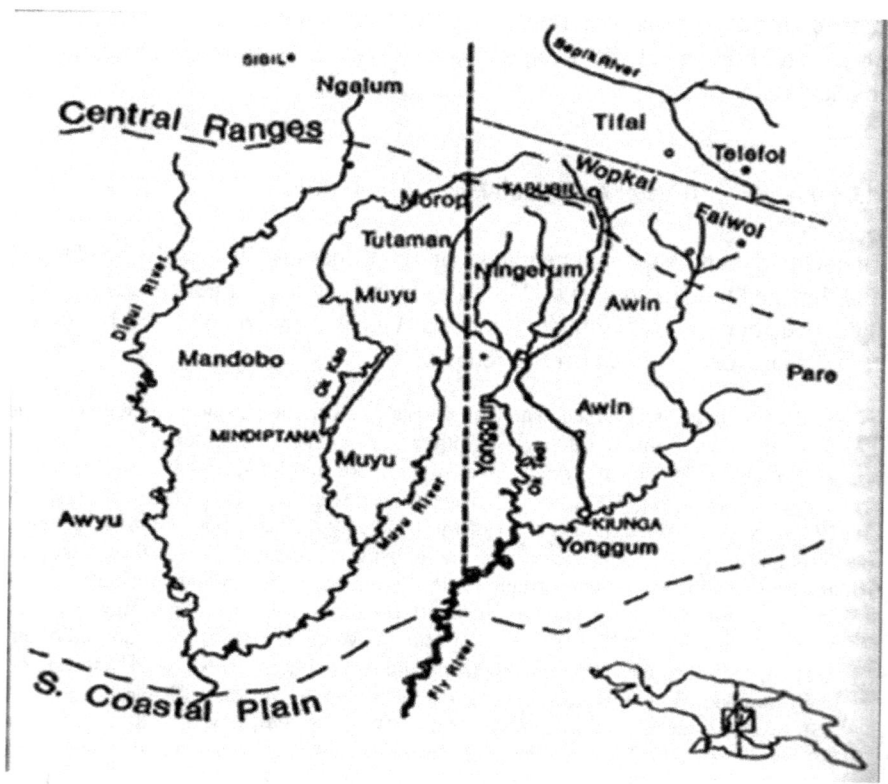

Map 3: The Upper Fly-Digul plain (from Welsch 1994: 86).

Mandobo, Muyu and so on). Those labels reflect arbitrary sections of dialect continua and do not correspond to social groups distinguished by Greater Awyu speakers themselves.

It is patriclans and individuals within those clans, that define the network of exchange, contact and diffusion. So, a Kombai speaking clan living close to the Becking River may have received brides from Korowai speaking clans whereas Kombai clans living close to the Digul river, for example in Kouh, will have contacts and exchange with Mandobo or Wambon speaking clans. Korowai clans close to Asmat-Kamoro speaking areas frequently established marriage connections with those groups, especially Citak groups. Language boundaries and boundaries between language families, are irrelevant to these networks of clans and individuals and it is those networks that determine the different lexical inventories of speakers. Much more research is needed, though, good dictionaries and above all detailed studies of lexical repertoires at the level of clans and individuals, to understand these patterns of contact and its linguistic consequences.

Van den Heuvel and Fedden (2014) first compare the two families that Muyu (Greater Ok) and Mandobo (Awyu-Dumut branch of Greater Awyu) are part of. This comparison is based on the bottom up comparative method and therefore they compare the languages on the level of proto forms of each family. Their tentative conclusions are that the two families have a distant genetic relation (both are Trans New Guinea) but that there is insufficient evidence for a subgroup of the two families defined by shared innovations (see §7.2.3). If Greater Awyu and Greater Ok are only distantly related via Trans New Guinea, reflected in some of the pronouns and in a handful of good correspondences to Trans New Guinea etyma, then the other correspondences in lexical items noted by Voorhoeve (2005) must be the result of contact, probably ancient contact, because the shared items occur in many languages of both families, not just in neighboring languages (van den Heuvel and Fedden 2014: 15).

Second, they looked at the relationship between Mandobo and Muyu from an areal and contact point of view. Typologically, both languages fit the profile of the two families they belong to and since these profiles are very distinct, there is no evidence for structural convergence due to contact (van den Heuvel and Fedden 2014: 19). Using cognation percentages calculated by Healy (1964) and by the Automated Similarity Judgment Program (Brown et al. 2008), van den Heuvel and Fedden (2014: 26) conclude that the lexical similarity between Mandobo and Muyu is remarkably low, given the combined force of co-residence, intermarriage, linguistic ideologies, high Muyu-Mandobo bilingualism (Welsch 1994: 111) and intensive cultural and economic interaction: Muyu Metomka-Mandobo: 8% (ASJP)/11% (Healy 1964); Muyu Ninati-Mandobo: 8% (ASJP)/7% (Healy 1964) and just a little bit higher than the lexical similarity percentages between Mandobo and a number of other Greater Ok languages, suggesting a weak correlation between linguistic similarity and geographic proximity (see Map 4).

Finally, van den Heuvel and Fedden (2014: 26–27) address the question of the striking discrepancy between the cultural continuity and intensive contact between Mandobo and Muyu on the one hand and the linguistic discontinuity (both lexical and grammatical) on the other. They suggest that "The low percentage might be explained as evidence that the groups have come to live in closer contact with each other only recently, possibly only several generations ago. We do know from several sources (e.g. Schoorl 1988, referring to Swadling 1983) that the movement of Ok speakers from the mountains southwards was a process which was still going on in the 1950s. The low percentage of borrowings, then, can be seen

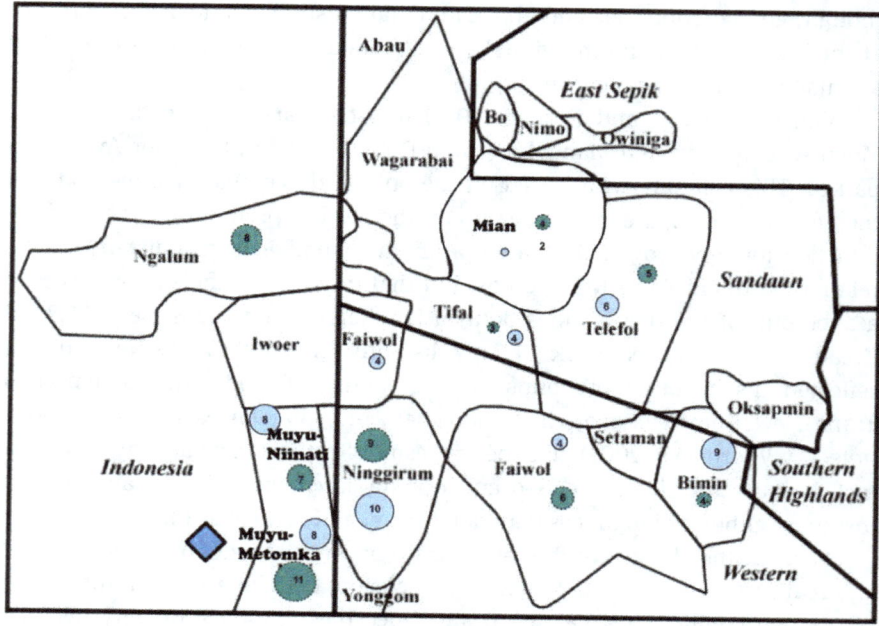

Map 4: Circles with a closed line express ASJP percentages, those with a dotted line are based on Healey (1964) (from van den Heuvel and Fedden (2014: 25).

as a sign that this process had started only a short period before this, so that contacts between Ok and Awyu-Dumut speakers are of recent date" (van den Heuvel and Fedden 2014: 26).

The other possible explanation has to do with the cultural contexts in which Greater Awyu languages functions (see chapter 6). Van den Heuvel and Fedden (2014: 26) write:

> As can be deduced from Stasch (2009), Welsch (1994) and de Vries (2012a), multilingualism is high but very much centered around individuals, in that each individual has his own repertory of languages. There is no strong link between language and group identity and one cannot speak of, for example, a general Muyu-Mandobo bilingualism. On the contrary, some Mandobo-speaking individuals may have contacts with Digul Wambon and with Muyu speakers, others may know Marindic-Jaqajic and Shiagha, while again others might have contacts with speakers of Yonggom Wambon and Aghu. One might claim that this 'ego-centered' form of multilingualism prevents the massive spreading of linguistic forms, as some typical incentives for change are lacking in such a context. There is no such thing as a group attitude towards the group's own language or towards

the other group's language, attitudes that might further diffusion of typological patterns or actual forms in one direction or the other. In order to sustain the claim, one would need more data on individuals' histories of contact, combined with individual's varieties of speech.

It is certainly true that more data and research is needed on cultural and linguistic practices of "ego-centered" multilingualism, linguistic exogamy and identity construction through language and patterns of contact in Greater Awyu clan communities. For the time being it seems that the best comparative practices in these contexts would prioritize the reconstruction of proto morphologies and morphological innovations, especially pertaining to bound, inflectional morphology.

7.3.5 Counting, numerals and areal diffusion

Counting systems and numerals are particularly sensitive to borrowing and diffusion in the New Guinea context, because they travel with the cultural practices that they are embedded in, practices of trade and money systems and practices of accumulating wealth or harvest items during feasts and rituals (Laycock 1975).

This is also true for the Greater Awyu family. For example, Yonggom Wambon speakers may also use *kumuk-kumuk* "wrist-wrist", i.e. six-six for 12, as an alternative to *turutop* 'ear; twelve', the body part with the numerical value of 12. Yonggom Wambon has Muyu, a Greater Ok language with a base 6 system, as its eastern neighbour. Drabbe (1959: 123) remarks that this seems to suggest influence from Muyu. The Awyu subgroup borrowed the hands-and-feet system from their Marindic neighbors (see §3.9). Greater Awyu groups borrowed Malay numerals along with the introduction of modern currencies, first the Dutch guilder, later the Indonesian rupiah.

The body part tally counting systems of the type found in Greater Awyu languages occur only in New Guinea (and to a limited extent in Australia, Lean 1992). Moreover, within New Guinea they have a restricted geographical distribution: they occur only in central New Guinea with some diffusion into adjacent lowland areas, occurring in a subsection of languages deemed to be Trans New Guinea and non-Trans New Guinea. It is this geographical distribution that led Pawley and Hammarström (2018: 130) to the conclusion that body part tally systems diffused out of central New Guinea, probably from the Greater Ok family. Since the Greater Awyu languages border on that family, they may have acquired it from their neighbors, either after of before their descent into the lowlands.

The distinctive feature of such systems are the use of hands, arms and head, with the body part nouns doubling as numerals, the absence of a distinction between base and derived numbers and the restriction to body parts of the upper half of the body. The Awyu subgroup is the only Greater Awyu group that does not have a body part tally system but a hands-and-feet system with base numbers 5, 10 and 20, based on the hand (5), two hands (10) and hands-and-feet (20, the whole body). Since they live among Marindic-Jaqajic groups, they will have adopted the hands-and-feet counting practices from their new neighbors, although they adopted just the system, not the lexical items for the body parts involved in the system. Both the hands-and-feet and the body part tally system are a kind of add-on in Greater Awyu languages to an elementary numeral system with the numbers 1 and 2 (and compounds of these to produce 3 (=two-one) and 4 (=two-two)).

Cross-linguistically, numerals have either a somatic or a transactional origin (Comrie 1997). The somatic basis is exceptionally transparent in Greater Awyu languages with their body part tally systems. But alongside those somatic numerals we also find numerals in Greater Awyu languages with a transactional basis, e.g. the Yonggom Wambon numeral *tikmae* 'ten' that means 'rattan string'. Rattan strings with ten *kauri* shells were used in transactions (Drabbe 1959: 123). When I lived in the Korowai and Kombai area in the early 1980s, transactions based on dog teeth, pig teeth and shells were still in use, for example in bride wealth payments. Verbs that denote buying or selling tend to be derived from the noun for *kauri* shell, e.g. Digul Wambon *taxet* '*kauri* shell' and *taxi-mo-* 'to buy/sell'. But Indonesian money rapidly replaced traditional money systems.

7.4 Typological context

7.4.1 Introduction

Bayesian phylogenetic clustering methods as applied by Reesink, Singer and Dunn (2009: 4) are based on large numbers of typological characteristics of languages. Bayesian statistics calculates probabilities for different hypotheses about clusters of languages. Using such methods, Reesink, Singer and Dunn (2009) distinguish Trans New Guinea and non-Trans New Guinea languages on the southern plains.

Notice that although they use the term 'Trans New Guinea' and 'non-Trans New Guinea', these terms have a somewhat different meaning in these quantitative top-down methods than in the qualitative genetic top-down reconstructions of Pawley (2005) and Ross (2005). Trans New Guinea is a genetic term in the latter but a statistical-typological term in the former method: the statistics reveals clusters of languages that look very much like each other, whether because of shared origin or because of contact, or both, in the words of Reesink, Singer and Dunn (2009: 2): "Borrowing of features presented a different set of issues. Given the social demographics of the area, horizontal transmission of features must be considered part of the historical signal, rather than noise. We thus adopt a model that allows one to reconstruct population history given a current signal that encodes both phylogeny and hybridization". This does not mean that these statistical methods based on typological features cannot be used to make claims about genetic groupings. They can to some extent, but always in combination with independent other evidence.

The terms Trans New Guinea and non-Trans New Guinea also refer to different sets of languages in both approaches. For example, Marind is seen as a Trans New Guinea language in the genetic top-down approach of Pawley (2005) and Ross (2005) but as non-Trans New Guinea in the typological-statistical top down approach of Reesink, Singer and Dunn (2009). Typologically, Marind is placed by the Bayesian calculation in a cluster of non-Trans New Guinea languages on the New Guinea south coast, from the Trans Fly region all the way to the Bird's Head, a cluster that also includes Arammba, Gizzra, Meriam Mir, Kiwai, Inanwatan (Reesink, Singer and Dunn 2009: 4). The only Greater Awyu language in their sample, Korowai, is placed in the Trans New Guinea group (Reesink, Singer and Dunn 2009: 5).

Bayesian statistics, if applied to large numbers of typological features in large sets of languages as Reesink, Singer and Dunn (2009) did, allows us to be less impressionistic and intuitive in the characterization of the typology of Papuan languages. They show that it is possible to speak of various types of non-Austronesian languages of New Guinea, for example a Trans New Guinea or mountain type (Reesink, Singer and Dunn 2009: 4), a south New Guinea coast type (Reesink, Singer and Dunn 2009: 5, Trans-Fly, Marindic-Jaqajic, Inanwatan), a West Papuan/Bird's Head type and so on, in ways that are still not exact but often seem to be more informative than "Papuan" as a typological term.

The tension between classifying Marind genetically as Trans New Guinea and typologically as non-Trans New Guinea has traditionally been resolved in Papuan linguistics by assuming that Marind had intense contact with non-Trans New Guinea languages on the coastal plain for a long time (Wurm 1982: 94; Evans and Klamer 2012: 6). That long time contact presumably caused its typological profile to switch to the non-Trans New Guinea South Coastal type. For example, Wurm regarded Marind as a member of the Trans New Guinea family but noticed the "aberrant features [. . . .] which are probably attributable to a strong substratum" (Wurm 1982: 94).

Typologically, Greater Awyu languages resemble languages of the mountain Trans New Guinea type families, to their north and not their southern neighbors such as Marindic-Jaqajic. But their clause chaining, switch reference and relative tense are relatively underdeveloped when compared to canonical clause chaining languages of the mountain Trans New Guinea families, perhaps the result of convergence with clause combining syntax of their southern neighbours that completely lack clause chaining and switch reference. In terms of counting systems, Greater Awyu languages also follow their northern mountain neighbors rather than their southern Marindic-Jaqajic neighbors, with the exception of languages of the Awyu subgroup that migrated downriver and settled among Marindic-Jaqajic speaking groups.

We will now discuss features of Greater Awyu languages from a typological perspective in somewhat more detail.

7.4.2 Phonology

The vowel systems of Greater Awyu languages relatively complex, seen in the context of Trans New Guinea phonologies that tend to have symmetrical 5 vowel systems (Pawley and Hammarström 2018: 85). Some Greater Awyu languages added the tense, rounded high vowel /y/ (§2.1.1) to the 5 vowel system. The /y/ is cross-linguistically and in New Guinea rather rare (Foley 2000: 368). Kombai added both the front vowel /y/ and the back vowel /ɯ/. Aghu added nasal vowels.

The consonantal systems of Greater Awyu languages are of a type found in many Trans New Guinea languages that tend to have between 11 and 15 consonants, series of plosives, two or three nasals in bilabial, alveolar or velar positions, semivowels /j/ and /w/, and very small classes of rhotics and fricatives (Pawley and Hammarström 2018: 82). The contrast between voiceless stops and voiced prenasalized stops is particularly widespread in Trans New Guinea languages (Pawley and Hammarström 2018: 82; Foley 2000: 368). The Awyu subgroup lost this prenasalization feature of voiced stops and Korowai, of the Becking-Dawi branch, has a three way contrast of oral voiced stops, prenasalized voiced stops and voiceless stops, not so common in New Guinea according to Foley (2000: 369). It occurs also in Marindic-Jaqajic and Lower Sepik families of Papuan languages.

The simple (C)V(C) syllables of Greater Awyu languages tie them to Papuan languages of the Trans New Guinea type (Foley 2000: 369). Of course, cross-linguistically, that is also a very much preferred syllable type (Dixon 2010 vol.I: 9).

A number of Greater Awyu languages (e.g. Korowai, Kombai) developed a contrastive pitch accent.

Greater Awyu languages each have their own distinctive sound profile because of different patterns of allophony and allomorphy. For example, only Korowai has implosive realizations of oral voiced stops and only Kombai has lateralized allophones of voiceless fricatives. Mandobo pronounce their voiceless stop word finally completely unreleased (Drabbe 1959: 5). Jang (2008: 10) formulated some of the complex and interacting morphophonological rules of Wambon that turn the underlying phonological forms into surface realization, explaining the remarkable distance between the two.

7.4.3 Morphology

Foley (2000: 370) observed that "Morphological types in the languages of New Guinea vary enormously, from the simple, almost isolating languages of the West Papuan, Lakes Plain and Sepik families, to the typically agglutinative, mildly synthetic languages of the Trans New Guinea family, to the highly complex polysynthetic languages of the Kiwai or Lower Sepik–Ramu families". The morphologies of the language families of the southern plains differ widely from each other, in patterns and matter. Morphologies, especially bound verb morphology, form the inherited, relatively most stable, distinctive core of Papuan language families.

Typical for Greater Awyu verb morphology is the fundamental importance of the realis-irrealis distinction in verbs (§3.6.1.4), in combination with a three way opposition of verb types (non-finite same subject verbs, semi-inflected verbs and fully inflected verbs), §3.6.1.3).

Greater Awyu tense is secondary to the basic mood opposition of realis and irrealis and this feature links Greater Awyu typologically to many other Papuan languages, especially of central New Guinea, in the words of Foley (2000: 381): "In many languages and especially those of the Trans New Guinea family, the modal distinction between realis and irrealis is fundamental and tense, if present, functions as a subsidiary of that (Roberts 1990)". The Awyu-Dumut branch has a cross-linguistically unexpected pattern of irrealis as formally unmarked (zero-marked) and realis as marked with a suffix. This is indeed striking in the light of the statement by Dixon (2012: 25) that "if one term may have zero realization, or a zero allomorph, this is always realis" (see also Aikhenvald 2015: 140). The Becking-Dawi branch marks irrealis forms with a suffix and leaves the realis forms unmarked.

Greater Awyu fully inflected verbs are marked: speakers tend to use them sparingly, often discourse-final or at the end of (long) strings of mini clauses, to indicate the time framework of larger chunks of text. The tense systems of Greater Awyu languages (§3.6.1.7) vary widely, in forms and distinctions (Wester 2014: 105–116). Fully inflected verbs, with three slots for suffixes, a modality slot, a person-number and a tense slot, are only used sparingly. Much more frequent are verbs with two slots, one for subject person-number and one for modality (realis or irrealis). Often the relation between fully inflected verbs and the semi-inflected verbs is transparent: leave out the tense suffix and the result is a realis or irrealis verb (de Vries 2010).

Same subject verbs consist of just a verb stem or a verb stem plus a switch reference suffix or a temporality suffix (sequence versus simultaneity). These switch reference and temporality suffixes often look suspiciously similar to coordinating conjunctions and some of them clearly originated as conjunctions with meanings as 'and', 'and then' or 'first' (de Vries 2010: 341).

Apart from same subject verb forms, Greater Awyu languages did not develop much more dedicated switch reference verb morphology (§3.6.1.5). Greater Awyu languages have four ways to indicate switch reference (DS). First, the use of switch reference conjunctions that cliticize to independent verbs (e.g. Korowai). Second, the chain medial use of independent verb forms *per se* implies that the next clause has a different subject (e.g. Kombai). Third, a specific independent verb became strongly associated with switch reference (e.g. Digul Wambon *t*-forms became realis and different subject verbs in non-final contexts, §3.6.1.4). Fourth, a combination of these ways is used (e.g. Aghu). As in so many Papuan languages (Reesink 1983), semantic and pragmatic factors also play a role in what counts as same subject referents or different subject referents in Greater Awyu languages, with the usual 'false' SS forms preceding experiential clauses, weather clauses and other clauses with inanimate subject of low discourse importance (de Vries 1989: 62–64).

The relative absence of medial-final verb morphology and the emergent nature of clause chaining in Greater Awyu languages makes Greater Awyu languages less similar to the canonical clause chaining languages of central New Guinea, of the Trans New Guinea type, and more similar to their western and southern neighbors (Asmat-Kamoro, Marindic-Jaqajic).

Verb paradigms of Greater Awyu languages conflate second and third person. Subject person-number suffixes express two oppositions, speaker (marked) versus non-speaker (formally unmarked, zero) and singular (unmarked) versus plural (formally marked) (§3.6.1.6). Cysouw (2003: 49) observes that homophony in the marking of singular participants is cross-linguistically rare (estimated to occur in less than 1% of the world's languages). The Greater Awyu type of 2/3 homophony, though, is not uncommon in the Papuan context (Cysouw 2003: 42). Within the group of languages that do have a form of singular participant homophony, Greater Awyu languages stand out because they have a very systematic 2/3 homophony in singular and plural and, crucially, in all verb paradigms, with the exception of one verb paradigm in Korowai, the adhortative paradigm. Since Greater Awyu languages have anaphoric agreement (sometimes called 'pro-drop') and since speakers tend to avoid the use of personal pronouns to identify participants, the systematic conflation of second and third person frequently creates ambiguities in subject reference that can only be resolved in context.

A feature that does link Greater Awyu morphologies to wider Papuan contexts is the clear distinction between nouns and verbs (with derivational morphology to indicate change of word category from verb to noun). This sharp morphological boundary between nouns and verbs is lacking in the Austronesian languages of New Guinea (Foley 2000: 370). Greater Awyu languages verbalize members of other word categories on a grand scale, in order to create mini clauses of the preferred structure (a verb with maximally one overt argument) by distributing core and peripheral arguments of verbs over series of clauses (§3.6.1 and §5.5).

As in most other Papuan languages (with important exceptions such as Torricelli and Sepik-Ramu languages, Foley 2000: 371), nouns are morphologically very simple in Greater Awyu languages, compared to verbs. The only noun-related morphology are possessive pronominal prefixes, plural suffixes with kinship nouns (and a few other nouns) and derivational suffixes to derive verbal nouns. In texts, the overwhelming majority of nouns occurs in the form of bare noun stems. In Greater Awyu languages, as in many central highland languages, nouns are covertly categorized by posture verbs (Foley 2000: 372) according to culturally perceived default postures of referents, e.g. trees typically stand, pigs lie and so on.

Greater Awyu adjectives are an open, small class with plural forms and adjectival suffixes. Greater Awyu languages, just like many other Papuan languages, do not have dedicated grammatical comparatives or superlatives. Speakers use a range of strategies to indicate their comparative intentions, strategies shaped by the general preference for clauses of the [(XP) V] form (§5.5): speakers either leave the standard argument unexpressed in clauses with comparative readings, or comparee and standard are distributed over two clauses (§5.5.).

7.4.4 Discourse preferences and syntactic continuities

Greater Awyu speakers share a number of distinct preferences with various other speech communities of New Guinea, as we saw in chapter 5: recapitulative linkage of clause chains by tail-head linkage and generic deictic verb linkage, quotative framing of thoughts, intention, emotions and other inner movements within persons, the use of extra-clausal theme phrases and theme clauses followed by comment clauses, distribution of arguments over a series of mini-clauses and other strategies aimed at creating clauses with just a verb or maximally one overt argument.

These preferences of speakers led to high frequency of usage of certain patterns which then further froze or conventionalized into grammatical patterns and constructions that occur in many Papuan languages in some form. For example, the tendency to distribute arguments of a verb over multiple clauses led to conventionalized argument distribution that we find in many Papuan languages, with verbs of causation (§5.5), perception (§ 5.5) and in the form of comparative and superlative expressions (§5.5). Quotative framing conventionalized into obligatory grammar in certain contexts of Greater Awyu languages, for example in Kombai purposive constructions. Again, this ties Greater Awyu languages to many other Papuan languages with similar quotative constructions in the domain of intention and purpose (§5.3).

Thematization tendencies also led to a number of constructions and grammaticalization paths in Greater Awyu languages that have been reported for many languages of New Guinea: the conflated 'adverbial/relative clause' construction (§4.2.5.4) and §5.6), the development of demonstrative-based topic markers (§3.5.2) and experiential constructions with the human experiencer expressed as topic (§5.6).

It is not only with well-known and widespread constructions in New Guinea (thematization, quotative framing, recapitulative linkage) that understanding discourse preferences may help to explain aspects of Greater Awyu grammars. For example, Kombai has a typologically very marked construction, also never reported for a Papuan language, a relative clause construction with the common argument expressed twice, within the relative clause and as the head noun that is modified by the relative clause (see chapter 4). Compare (286) and (287), repeated from chapter 4:

(286) [[*Doü adiya-no-n=o*] MOD [*doü*]] HN, *deyalu-xe*
   sago give-[RLS]NON1PL-LNK=MOD sago finished-ADJ
   'The sago they gave, is finished.'   (Kombai, de Vries 1993a: 78)

(287) Yare   Gamo xereja b-o-gi-n=o   Rumu
       old.man   Join work   DUR-do-RLS[NON1SG]-LNK=MOD   Son
       na-momof=a.
       my-uncle=COP
       'The old man who is joining the work, is my uncle.'
                                           (Kombai, de Vries 1993a: 77)

If we view *yare* 'the old man' and the first occurrence of *doü* 'sago' in (286) and (287) as former extra-clausal themes, followed by a canonical prenominal relative clause (The old man, the person who joined the work, is my uncle), then these structures make sense. Just like the extra-clausal experiencer theme ended up as initial topic constituent of the experiential clause, the extra-clausal thematic common argument became integrated in the following prenominal relative clause that modifies the co-referential head noun *doü* 'sago' in (286) and *rumu* 'person' in (2.8.7). Mandobo also has a double-headed relative clause construction, and interestingly, it is far less grammaticalized than the Kombai one where co-referential dummy heads form the syntactic head of the relative NP and syntactic modifier-head connectives link relative clauses and head. In Mandobo, the first antecedent 'head' is an extra-clausal theme, separated intonationally and syntactically from the next clause. In other words, the Mandobo construction looks like an earlier stage of development than the Kombai one. The Mandobo type still relies heavily on pragmatic relevance relations between juxtaposed utterances (see §4.2.5.4).

7.5 Where did Greater Awyu speakers come from?

Under a scenario that has Greater Awyu speakers entering the lowlands from the mountains and meeting Marindic-Jaqajic groups on the southern plains that were already well-established and had developed technologies related to lowland ecology (e.g. canoe technology, processing sago, using coconut and sago palm for clothing and building houses), we would expect them to borrow words from their new neighbors (and marriage partners) that relate to key aspect of living on the plains and that are not found in the mountains. Indeed, the Marindic-Jaqajic languages supplied Greater Awyu speakers with words for things at the very heart of life on the plains: words related to swamps, travel via waterways and the two coastal palms with huge significance, ecologically, culturally and ritually: coconut and sago (§7.3.2).

Evidence from archeology is consistent with a migration scenario of descent from the mountains. Archeological evidence points to the development of agriculture in the central highlands of New Guinea around 8000 year B.C. followed by intensification of agriculture in the Wahgi and Baliem Valley around 4000 B.C. (Pawley et al. 2005: 5; Golson et al. 2017). It is this agriculture that may have fueled the expansion of mountain groups. When the mountain valleys became too full gradually groups of speakers were pushed into lower and lower valleys, eventually reaching the lowlands south of the central ranges. The ancestors of Greater Awyu speakers will have been part of this descent from the central mountain ranges.

The northernmost part of the Greater Awyu speaking area, close to the central mountain range and partly in the foothills, between the Upper Digul and Upper Becking river, shows the greatest internal diversity. There we find two branches, the Becking-Dawi and Awyu-Dumut branch and two subgroups of the Awyu-Dumut branch, the Ndumut subgroup and the Ndeiram subgroup (de Vries, Wester and van den Heuvel 2012). One subgroup of the Awyu-Dumut branch, the Awyu subgroup, followed the Digul river southward until they reached the coastal area and settled amidst Marindic-Jaqajic speaking groups that were already there. When ancestors of Greater Awyu speakers descended to the Upper Fly-Digul plain, they probably stayed in the foothills and uppermost part of the plain long enough to diversify there before moving further down south.

The speakers of Greater Awyu languages together with adjacent highland groups of West New Guinea belong to the most isolated people groups of New Guinea in terms of population genetics, also completely isolated from genetic influence of Austronesian populations that arrived on the shores of northern, eastern and south-eastern parts of New Guinea 3,500 years ago (Kayser et al. 2003: 281).

In the oral traditions of Greater Awyu peoples so far we have not found references to a mountain origin of ancestors. But the evidence from Marindic-Jaqajic loans for lowland items in Greater Awyu languages, makes its very likely that the Greater Awyu ancestors were part of the a larger Trans New Guinea descent scenario proposed by Pawley (2005: 101), a descent into the southern lowlands after population numbers increased through horticultural developments in the central mountain valleys. The Greater Awyu must have come down to the lowlands much later than the Marindic-Jaqajic, their Trans New Guinea neighbors (Usher and Suter 2015) not only because the Marindic-Jaqajic gave them the terms for essential features of lowland life but also because the Marindic-Jaqajic are typologically non-Trans New Guinea (Reesink, Singer and Dunn 2009: 4) and must have been there in contact with non-Trans New Guinea languages of south coast New Guinea for a long time (Evans and Klamer 2012: 6).

7.6 Summary

The two parallel worlds that Greater Awyu languages function in, the clan worlds and the world of the *kampungs*, shaped these languages in many ways, for example in terms of linguistic ideologies, language and identity, patterns of language contact, language attitudes, multilingualism, language names, and speech registers (see chapter 6).

The southern lowlands are recent products of sea level changes and the Greater Awyu family cannot have been a neighbor of the other coastal families for a very long time. The ancestors of Marindic-Jaqajic speakers must have descended to the southern plains long before those of Greater Awyu speakers did because Marindic-Jaqajic because their typological profile is distinctly non-Trans New Guinea (Reesink, Singer and Dunn 2009).

A mountain origin seems the most likely scenario for the Greater Awyu family. After their descent they resided first a prolonged period in the area of the upper part of the Digul river since there we find the greatest diversity of subgroups. In the course of time some Greater Awyu groups followed the Digul river down to the south coastal zone, where they settled amidst Jaqaj and Marindic-Jaqajic that were already well-established there and that had adapted to the ecology of swamps and rainforests, so that Greater Awyu speakers adopted their technologies of canoe building and of the many kinds of utilization of coconut and sago palm trees and they borrowed the words that were embedded in those cultural practices.

In the areas of syntax and discourse the Greater Awyu languages show clear continuities with other Papuan language families but these do not point into a specific direction and seem to be for the most part the result of general preferences of language use that are not specific to New Guinea (quotative framing, thematization, recapitulative linking, verby single argument clauses of the [[XP] V] type) and that tie Greater Awyu languages typologically also to oral languages outside New Guinea, e.g. to native languages of the Americas.

Greater Awyu languages have a distinctive morphological profile of inherited patterns and matter which set it apart from its neighbors, including a division into three basic verb types, a basic realis and irrealis distinction, a very systematic 2/3 homophony in verb paradigms and a verbal negation pattern that combines a prefix *bV/fV-* with a suffix *–dV*. Yet, within that inherited morphological framework, there is incredible diversity, for example in the way Greater Awyu languages give the three verb types different grammatical functions and usages and in the variation of tense patterns and matter, all within a family of 35,000 speakers. For example, the Awyu subgroup has four past tenses (hodiernal past, a hesternal past, a distant past and an historical past),

Kombai does not have a past tense and the Dumut subgroup has one general past tense. The diversity is also visible in the dialect chains where we see different stages of diachronic paths synchronically represented, for example in the development from relational nouns to case marking postpositions (§4.2.4), from demonstrative to topic marker (§3.5.2) and from clause conjoining to clause chaining (§3.6.1.5).

The absence of writing, the fact that language does not represent clan identity, the extreme high degree of political fragmentation in small, autonomous clans, linguistic ideologies that favor imitation of speech practices of related individuals or clans, the very small numbers of speakers per language, all these factors contributed to variation and change that created internal diversity within the Greater Awyu family. Greater Awyu speech varieties are unstable, open, porous and quickly changing forms of verbal communication in clan communities, sections of long dialect continua, without clear borders or cultural recognition as discrete and named entities.

The situation strongly resembles the way in which Heeschen (1998: 24) characterized the Eipo speech variety, as "perhaps only a passing phenomenon in the history of the Mek languages". Heeschen (1998: 24) writes about grammatical patterns: "When it is stated: 'the Eipo language has the rule x', the reader should bear in mind what has been stated here about the smallness of the speech community and its norms. The rule should properly read: the speaker y or the group of men from such or such a clan . . . say "x" under certain circumstances".

The goal of this book was to offer readers a glimpse of the fascinating passing phenomena of Greater Awyu languages of West Papua, languages that were vital in the 1950s till 1990s, when they were described, and most of them are still vital today. But coastal Papuan languages of New Guinea, especially in the vicinity of urban centers, are dying on a grand scale and this process is steadily moving upriver, into the interior, with more and more non-Papuan newcomers settling in the interior, going up the same rivers that the ancestors of Greater Awyu speakers once followed downward, when they migrated from the mountains into the plains.

References

Adelaar, Willem. 1990. The role of quotations in Andean discourse. In Harm Pinkster and Inge Genee, (eds.), *Unity in Diversity: Papers Presented to Simon C. Dik on his 50th Birthday*, 1–12. Dordrecht: Foris Publishers.

Aikhenvald, Alexandra Y. 2008. *The Manambu language of East Sepik, Papua New Guinea*. Oxford: Oxford University Press.

Aikhenvald, Alexandra Y. 2015. *The Art of Grammar. A Practical Guide*. Oxford: Oxford University Press.

Aikhenvald, Alexandra Y. 2008. *The Manambu languages of East Sepik, Papua New Guinea*. Oxford: Oxford University Press.

van Baal, Jan. 1966. *Dema. Description and analysis of Marind-anim culture*. The Hague: Nijhoff.

van Baal, Jan. 1982. *Jan Verschueren's description of Yéi-Nan culture. Extracted from the posthumous papers*. The Hague: Martinus Nijhoff.

van Baal, Jan. 1984. The dialectics of sex in Marind-anim culture. In Gilbert Herdt (ed). *Ritualized homosexuality in Melanesia*, 128–166. Berkeley: University of California Press.

Baas, Peter. 1981. *Tsakwambo Taalstudie*. Unpublished language survey and language learning notes by missionary Peter Baas.

Barclay, Pete. 2008 *A Grammar of Western Dani*. München: Lincom.

Boelaars, Johan H.M.C. 1970. *Mandobo's tussen de Digoel en de Kao, bijdragen tot een etnografie*. Assen: Van Gorcum.

Bromley, H. Myron. 1981. *A Grammar of Lower Grand Valley Dani*. Canberra: Australian National University Press.

Brown, Cecil H., Eric W. Holman, Sören Wichmann and Viveka Vellupilai. 2008. Automated classification of the world's languages: a description of the method and preliminary results. *Language Typology and Universals* 61(4): 285–308.

Burenhult, Niclas. 2008. Spatial coordinate systems in demonstrative meaning. *Linguistic Typology* 12: 99–142.

Chafe, Wallace. 1994. *Discourse, Consciousness, and Time: The flow and displacement of conscious experience in speaking and writing*. University of Chicago Press.

Chappell, John. 2005. Geographic changes of coastal lowlands in the Papuan past. In Andrew Pawley, Robert Attenborough, Jack Golson and Robin Hide (eds.), *Papuan Pasts: cultural, linguistic and biological histories of Papuan-speaking peoples*, 525–541. Canberra: Australian National University Press.

Comrie, Bernard. 1997. Some problems in the theory and typology of numeral systems. In Bohumii Palek (ed.), *Typology: Prototypes, Item Orderings and Universals*, 41–56. Prague: Charles University Press.

Cysouw, Michael. 2003. *The paradigmatic structure of person marking*. Oxford: Oxford University Press.

Daniels, Don. 2014. Complex coordination in diachrony. Two Sogeram case studies. *Diachronica* 31(3): 379–406.

Dixon, Robert M.W. 1994. *Ergativity*. Cambridge: Cambridge University Press.

Dixon, Robert M.W. 2010. *Basic linguistic theory*. Vol. I. Methodology. Oxford: Oxford University Press.

Dixon, Robert M.W. 2010. *Basic Linguistic Theory. Vol II. Grammatical Topics.* Oxford: Oxford University Press.
Dixon, Robert M.W. 2012. *Basic Linguistic Theory. Vol III. Further Grammatical Topics.* Oxford: Oxford University Press.
Döhler, Christian. 2016. *Komnzo. A language of Southern New Guinea.* Canberra: Australian National University dissertation.
Dol, Philomena. 1999. *A grammar of Maybrat, A language of the Bird's Head, Irian Jaya, Indonesia.* Leiden: University of Leiden dissertation.
Donohue, Mark. 1999. *Warembori.* Languages of the World/ Materials, vol. 341. Munich: Lincom Europa.
Drabbe, Petrus. 1937. *Woordenboek der Kamoro taal.* In KITLV-inventaris 157. Collectie Petrus Drabbe M.S.C.
Drabbe, Petrus. 1950. Twee dialecten van de Awju-taal. *Bijdragen tot de Taal-, Land- en Volkenkunde* 106: 92–147.
Drabbe, Petrus. 1955. *Spraakkunst van het Marind. Zuidkust Nederlands Nieuw-Guinea.* Wien-Moedling: Drukkerij Missiehuis St. Gabriël.
Drabbe, Petrus. 1957. *Spraakkunst van het Aghu-dialect van de Awju-taal.* Den Haag: Nijhoff.
Drabbe, Petrus. 1959. *Kaeti en Wambon. Twee Awju-dialecten.* Den Haag: Nijhoff.
Du Bois, John. 1987. The discourse basis of ergativity. *Language* 63: 805–855.
Dryer, Matthew S. 2013. Order of Relative Clause and Noun. In Matthew S. Dryer and Martin Haspelmath (eds.). *The World Atlas of Language Structures On line.* Leipzig Max Planck Institute for Evolutionary Anthropology. http://wals.info/chapter/90
van Enk, Gerrit J. and Lourens de Vries. 1997. *The Korowai of Irian Jaya. Their language in its cultural context.* Oxford: Oxford University Press.
Evans, Nicholas, Wayan Arka, Matthew Carroll, Yun Jung Choi, Christian Döhler, Eri Kashima, Emil Mittag, Bruno Olsson, Kyla Quinn, Jef Siegel, Philip Tama, Dineke Schokkin and Charlotte van Tongeren. 2018. The Languages of Southern New Guinea. In Bill Palmer (ed.), *The Languages and Linguistics of the New Guinea area*, 641–796. Berlin: De Gruyter Mouton.
Evans, Nicholas and Marian A.F. Klamer. 2012. Introduction: Linguistic challenges of the Papuan region. In Nicholas Evans and Marian A.F. Klamer (eds). Language Documentation & Conservation Special Publication No. 5 (December 2012) *Melanesian Languages on the Edge of Asia: Challenges for the 21st Century*, pp. 1–12. http://nflrc.hawaii.edu/ldc/sp05/ http://hdl.handle.net/10125/4558
Farr, Cynthia J.M. 1999. *The interface between syntax and discourse in Korafe, a Papuan language of Papua New Guinea.* Canberra: Australian National University Press.
Fedden, Sebastian O. 2007. *A Grammar of Mian. A Papuan language of New Guinea.* Melbourne: University of Melbourne dissertation.
Foley, William A. 1986. *The Papuan languages of New Guinea.* Cambridge: Cambridge University Press.
Foley, William A. 1991. *The Yimas language of New Guinea.* Stanford: Stanford University Press.
Foley, William A. 1997. *Anthropological Linguistics. An introduction.* Oxford: Blackwell.
Foley, William A. 2000. The languages of New Guinea. *Annual Review of Anthropology* 29: 357–404.
Foley, William A. 2005a. Personhood and linguistic identity, purism and variation. *Language Documentation and Description* 3: 157–180.

Foley, William A. 2005b. Linguistic prehistory in the Sepik-Ramu basin. In *Papuan Pasts, cultural, linguistic and biological histories of Papuan-speaking peoples*, ed. A. Pawley, R. Attenborough, J. Golson, and R. Hide, 109–144. Canberra: Australian National University Press.

Gravelle, Gilles. 2010. *A Grammar of Moskona, an East Bird's Head Language of West Papua*. Amsterdam: Vrije Universiteit dissertation.

Golson, Jack, Tim Denham, Philip Hughes, Pamela Swadling & John Muke (eds.). 2017. *Ten thousand years of cultivation at Kuk Swamp in the highlands of Papua New Guinea* (Terra Australis 46). Canberra: Australian National University Press.

Hammarström, Harald. 2012. Pronouns and the (Preliminary) Classification of Papuan languages. Language and linguistics in Melanesia, Special issue 2012 Part 2, 428–539. http://www.langlxmelanesia.com/hammarstrom428-539.pdf]

Haiman, John. 1978. Conditionals are topics. *Language* 54: 564–589.

Haiman, John. 1980. *Hua: a Papuan language of the Eastern Highlands of New Guinea*. Amsterdam: Benjamins.

Haiman, John. 1985. *Natural syntax: iconicity and erosion*. Cambridge: Cambridge University Press.

Harley, Nerida, Robert Attenborough, Michael P. Alpers, Charles Mgone, Kuldeep Bhatia and Simon Easteal. 2005. The importance of social structure for patterns of human genetic diversity: Y-chromosome and mitotchondrial genome variation in Papuan-speaking people of mainland Papua New Guinea. In Andrew Pawley, Robert Attenborough, Jack Golson and Robin Hide (eds.), 2005. *Papuan Pasts: cultural, linguistic and biological histories of Papuan-speaking peoples*, 723–753. Canberra: Australian National University Press.

Healey, Phyliss M. 1964. *Teelefool quotative clauses*. Canberra: Australian National University Press.

Healey, Allys. 1970. Proto Awyu-Dumut phonology. In Stephen A. Wurm and Don C. Laycock (eds.). *Pacific Studies in Honour of Arthur Capell*, 997–1062. Canberra: Australian National University Press.

Heeschen, Volker. 1998. *An ethnographic grammar of the Eipo language*. Berlin: Dietrich Reimer Verlag.

van den Heuvel, Wilco. 2016. *Aghu. Annotated texts with grammatical introduction and vocabulary lists*. Asia-Pacific Linguistics A-PL 33. Canberra: Australian National University Press.

van den Heuvel, Wilco and Sebastian Fedden. 2014. Greater Awyu and Greater Ok: inheritance or contact? *Oceanic Linguistics* 54 (1): 1–35.

Hughes, Jock. 2009. *Upper Digul survey*. Dallas: SIL International.

Jacobsen, William A. 1967. Switch-reference in Hokan-Coahuiltecan. In Dell Hymes and W. Bittle (eds), *Studies in Southwestern Ethnolinguistics: Meaning and History in the Languages of the American Southwest*, pp. 238–63. The Hague: Mouton.

Jang, HongT. 2003. *Survey Report on Languages of Southeastern Foothills in Papua, Merauke Regency of Papua, Indonesia*. Dallas: SIL International.

Jang, Hong-Tae. 2008. *Morphology and syntax of Wambon. A grammar sketch*. Unpublished grammar sketch. SIL International Indonesia Branch.

Kayser, Manfred, Silke Brauer, Gunter Weiss, Wolf Schiefenhövel, Peter Underhill. Peidong Shen, Peter Oefner, Mila Tommaseo-Ponzetta and Mark Stonekin. 2003. Reduced

Y-chromosome, but not mitochondrial DNA, diversity in human populations from West New Guinea. *American Journal of Human Genetics* 72: 281–302.
van Kessel, Daphne. 2011. *Spatial deixis in Awyu-Dumut languages*. Amsterdam: Bachelor Thesis Vrije Universiteit.
Knauft, Bruce M. 1993. *South coast New Guinea cultures: history, comparison, dialectic*. Cambridge: Cambridge University Press.
Kriens, Ron and Randy Lebold. 2010. *Report on the Wildeman River Survey in Papua, Indonesia*. Dallas: SIL International.
Lang, Adrienne J. 1975. *The semantics of classificatory verbs in Enga (and other Papua New Guinea Languages)*. Canberra: Australian National University Press.
Laycock, Don C. 1975. Observations on number systems and semantics. In Stephen A. Wurm (ed.), *New Guinea area languages and language study, vol.1: Papuan languages and the New Guinea linguistic scene*, 219–233. Canberra: Australian National University Press.
Larson, Mildred L. 1978. *The functions of reported speech in discourse*. Arlington, USA (SIL and University of Texas).
Lean, Geoffrey. 1992. *Counting systems of Papua New Guinea and Oceania*. Port Moresby: University of Technology dissertation.
Levelt, Willem J.M. 1989. *Speaking. From intention to articulation*. Cambridge, Mass. MIT Press.
Loughnane, Robyn, and Sebastian Fedden. 2011. Is Oksapmin Ok? A study of the genetic relatedness of Oksapmin and the Ok languages. *Australian Journal of Linguistics* 31(1):1–41.
Lounsbury, Floyd. 1964. A formal account of the Crow- and Omaha-type kinship terminologies. In Ward H. Goodenough, *Explorations in cultural anthropology*, 351–391. New York: McGraw-Hill.
Merrifield, William R. 1983a. Comments on Kinship Notation. In William R. Merrifield, Marilyn Gregerson and Daniel C. Ajamiseba, *Gods, Heroes, Kinsmen. Ethnographic Studies from Irian Jaya, Indonesia* (eds), 177–188. Dallas/Jayapura: The International Museum of Cultures/Cenderawasih University.
Merrifield, William R. 1983b. Some Typological Comments. In William. R. Merrifield, Marilyn Gregerson and Daniel C. Ajamiseba, *Gods, Heroes, Kinsmen. Ethnographic Studies from Irian Jaya, Indonesia* (eds.), 291–296. Dallas/Jayapura: The International Museum of Cultures/Cenderawasih University.
Murane, Elizabeth. 1974. *Daga Grammar: From Morpheme to Discourse*. Dallas: Summer Institute of Linguistics Publications in Linguistics and related Fields, 43.
Palmer, Bill. 2018. Language families of the New Guinea Area. In Bill Palmer (ed.), *The Languages and Linguistics of the New Guinea area*, 1–16. Berlin: De Gruyter Mouton.
Pascual, Esther. 2014. *Fictive interaction. The conversation frame in thought, language and discourse*. Amsterdam: John Benjamins.
Pawley, Andrew, Robert. Attenborough, Jack Golson and Robin Hide (eds.). 2005. *Papuan Pasts: cultural, linguistic and biological histories of Papuan-speaking peoples*. Canberra: Australian National University Press.
Pawley, Andrew R. 2005. The chequered career of the Trans New Guinea hypothesis. In Andrew Pawley, Robert Attenborough, Jack Golson and Robin Hide (eds.). 2005. *Papuan Pasts: cultural, linguistic and biological histories of Papuan-speaking peoples*, 67–108. Canberra: Australian National University Press.
Pawley, Andrew. 2012. How reconstructable is Proto Trans New Guinea? *Language and Linguistics in Melanesia*, 2012: 88–164.

Pawley, Andrew and Harald Hammarström. 2018. The Trans New Guinea Family. In Bill Palmer (ed.), *The Languages and Linguistics of the New Guinea area*, 21–156. Berlin: De Gruyter Mouton.

Pilhofer, Gerhard. 1933. *Grammatik der Kâte-Sprache in Neu Guinea*. Berlin: Dietrich Reimer Verlag.

Reesink, Ger P. 1983. Switch reference and topicality hierarchies. *Studies in Language* 7(2): 215–246.

Reesink, Ger P. 1987. *Structures and their functions in Usan, a Papuan language of Papua New Guinea*. Amsterdam: John Benjamins.

Reesink, Ger P. 1993. Inner speech in Papuan languages. *Language and Linguistics in Melanesia* 24: 217–225.

Reesink, Ger P. 1994. Domain-creating constructions in Papuan languages. In Ger P. Reesink (ed.), *Topics in descriptive Papuan linguistics*. Semaian 10, 98–121. Dept. of Languages and cultures of South-east Asia and Oceania, Leiden University.

Reesink, Ger P. 2008. Lexicon and syntax from an emic viewpoint. *Studies in Language* 32, (4): 866–893.

Reesink, Ger P., R. Singer and M. Dunn. 2009. Explaining the linguistic diversity of Sahul using population models. *PloS Biology* 7 (11): e10000241. Doi: 10.1371/journal.pbio.1000241

Riesberg, Sonja. 2018. Optional ergative, agentivity and discourse prominence – Evidence from Yali (Trans-New Guinea). *Linguistic Typology*, vol. 22(1): 17–50.

Roberts, John. 1987. *Amele*. London: Croom Helm.

Roberts, John. 1997. Switch reference in Papua New Guinea. *Papers in Papuan linguistics* 3: 101–241. Australian National University Press.

Roberts, John R. 1990. Modality in Amele and other Papuan languages. *Journal of Linguistics* 26: 363–401.

Robbins, John and Alan Rumsey (eds.). 2008. Cultural and Linguistic Anthropology and the Opacity of Other Minds. *Anthropological Quarterly* 81.

Ross, Malcom. 2005. Pronouns as a preliminary diagnostic for grouping Papuan languages. In Andrew Pawley, Robert Attenborough, Jack Golson and Robin Hide (eds.), *Papuan Pasts: cultural, linguistic and biological histories of Papuan-speaking peoples*, 15–65. Canberra: Australian National University Press.

San Roque, Lilian. 2008. *An Introduction to Duna Grammar*. Canberra: Australian National University dissertation.

Sarvasy, Hannah. 2015. Breaking the clause chains. Non-canonical medial clauses in Nungon. *Studies in Language* 39 (3): 664–696.

Schachter, Paul and Timothy Shopen. 2007. Parts-of-speech-systems. In Timothy Shopen (ed.), *Language typology and syntactic description, Volume I: clause structure*. Cambridge: Cambridge University Press.

Schapper, Antoinette and Lourens de Vries. 2018. Comparatives in Melanesia: concentric circles of convergence. *Linguistic Typology* 22 (3): 437–494.

Schoorl, Jan W. 1988. Mobility and Migration in Muyu culture. *Bijdragen tot de Taal-, Land- en Volkenkunde*, 144 (4): 540–556.

Stasch, Rupert. 2001. *Figures of alterity among Korowai of Irian Jaya. Kinship, mourning and festivity in a dispersed society*. Chicago: dissertation University of Chicago dissertation.

Stasch, Rupert. 2007. Demon language. The otherness of Indonesian in a Papuan community. In Miki Makihara and Bambi B. Schieffelin (eds.), *Consequences of contact: Language ideology and sociocultural transformations in Pacific societies*, 96–124. Oxford: Oxford University Press.

Stasch, Rupert. 2008a. Referent-wrecking in Korowai: A New Guinea abuse register as ethnosemiotic protest. *Language in Society* 37(1): 1–25.

Stasch, Rupert 2008b. Knowing minds is a matter of authority: political dimensions of opacity statements in Korowai moral psychology. In Joel Robbins and Alan Rumsey (eds.), Cultural and Linguistic Anthropology and the Opacity of Other Minds. *Anthropological Quarterly* 81: 443–453.

Stasch, Rupert. 2009. *Society of others: Kinship and mourning in a West Papuan place*. Berkeley: University of California Press.

Stassen, Leon. 2000. AND-languages and WITH-languages. *Linguistic Typology* 4: 1–54.

Susanto, Yanti. 2004. *Report on the Mapi River survey. South coast of Irian Jaya*. Indonesia. Dallas: SIL International.

Usher, Timothy & Edward Suter. 2015. The Anim languages of southern New Guinea. *Oceanic Linguistics* 54(1): 110–142.

Suter, Edward. 2018. *Comparative Morphology of the Huon Peninsula Languages (Papua New Guinea)*. Cologne: Cologne University dissertation.

Swadling, Pamela. 1983. *How have people been in the Ok Tedi impact Region?* PNG National Museum Record no. 8. Boroko: Papua New Guinea.

Trudgill, Pete. 2011. *Sociolinguistic Typology: Social Determinants of Linguistic Complexity*. Oxford: Oxford University Press.

Usher, Timothy. 2018. Newguineaworld. Online manuscript. https://sites.google.com/site/newguineaworld/

Versteeg, Henry. 1983. Zijn stam en taal. In Tjerk S. de Vries (ed.), *Een open plek in het oerwoud*, 21–25. Groningen: De Vuurbaak.

van der Voort, Hein. 2002. The quotative construction in Kwaza and its (de)grammaticalisation. In Milly Crevels, Simon van de Kerke, Sérgio Meira & Hein van der Voort (eds.), *Current Studies on South American Languages: Indigenous Languages of Latin America* (ILLA) 3, 307–328.

Voorhoeve, Clemens L. 1965. *The Flamingo Bay Dialect of the Asmat Language*. 'S Gravenhage: Martinus Nijhoff.

Voorhoeve, Clemens L. 1971. *Miscellaneous notes on Languages of West Irian, New Guinea*. Canberra: Australian National University Press.

Voorhoeve, Clemens L. 1977. Ta-poman: metaphorical use of words and poetic vocabulary in Asmat songs. In Stephen A. Wurm (ed.), *New Guinea Area Languages and Language Study*, vol. 3: *Language, Culture, Society and the Modern World*, 19–38. Canberra: Australian National University.

Voorhoeve, Clemens L. 1980. *The Asmat languages of Irian Jaya*. Canberra: Australian National University Press.

Voorhoeve, Clemens L. 1999. *Dictionary of Central Asmat (Flamingo Bay dialect)*. Unpublished manuscript.

Voorhoeve, Clemens L. 2001. Proto Awyu-Dumut phonology II. In A. Pawley, M. Ross and D. Tryon (eds), *The Boy from Bundaberg. Studies in Melanesian Linguistics in Honour of Tom Dutton*, 361–381. Canberra: Australian National University Press.

Voorhoeve, Clemens L. 2005. Asmat-Kamoro, Awyu-Dumut and Ok: an enquiry into their linguistic relationships. In A. Pawley, R. Attenborough, J. Golson and R. Hid (eds.), *Papuan

Pasts: cultural, linguistic and biological histories of Papuan-speaking peoples, 145–166. Canberra: Australian National University Press.
de Vries, Klaas. 2007. *Tussen Boomhuis en Vliegveld. De Korowai van Papoea in aanraking met de buitenwereld*. Utrecht: Utrecht University thesis.
de Vries, Lourens. 1986. The Wambon relator system. *Working Papers in Functional Grammar*. Vol. 17. Amsterdam: University of Amsterdam.
de Vries, Lourens. 1987. Kombai kinship terminology. *Irian. Bulletin of Irian Jaya*, volume XV: 105–126.
de Vries, Lourens. 1989. *Studies in Wambon and Kombai. Aspects of two Papuan languages of Irian Jaya*. Amsterdam: University of Amsterdam dissertation.
de Vries, Lourens. 1993a. *Forms and Functions in Kombai, an Awyu language of Irian Jaya*. Canberra: Australian National University Press.
de Vries, Lourens. 1993b. Notional and coded information roles. *Working papers in Functional Grammar*, Issue 52. Amsterdam: University of Amsterdam.
de Vries, Lourens. 1995. Demonstratives, referent identification and topicality in Wambon and some other Papuan languages. *Journal of Pragmatics* 24: 513–533.
de Vries, Lourens. 2004. *A short grammar of Inanwatan, an endangered language of the Bird's Head of Papua, Indonesia*. Canberra: Australian National University Press.
de Vries, Lourens. 2005. Towards a typology of tail-head linkage in Papuan languages. *Studies in Language* 29 (2): 363–384.
de Vries, Lourens. 2006. Areal pragmatics of New Guinea: Thematization, distribution and recapitulative linkage in Papuan languages. *Journal of Pragmatics* 38: 811–828.
de Vries, Lourens. 2010. From clause conjoining to clause chaining in Dumut languages of New Guinea. *Studies in Language* 34 (2): 327–349.
de Vries, Lourens. 2012a. Speaking of clans: language in Awyu-Ndumut communities of Indonesian West Papua. *International Journal of the Sociology of Language*, 2012 (214): 5–26.
de Vries, Lourens. 2012b. Some notes on the Tsaukambo language of West Papua. *Language and Linguistics in Melanesia*, 2012: 165–193.
de Vries, Lourens. 2013. Seeing, hearing and thinking in Korowai, a language of West Papua. In Alexandra Y. Aikhenvald and Anne Storch (eds.), *Perception and Cognition in Language and Culture*, 111–136. Leiden: Brill.
de Vries, Lourens. 2014. Numerals in Papuan languages of the Greater Awyu family. In Anne Storch and Gerrit J. Dimmendaal (eds.), *Number- Constructions and Semantic*, 329–355. Amsterdam: John Benjamins.
de Vries, Lourens. 2017. Greater Awyu Languages of West Papua in Typological Perspective. In Alexandra Aikhenvald and Robert M. W. Dixon (Eds.), *The Cambridge Handbook of Linguistic Typology*, 911–941. Cambridge: Cambridge: Cambridge University Press. https://doi.org/Chapter DOI: https://doi.org/10.1017/9781316135716.030
de Vries. Lourens. 2019. Online and offline bridging constructions in Korowai. In Valérie Guérin (ed.), *Bridging constructions*, 185–206. Berlin: Language Science Press. DOI:10.5281/zenodo.2563690
de Vries, Lourens, Ruth Wester and Wilco van den Heuvel 2012. The Greater Awyu language family of West Papua. *Language and Linguistics in Melanesia*, 2012: 269–312.
de Vries, Lourens. and Robinia de Vries-Wiersma. 1992. *An Outline of the Morphology of Wambon of the Irian Jaya Upper-Digul Area*. Royal Institute of Linguistics and Anthropology. Leiden: KITLV Press.

Welsch, Roger L. 1994. Pig feasts and expanding networks of cultural influence in the Upper–Fly–Digul plain. In Andrew J. Strathern and Gabriele Sturzenhofecker (eds.), *Migration and Transformations, regional perspectives on New Guinea*, 85–119. Pittsburgh: University of Pittsburgh Press.

Wegener, Claudia. 2008. *A Grammar of Savosavo, a Papuan Language of the Solomons Islands*. Nijmegen: Radboud University dissertation.

Wester, Ruth. 2014. *A linguistic history of Awyu-Dumut. Morphological study and reconstruction of a Papuan Language Family*. Amsterdam: Vrije Universiteit dissertation.

Wilson, John D. 1988. *Scripture in an oral culture: the Yali of Irian Jaya*. MA Thesis Faculty of Divinity. University of Edinburgh.

Wundt, Wilhelm. 1911–1912. *Völkerpsychologie. Eine Untersuchung der Entwicklungsgesetze von Sprache, Mythus und Sitte*. Zweiter Band: die Sprache, Teil 1–2. Leipzig: Engelmann.

Wurm, Stephen A. 1982. *Papuan languages of Oceania*. Gunter Narr Verlag: Tübingen.

9 Appendix: Texts

9.1 Introduction

Greater Awyu text collections, transcribed and edited in English, can be found in van Enk and de Vries (1997) (Korowai), de Vries 1993a (Kombai), de Vries and de Vries-Wiersma 1992 (Digul Wambon) and van den Heuvel (2015) (Aghu). Van den Heuvel (2016) is an annotated edition of all the Aghu texts published in Dutch by Drabbe (1957). The Yonggom Wambon and Mandobo texts collected and published by Drabbe (1959) are only accessible for readers who know Dutch and understand the terminology and transcription conventions that Drabbe followed. That is why some Mandobo and Yonggom Wambon texts of Drabbe (1959) are published as an appendix to this book. Dr. Ruth Wester transcribed and glossed the Yonggom Wambon and Mandobo texts of this appendix.

These two texts are added also to exemplify many aspects of Greater Awyu languages described in this book: discourse patterns, e.g. the role of secondary deictic motion verbs in spatial orientation, tail-head linkage, quotative framing, argument distribution, and thematization; patterns of syntax (e.g. relative clause constructions, experiential clauses, clause chaining, the syntactic role of deictic-based topic markers), morphology (e.g. switch reference based on non-finite-finite distinctions, the three verb types). The two texts are versions of the same story of the origin of the canoe, the first (§9.2.2) is a Mandobo text, the second a Yonggom Wambon text (§9.3).

9.2 Origin of the Ndumut river and the canoe

9.2.1 Introduction

This narrative is part of a cycle of sacred and secret origin stories of the Mandobo clan Omba. The narrator is Jatüp, 50 years old (which makes him an old man in the Mandobo context). He told these origin stories to Father Drabbe in the 1950s and Drabbe transcribed them with the help of some younger Mandobo speakers (Drabbe 1959: 3).

The main character in the story cycle is Nggou, who lives with his wives and offspring in the *etot*, the longhouse where pig festivals and pig markets are held. Nggou is his *ketpon* name, his taboo name, not meant to be told either to or by women, children (see §6.3). He is an ancestral culture hero, involved in one way or another with the origin of all things that matter most to Mandobo:

the first pig, the first *etot* longhouse, the sacred pig Mutut, the bullroarer, cross-cousin marriage and the river Ndumut (Mandobo river). Secrecy distinctions between genres of texts play an important role in Greater Awyu oral literature (van Enk and de Vries 1997). Some stories, songs and formulae can be performed by all people of a clan, other texts just by the adult men and yet other others are for everyone, including foreigners. The secret part of the myth of origin of people and animals starts when the sacral name Nggou is used after an introduction in which he is called *Tomorüp* with a non-taboo name (Drabbe 1959: 14).

Rivers and streams are often the only named features of the landscape (cf. Stasch 2001: 35) and the names of *kampongs* are almost always derived from river names (Stasch 2001: 35) or combinations of river names and river features (Drabbe 1959: 14). The terminology for river features is rich and detailed. For example, Mandobo has two nouns denoting a part of a river where the river had widened and deepened because now or in the past another river joined that river: a *wage* is such wide and deep place in a big river and a *türop* in a small river. Place names such as Kawagit are Indonesianised versions of Kao wage: wide and deep place where the Kao river meets the mighty Digul river.

The central place of streams in Greater Awyu fysical and cultural worlds is reflected in the following Mandobo myth about the origin of the river Ndumut (=Mandobo river) and the origin of the dug-out canoe. Although the origin of the Mandobo river and the canoe are the central themes, the myth contains a lot of foundational references to cultural practices and institutions of the Mandobo (and many other Greater Awyu groups): avoidance and taboo practices related to menstrual blood, compensation practices based on pigs, pork and dog teeth, practices around conflict management caused by sexual activities that infringe on the rights of fathers, the opacity of the other's mind and trickster practices (Nggou is tricked by the crocodile to become his friendly neighbor, the crocodile uses the sound of heavy tropical rains on the foliage so that he can stealthily approach the daughter of Nggou without being heard and the separation of the men's section and women's section in the tree house so that Nggou cannot see him approaching.)

An important theme in this myth is the foundational and creational roles of mythical pigs, a key theme in Greater Awyu mythology. In this story it is contact between the sacred pig's stomach (=the emotional and cognitive center) and a little bit of water that creates the big water, the river Ndumut (=Mandobo river in Indonesian).

The section about the origin of the Mandobo river in this appendix continues the story cycle at the point where Nggou, with his second wife and daughter, is on the return journey home after he tracked one of his three domesticated pigs that had wandered off into the jungle to live there. The three pigs, one white, one brown, one black, originated from a hollow tree in which his axe dropped and from which a voice came (the tree spirit Jomkimop) who told him that the three pigs were his children and Nggou should raise them and slaughter them. Nggou fattens the pigs, invites guests for a pig festival in his *longhouse* but when he wants to slaughter them for the guests to eat, he finds them gone. He demands an explanation of his first wife (women have the task to take care of domesticated pigs). She tells him that when she menstruated, his sister's son had sex with her and that the pigs had run off to the jungle when they smelled her menstrual blood. Nggou is very upset with his first wife and accuses her of adultery. He hits her and says that her adultery is the cause of the (sacral) pigs running off.

Three transgressions co-incide in her sexual relations with his sister'son: the pollution taboo and avoidance obligation in relation to female blood originating in the uterus (childbirth, menstruation), theft and incest, because in the avuncular dyad mother's brother-sister's son, the latter calls his maternal uncle's wife 'mother'. The avunculate is perhaps the most significant and valued kinship dyad in Greater Awyu Omaha-based kinship practices (see §6.7.2): they highly value each other as parent and child, they rely on each other in conflicts and the sister's son depends on his uncle for his sexual education and to acquire a bride. Adultery is called theft in Greater Awyu languages because the rights of the husband (and his clan) are violated, no so much property rights, but procreational rights: after paying the bride price, the children to be born count as members of the husband's clan, not of the mother's clan of origin. After each childbirth gift and wealth items are (often) given to the maternal clan.

Nggou leaves his first wife behind and takes his second wife (and the daughter of his second wife) into the jungle to track down one pig (telling his first wife to track the other pigs). At this point, our section of the myth begins, and the same theme of transgression by illicit sex and violation of pollution taboos returns: Nggou's daughter menstruates and her blood falls on the snout of a trickster-crocodile. Now Nggou is the guilty party: his daughter has caused lethal danger to the crocodile (who had offered to take her across on his back to the other side of the Mandobo river) and Nggou is responsible for her. Nggou behaves as a good Mandobo man should: he pays a compensation fee to the crocodile.

But the crocodile is a bad person: he accepts the compensation and speaks friendly words (implying that the balance is restored and that all is good between them) but in fact executes a plan to rape Nggou's daughter to satisfy his deep offense and anger (the menstrual blood sticks to his nose, whatever he does to wash it off). But the good and exemplary behavior of Nggou shows what a proper culture hero does: he kills the deceptive crocodile (and turns him at the request of the croc into the first canoe), retrieves his pigs and returns home where he finds that his first wife Fingon (whom he had hit before he left her) has been taken by his mate Kimitponop. He kills Kimitponop, takes all his shell-money and takes his first wife home to his longhouse.

The order of things has been restored: the good Nggou is fully compensated for the extreme and heinous taboo-breaking violations of his rights by those he had very good reason to trust most: his own his sister's son, his friend Kimitponop, his first wife and the crocodile that had accepted his compensation payment.

This fascinating myth evokes many scenes of daily life that I witnessed when I lived in the area in the 1980s: the chanted calling by women who look for stray domesticated pigs that they have raised and have become very attached to (by calling the names of the pigs), the clever negotiations of compensation payments in pork and dog-teeth strings after cases of illicit sex, felling trees to form bridges when small streams have swollen by persistent rain, the sound of endless tropical rains smothering all other sounds, the binding of pigs or people by jamming them between sticks, bending the sticks and tying them up with rattan tightly, so they cannot move, the quick construction of a temporary shelter when travellers have to sleep in the jungle.

9.2.2 Annotated Mandobo text (Drabbe 1959: 50–60)

(1) Orumop   me-gen-on   wüop   me-gen-on
     back   come-RLS-NON1PL   middle   come-RLS-NON1PL
     do, wemin ge-gen.
     CNJ night be-RLS[NON1SG]
     'They (=Nggou, his second wife and their daughter) came back, they came halfway and the night fell.' (=In the middle of their return journey home, the night fell (and this forced Nggou to make a shelter for the night.))

(2) Rogo   rüo   mbügiarop tarap ti-gen.
     go.downhill go.down   valley   hut   build-RLS[NON1SG]
     'He went down to a valley and built a hut.'

(3) Tarap ti   amboto e-metip   e-aŋgen   in
     hut   build finish 3SG.POSS-daughter 3SG.POSS-wife firewood
     küomo-ro- me-ro   in   mbo köŋ-gen-on.
     break-take- come-ss   fire   TOP build-RLS-NON1PL
     'When he finished building a shelter, his daughter and his wife collected firewood, brought it and built a fire.'

(4) Ege mbo⁴⁶   u-j-ogömö   tiri   korö   mbügiarop wüop
    he   TOP   pig-LNK-stomach clean   go.down   valley   middle
    ro   kaoma-gen.
    put.down   divide.in.two-RLS[NON1SG]
    'But he went to rinse the pig stomach,⁴⁷ went down to the middle of the valley, put it (stomach) down and divided it in half.'

(5) Ro   matere   go   me-re   tarap   ot-ken.
    hold   come/get.up   go   come-SEQ⁴⁸   hut   go.in-RLS[NON1SG]
    'He carried it back and entered the hut.'

(6) Tarap   togo   mba-gen   do,   wemin   ge-r-an
    hut   go.in   stay-RLS[NON1SG]   CNJ   night   be-RLS[NON1SG]-PAST
    do,   ndu   ane   raŋ-gen   do   wemin   ge-r-an
    CONN   sago   eat   lie-RLS[NON1SG]   CNJ   night   be-RLS[NON1SG]-PAST
    do   komöt   ŋgoŋwan-gen,   murüp   ke-gen.
    CNJ   thunderstorm   break.out-RLS[NON1SG]   rain   be-RLS[NON1SG]
    'He went into the hut, it became night, they ate sago, slept, and in the night, there was a thunderstorm and it rained.'

---

46 There is a distal deictic element *mbe* (allomorphs *mbere* and *mbo* (in vowelharmony) and *po* (after wordfinal voiceless stops)) 'there (where you are)' in Mandobo that occurs as an adverb 'there', as a demonstrative 'that', as a definite article, as a marker of topicality (Drabbe 1959: 18–20) with personal pronouns, noun phrases and subordinate clauses, for example conditional clauses (Drabbe 1959: 37) and relative clauses (Drabbe 1959: 53). It also functions as discourse connective 'thus; in that way'. See section 3.5 for the roles of deictics in Greater Awyu grammars. There is an unrelated durative maker *mbo* that always occurs immediately before finite verbs, derived from the verb *mba* 'to sit'.

47 In the previous story of the Nggou cycle (Drabbe 1959: 43–50) Nggou had slaughtered one of his pigs that had run away and was killed by his comrade. The intestines and stomach of slaughtered pigs are cleansed with water, from a small stream or pool. The contact between the intestines or stomach of the mythical pig with the water of a small stream or rain pool in which it is washed is the cause of the origin of the big river (left implicit in the story). Drabbe (1959: 51) observes that this theme of the origin of big rivers as a result of cleansing the insides of a pig belly with water from a small source occurs also in the Aghu story of origin of the Digul river where the contact between the faeces of the pig and a small river is the basis for the Digul. In this story it is the rain of one night collected in a pool at the lowest point of the valley that comes into contact with the insides of the pig's belly.

48 Drabbe (1959: 15) describes – *re* (subject to vowel harmony) as an anteriority marker (glossed as SEQ in this book) with non-finite medial verbs that is restricted to verbs of motion and posture. Its Yonggom Wambon counterpart is described by Drabbe (1959: 132) as optionally occuring with all SS verbs, in sequence and simultaneity conditions. It is glossed as SS in the Yonggom Wambon text.

(7) *Ke-gen   do mbo teet ke-gen.*
be-RLS[NON1SG] CNJ DUR day be-RLS[NON1SG]
'It kept raining until the next day.'

(8) *Matero itigio-gen   do mbügiarop   mbo og goneni*
get.up see-RLS[NON1SG] CNJ valley.middle TOP river big
anema-gen.
block.off- RLS[NON1SG]
'When he got up, the valley, a big river blocked it.'

(9) *Anema-gen*[49]   *doro*[50] *irupma-gen   kenemop kej'o*
block.off-RLS[NON1SG] CNJ   be.amazed- RLS[NON1SG] what   Q
ne-gen.[51]
say-RLS[NON1SG]
'It was blocked and this amazed him.'
(Lit. it (the valley) was blocked and so he was amazed, What is this, he said/thought.)

(10) *E-aŋgen   de*[52] *e-metip   te   u*
3SG.POSS-wife COORD 3SG.POSS-daughter COORD pig
kweti mbo-gen.
guard stay-RLS[NON1SG]
'His wife and his daughter stayed behind to guard the pig(meat).'

(11) *Ege mbo matero ok   Po kurümü-rü küm   go-gen,*
He TOP get.up river TOP follow-SEQ upstream go-RLS[NON1SG]
korümü-rü go itigio-gen   do ok   po ŋguruop to
follow-SEQ go see-RLS[NON1SG] CNJ river TOP far   CNJ

---

49 This is one of the many tail-head linkages between sentences, see §5.2.1 for tail-head linkage.
50 Drabbe (1959: 18) describes *doro* (allomorph *tore*) as a causal conjunction that is also frequently used as a connective in tail-head linkage without cause or reason meanings.
51 This is an example of highly conventionalized quotative framing in the domain of emotion. Verbs that express inner states such as 'to be amazed', 'to be surprised' are almost always accompanied by a verb of saying and a direct quote. An idiomatic translation would be 'he was amazed and wondered what what going on' (see §5.3).
52 *De* (allomorphs *do/ te/to*) is described by Drabbe (1959: 12) as a predicative element that functions as copula with nominal and adjectival predicates. It also functions as a coordinating conjunction with nouns and it conjoins clauses. Wester (2014: 165) argues that *te* is a subordinating conjunction when it links clauses.

```
       ko-gen              doro,  orümop oro    me-gen.
       go-RLS[NON1SG]  CNJ  back    hold   come-RLS[NON1SG]
```
'But he got up, followed the river upstream and saw that the river is long (goes far) and so he returned.'

(12)   *Me-ro   e-aŋen   e-metip   tagamo   kinokmo*
       come-SEQ   3SG.POSS-wife   3SG.POSS-daughter   say   decide
       mba-nog-i-n-in   de   no, no mbo kerok nekem   kea-ep
       say-IMP-LNK-NON1PL   CNJ Say I   TOP go.by downstream   go-1SG
       naŋaŋo   Tagamo kem   ko-gen   kem   ko-ro
       Say   Say   downstream   go-RLS[NON1SG]   downstream   go-SEQ

(13)   *kurümü-rü go-gen   do,   ok   po   ŋuruop to*
       follow-SEQ go-RLS[NON1SG]   CNJ   river TOP far   CNJ
       go-gen   do, kurüma-gen   do   eren
       go-RLS[NON1SG]   CNJ follow-RLS[NON1SG] CNJ impossible
       ge-gen   doro regimbörö gö   orümop me-gen.
       be-RLS[NON1SG]   CNJ   other.way be   back   come-RLS[NON1SG]

'He returned and said to his wife and daughter: stay here! I am going downstream, I am going he said and went downstream, he went downstream following (the river), the river was long, and he followed it but because it was impossible he returned the other way.'

(14)   *Me-ro   tarap togo   e-metip   e-aŋen   tagaŋ-gen,*
       come-SEQ   hut   go.in   3SG.POSS-daughter 3SG.POSS-wife   say-RLS[NON1SG]
       ko-gen-ep   te   eren   ge-gen   doro, orümop oro
       go-RLS-1SG CNJ   impossible   be-RLS[NON1SG]   CNJ   back   hold
       me-gen-ep   ne-gen.
       come-RLS-1SG say-RLS[NON1SG]

'He returned and entered the hut and said to his wife and daughter: I went but it was impossible and so I have come back.'

(15)   *Wemin ge-gen   doro kinum reŋi-re ö   itigio-gen*
       night   be-RLS[NON1SG]   CNJ   sleep lie-SEQ dream   see-RLS[NON1SG]

'It was night and he was asleep and he had a dream.'

(16)   *ö   reŋi-ri itigio-gen   do: orat   ke-n   do, in*
       dream   lie-SEQ see-RLS[NON1SG]   CNJ   light do-[IRR]NON1.SG   CNJ tree

oru   ndokmo-nog   O   ne-gen.
chop.down lie.across-IMP[SG] CONN say-RLS[NON1SG]
'he had a dream in his sleep, when it becomes light, chop down a tree and lay it across, someone said.'

(17) Karemo orat   ke-r-an   do,   matero in   tomet
     obey   light   be-RLS[NON1SG]-PAST CNJ get.up tree   tomet
     oru-gon-gen.
     put.in-RLS[NON1SG]
     'He obeyed and it became light, he got up, chopped down a *tomet* tree, put it in (the river)'.

(18) In   tomet oru-goöŋ-gen   do   mbarane-gen.
     tree   tomet chop.down-put.in-RLS[NON1SG] CNJ be.too.short-RLS[NON1SG]
     'He chopped down the *tomet* tree and put it in the river, but it was too short.'

(19) Igia   in   kumuti   oru-goöŋ-gen
     Again tree   type.of.tree chop.down put.in-RLS[NON1SG]
     mbarane-gen.
     be.too.short-RLS[NON1SG]
     'Again, he chopped a *kumuti* tree, put it in (the river), it was too short.'

(20) Igia   kondep   ku   oru-goöŋ-gen,
     again another ku.tree   chop.down-put.in-RLS[NON1SG]
     mbarane-gen.
     be.too.short- RLS[NON1SG]
     'Again he chopped down another tree, a *ku* tree, put it in (the river), it was too short.'

(21) Igia   in   mbogot   oru   goöŋ-gen,
     again tree   type.of.tree chop.down   put.in-RLS[NON1SG]
     mbarane-gen.
     be.too.short-RLS[NON1SG]
     'Again, he chopped a *mbogot* tree, put it in (the river), it was too short.'

(22) Igia   in   ndambet   oru   goöŋ-gen,
     again tree   type.of.tree chop.down   put.in-RLS[NON1SG]

    mbarane-gen.
    be.too.short-RLS[NON1SG]
    'Again, he chopped a *ndambet* tree, put it in (the river), it was too short.'

(23) Igia   in   tiöŋjarenop   oru   goöŋ-gen,
     again tree type.of.tree chop.down put.in-RLS[NON1SG]
     mbarane-gen.
     be.too.short-RLS[NON1SG]
     'Again, he chopped a *tiöŋjarenop* tree, put it in (the river), it was too short.'

(24) Igia   in   kimit   oru   goöŋ-gen,
     again tree type.of.tree chop.down put.in-RLS[NON1SG]
     mbarane-gen.
     be.too.short-RLS[NON1SG]
     'Again, he chopped a *kimit* tree, put it in (the river), it was too short.'

(25) Wemin ge-gen.
     night   be-RLS[NON1SG]
     'It became night.'

(26) Wemin ge-gen   doro tarap koujap togo   kinum raŋ-gen
     night   be-RLS[NON1SG] CNJ   hut   again   go.in sleep lie-RLS[NON1SG]
     'it became night and he went into the hut again to sleep'

(27) ö   Koujap reŋgi-ri itigio-gen   do tagaŋ-gen,   mene
     dream again   lie-SEQ see-RLS[NON1SG] CNJ say-RLS[NON1SG] now
     mb' orat ke-n   do, tegep   mbo
     TOP light do-[IRR]NON.SG CNJ nibung.palm there
     ri-gin   mbo[53] oru   ko-non   ne-gen.
     stand-RLS[NON1SG] TOP   chop put.in-IMP[SG] say-RLS[NON1SG]
     'Again he had a dream in his sleep and someone said (in his dream): now when it will be light, chop down the *nibung* palm that stands there and put it in (the river)'

---

[53] The distal deictic *mbo (mbe/po)* 'that/there' acquired many functions in Mandobo (see note 1). The noun phrase *tegep mbo rigin mbo* is analysed by Drabbe (1959: 53) as relative NP headed by *tegep* 'nibung palm' followed by the relative clause *mbo rigin mbo*. Drabbe observes that there is a pause after the head *tegep* and that *mbo rigin mbo* is spoken in one breath, that the first *mbo* is part of the relative clause as distal locative adverb 'there' and that the second

(28) *Ne-gen doro ndare raŋ-gen do, orat ke-gen*
say-RLS[NON1SG] CNJ hear lie-RLS[NON1SG] CNJ light be-RLS[NON1SG]
doro, karemo matero tegep oru-gun.
CNJ obey get.up nibung.palm chop.down-RLS[NON1SG]
'When someone said that, he heard, slept and after it had become light, he obeyed, got up and chopped down the *nibung* palm.'

(29) *Oru ok koŋ-gen.*
chop.down river put.in-RLS[NON1SG]
'He chopped it down and put it in the river.'

(30) *Ri-gin do, kerima-gen doro, mbere ne*
stand-RLS[NON1SG] CNJ last.short-RLS[NON1SG] CJN, there GEN
ondut ngwane-gen doro, itigio-gen do, me-re
wave stop-RLS[NON1SG] CNJ see-RLS[NON1SG] CNJ, come-SEQ
ono-gen, itigio-gen do riwop
come.above.water-RLS[NON1SG] see-RLS[NON1SG] CNJ middle.of.river
mbogo ono-gen, ono muŋ-gun,
there come.above-RLS[NON1SG] come.above come.across-RLS[NON1SG],
e gap mba ro me-re kima-gen.
3SG self towards hold come-SEQ come.onto.land-RLS[NON1SG]
'He stood, it lasted only a short while, the waves (caused by the *nibung* palm he threw into the water) stopped and he saw that it (the *nibung*) came to the surface, he saw that it surfaced in the middle of the river there and that it came across towards himself, it approached and came onto the land'.

(31) *Ege itigi ŋgjotke towemo-gen.*
He see be.scared be.afraid-RLS[NON1SG]
'He saw, became scared and afraid.'

(32) *Kenemop te geja ne-gen kenemop te geja*
what FOC Q say-RLS[NON1SG] what FOC Q
ne tomamo-gen.
say ask-RLS[NON1SG]
'What is this? he said. What is this? he asked.'

---

mbo functions as a definite article "to be translated in Dutch as a relative pronoun". In our analysis, this last *mbo* is a topic marker that marks the preceding NP as a topical relative NP.

(33) ŋda-j-o,   tegep   mb' oru   komo-r-an
    not-LIG-CNJ nibung.palm that chop.down put.in-RLS[NON1SG]-PAST
    kiambot   kerema-gen-ew-a   ne-gen.   ge to,
    crocodile become-RLS-1SG-CNJ say-RLS[NON1SG] be CNJ,
    'Nothing, it is the *nibung* palm which you chopped down and put in (the river as a bridge), I became a crocodile, he said.'

(34) ŋgo mb' oru   komo-r-an   ge to joun keremo
    you TOP chop.down put.in-RLS[NON1SG]-PAST be CNJ canoe become
    ro   me-re   kimi-gian-ep   ŋgo meri-ro   nene mbuman
    hold come-SEQ come.unto.land-RLS-1SG you come-SEQ my   back
    tarok menemo meri   mba-nag   eta,
    on   here   come.down sit-IMP[SG] CONN,
    ro-undo-w=a   ne-gen.
    hold-go.across-[IRR]1SG=CONN say-RLS[NON1SG]
    'It was what you chopped down, put into the river, I became a canoe and came unto land; you come, come down here onto my back, sit and I will take you across' he said.'

(35) Ro-ndogo   eiga   ro-p   to,
    hold-go.across other.side put.down-[IRR]1SG CNJ,
    undo-nog-a   ne-gen.
    go.across-IMP[SG]-CNJ say-RLS[NON1SG]
    'I will take you to the other side and put you down, you must go across, he said.'

(36) Ne-gen   doro jok ne-gen.
    say-RLS[NON1SG] CNJ yes say-RLS[NON1SG]
    'He said so and the other[54] agreed.' (lit. he said (DS) and he said 'yes')

---

54 Drabbe (1959: 17) writes that Mandobo has a switch reference system built on the opposition finite verb (=DS)/non-finite verb (=SS). The first *negen* 'he said' is part of the tail-head linkage (35)/(36) and therefore the canoe/crocodile is the referent of the subject. By using a finite form in the recapitulated clause, the addressee expects a switch of subject, in this case to Nggou. However, Drabbe (1959: 34) points to cases where a series of conjoined finite verbs have the same subject. Wester (2014: 179–184) argues that independent verbs in all Dumut languages, including Yonggom Wambon, signal DS when used before another conjoined clause but that there are two specific conditions where independent verbs can occur before clauses with same subjects: (i) when one event is completed before the next event and the conceptual relation between the two events is not close (Wester 2014: 180) and (ii) when a clause is specified by the next clause (Wester 2014: 178).

(37) U   tiramba   tima-gen;   timo kiambot Ndagom
     pig   upper.body   take-RLS[NON1SG] take crocodile Upside
     korü-gen.
     go.down-RLS[NON1SG]
     'He took the pig's upper body, he took it and the crocodile's upside went down (into the river)'

(38) Korü-gun   ro-ndogo   ro-gen   aro,
     go.down-RLS[NON1SG]   hold-go.across   put.down-RLS[NON1SG]   SEQ
     igia   ro-muŋ-gun.
     again   hold-come.across-RLS[NON1SG]
     '(the crocodile) went down and took (him) across, and then he put him down, again took (someone) across.'

(39) Mandogo   e   metip   mbo ri-gin,   e   nou
     come.across   his   daughter   TOP stand-RLS[NON1SG]   her   mother
     mbo   u   gegeman   timo   ŋgane   korü-gun
     TOP   pig   lower.body   take   short.distance   go.down-RLS[NON1SG]
     'He came across and his daughter stood (there), her mother took the pig's lower body and went short distance, goes down.'

(40) ŋgane   korü-gun   dora,   ro-ndogo   e-anogomberi
     short.distance   go.down-RLS[NON1SG]   CNJ,   hold-go.across her-husband
     mba   ro-gen.
     at   put.down-RLS[NON1SG]
     'He went down a short distance, took her across and put her down where her husband was.'

(41) Igia   mandogo-ro   e   metip   tagaŋ-gen   doro,
     again   come.across-SEQ   his   daughter   say-RLS[NON1SG]   CNJ,
     mbonoma-gen.
     refuse-RLS[NON1SG]
     'Again he came across and spoke to his daughter, but she refused'

(42) ŋorug   o   ne-gen.
     go.down.IMP.SG   CONN   say-RLS[NON1SG]
     `You must go down' he said.

(43) *Ne-gen   doro   ŋgane   korü-gün.*
     say-RLS[NON1SG] CNJ, short.distance go.down-RLS[NON1SG]
     'He said (so) and went down a short distance.'

(44) *Korü-gün   doro   ene   ketambö⁵⁵   mbo   ŋgwane*
     go.down-RLS[NON1SG]   CNJ   her   menstruation.blood   TOP   come.loose
     kiambot   kuruguat   tereni-gen.
     crocodile   snout   stick-RLS[NON1SG]
     'He went down, and her menstruation blood came loose and stuck to the crocodile's snout.'

(45) *Oro   riwöp   ko-gen   doro,   a   gokmo   kumü*
     next   middle.of.river   go-RLS[NON1SG]   CNJ,   Inside   be.hot   dive
     gorü-gen   doro,   e   neti   matero   tagaŋ-gen,
     go.down-RLS[NON1SG]   CNJ   her   father   get.up   say-RLS[NON1SG]
     kiambor   o,   no   metip   tiri   öndö-nok
     crocodile VOC, my   daughter   take   come.above.water-IMP[SG]
     ne-gen.
     say-RLS[NON1SG]
     'And he went to the middle of the river and angrily submerged, her father got up and said: crocodile, come above water with my daughter,'

(46) *Jok   naŋgaŋo   önö-gen.*
     yes   say   come.above.water-RLS[NON1SG]
     'He consented and came up above water.'

---

55 Greater Awyu groups tend to have strong pollution taboos regarding menstruation blood. Men fear that contact with it makes them ill or kills them, especially through respiratory diseases, coughing and tuberculosis (van Enk and de Vries 1997: 43). Menstruating women are expected to prevent anyone coming into contact with their blood. If that happens, it is a transgression, and the male victim will demand compensation (in the form of pork, pigs, or other valuables). The crocodile is the victim in this story, he demands compensation and receives it after Nggou finds that his daugther indeed bled on the snout of the crocodile. In the tree house a wall separates the women's section and the men's section. Among Korowai, the tree house has the men's section 'upstream' and the women's section 'down stream'. If the women had their fireplaces (where they sleep and live with their dependent children) on the upstream part of the tree house, there is a fear thattheir menstrual blood could flow downstream to the men's section (Stasch 2001: 65).

(47) *Ro-ndogo   e   neti   mba kima-gen.*
hold-go.across her father at   come.onto.land-RLS[NON1SG]
'He took her across and came unto the land near her father.'

(48) *ŋgane   matere-gen.*
short.distance come.up-RLS[NON1SG]
'At a short distance he came to the surface'

(49) *Kiambot   tagaŋ-gen,   kea   nda-j-o   rigi-nog*
crocodile say-RLS[NON1SG] go[IRR][NON1SG] not-LIG-CONN stand-IMP[SG]
eten O   ne-gen.
CONN CONN[56] say-RLS[NON1SG]
'The crocodile said: do not go, stand! he said.'

(50) *Ne-gen   doro ri-gen.*
say-RLS[NON1SG] CNJ   stand-RLS[NON1SG]
'He said that and so she stood.'

(51) *Kiambot ege mbo ndombakne korü-gen.*
crocodile he TOP dive   go.down-RLS[NON1SG]
'The crocodile, he submerged.'

(52) *ndombakne korü-ro   ene kuruguat tombüma-gen.*
dive   go.down-SEQ   his snout   clean-RLS[NON1SG]
'He submerged and cleaned his snout.'

(53) *Eren   ge-gen,   me-re   önö-gen.*
impossible be-RLS[NON1SG] come-SS come.above.water-RLS[NON1SG]
'It was impossible; he came up above water.'

(54) *Mi   igia   korü-gen.*
again again go.down-RLS[NON1SG]
'Again and again he dived.'

---

[56] The connective *o* (allomorph *a*) signals the end of the quoted speech in speech reports (Drabbe 1959: 23) and links it to the generic verb of speaking *ne-*.

(55) *Tombüma-gen   doro   mep   eren   ge-gen.*
     clean-RLS[NON1SG] CNJ entirely impossible be-RLS[NON1SG]
     'When he tried to clean (his snout), it was entirely impossible.'

(56) *Igia me-re   önö-gen.*
     again come-SEQ come.above.water-RLS[NON1SG]
     'Again he came up above the water.'

(57) *Kiambot tagaŋ-gen: ŋgou-j-o,   ŋgo metip   tomamo-nog*
     crocodile say-RLS[NON1SG]   ŋgou-LIG-VOC   your Daughter ask-IMP[SG]
     o   ne-gen.
     CNJ say- RLS[NON1SG]
     'The crocodile said: Nggou, ask (interrogate) your daughter! he said'.

(58) *Ne-gen   doro, e   metip   tomamo-gen.*
     say-RLS[NON1SG]   CNJ, his daughter ask-RLS[NON1SG]
     'He_i (crocodile) said and he_j (Nggou) asked his daughter.'

(59) *Jog o,   no mbo nene ketambö   köp To*
     yes EXCL, I TOP my   menstruation.blood with CNJ
     ri-gin-iw   o   ne-gen.
     put-RLS-1SG CONN say-RLS[NON1SG]
     'yes, I am bleeding and I lost (some), she said.'

(60) *ŋgöp wakmo-gen   o   ne-gen.*
     you be.guilty-RLS[NON1SG] CONN say-RLS[NON1SG]
     'You are guilty, he said.'

(61) *Jog o,   kogoröm do, ene ketambö   Köp tore to,*
     yes EXCL, just   CNJ her menstruation.blood With CNJ CNJ
     ŋgwane   meri   o,   ŋgone kuruguat terendi-r-an
     come.loose come.down EXCL, your   snout   stick.to-RLS[NON1SG]-PAST
     o   ne-gen.
     CONN say-RLS[NON1SG]
     'Yes, that is right, her menstruation blood came loose, came down, stuck to your snout, he said.'

(62) *Tagaŋ-gen   o,   ŋgo-ano mbeta-gen   doro, nöp*
     speak-RLS[NON1SG] CONN, you-SBJ be.guilty-RLS[NON1SG] CNJ, me

waŋgöm   tokmo-nok   ne-gen.
compensation pay-IMP[SG] say-RLS[NON1SG]
'He$_j$ (Nggou) said (that), then he$_i$ (crocodile) said 'because you are guilty, you must pay me compensation.'

(63) *Ne-gen   doro, kenemop te   ndigio-p   Kejo*
     say-RLS[NON1SG]   CNJ, what   FOC[57] give-[IRR]1SG Q
     ne-gen.
     say.RLS[NON1SG]
     'He$_i$ (crocodile) said (so) and then he$_j$ (Nggou) said (to himself)[58] 'what shall I give?'

(64) *Ne-gen   doro kegeman   timo   kiambot   ndigio-gen.*
     say-RLS[NON1SG]   CNJ lower.body take   crocodile give-RLS[NON1SG]
     'He$_i$ said that, and he took the pig's lower body and gave (it) to the crocodile.'

(65) *U   gegeman   ome   mbe nda, meŋit   makmo To   men*
     pig lower.body   only that not   dog.teeth   add   CNJ give.IMP
     ne-gen.
     say.RLS[NON1SG]
     'Not only the pig's lower body, add dog teeth and give it to me, he$_i$ said.'

(66) *Ne-gen   doro, meŋit   karemo tik   komo   ndigio-gen.*
     say-RLS[NON1SG]   CNJ   dog.teeth   obey   rotan   thread give-RLS[NON1SG]
     'He$_i$ said that, and he$_j$ consented to the dog teeth and gave one rattan string (of dog teeth).'

---

57 Drabbe (1959: 55) describes *te* here as a predicative in a cleft-like construction (What is it that I should give?), observing that it always follows questionwords. Perhaps the construction is indeed historically a copula clause with a relative NP as topical subject and the question-word as focal nominal predicate. An alternative analysis is that the *de* added a function as focus marker through this historical process but that the construction no longer contains a relative NP (because it shows no signs of being one).

58 Drabbe (1959: 54) correctly translates this verb of speaking as 'he thought'. Mandobo (as other Greater Awyu languages and many Papuan languages in general) use speech reports as a frame to express inner processes such as thinking, emotions, considerations. This quotative framing occurs very frequently in Greater Awyu languages (see §5.3) and has become the conventional way to express such domains. In fact, the translation 'Nggou wondered what to give' is probably the best in this case.

(67) *Mene mbo urumo e-gen   doro migia kondep men*
     this TOP little be-RLS[NON1SG] CNJ, again another give.IMP
     do makmo to   agöp   ke-n   do timo-p
     CNJ add   CNJ much be-[IRR]NON1SG CNJ receive-[IRR]1SG
     'this is too little, again give me more, add (until) it is much and I will receive it.'

(68) *Timo-p   to   kare   e-gen   do, imban*
     receive-[IRR]1SG CNJ, enough be-RLS[NON1SG] CNJ, tooth
     keremo-n   o, u   mene ande-p.
     become[IRR]NON1SG CONN pig this eat-[IRR]1SG
     'I will receive, it will be enough, the teeth will be enough to eat this pig with.'

(69) *Wangöm   tokmo-gen   do, timi-gian-ep   toro ŋgo*
     compensation pay-RLS[NON1SG] CNJ receive-RLS-1SG CNJ you
     mbo kea-nda,   ok   tiritiop   mberemo tarap Ti   mbegi-ro
     TOP go[IRR]-NEG, river high.bank   thus   hut   build stay-SEQ
     mbutüp ti-nok.
     house   build-IMP[SG]
     'After you pay me compensation, after I receive it, you will not go, stay on the river's high bank, build a hut and stay there to build a (tree) house.'

(70) *Ne-gen   doro, jok ne-gen.*
     say-RLS[NON1SG] CNJ, yes say-RLS[NON1SG]
     'He_i said that, he_j said yes.'

(71) *Ndot-ken-ep   toro mbutüp⁵⁹ ti-j-ep   naŋgaŋgo- tagamo*
     listen-RLS-1SG CNJ   house   build-[IRR]LIG-1SG speak- say
     ŋgane   ndon⁶⁰   törö-rö   ti-gen.

---

59 The noun *mbutüp* means place, a place to live, clan territory. Making a place to live implies making a clearing in the rainforest by cutting downs trees and shrubs followed by the construction of a tree house. It is the custom to build a temporary hut, not in the trees, as a shelter to stay in during the clearing of the jungle and the construction of a tree house.

60 The crocodile tricks Nggou into believing that the compensation payments (pigmeat, dog-teeth) are enough to compensate for the damage done to him when the daugther broke the pollution taboo by letting her menstruation blood drip on his face, something that could cause his death. By accepting the compensation payment, the relationship between the crocodile and Nggou is restored and the crocodile invites Nggou to settle as his neighbor. In fact, he is still very angry and is making dangerous plans. The negotiation about compensation payments is very

       short.distance land.opposite.water go.up-SEQ build-RLS[NON1SG]
       'I listen (obey) and I will build a (tree) house, he said, and at a short distance from the river he went up and built (a tree house).'

(72) *Tarap ti   mbegi-ro mbutüp[61] orü- ŋgwamo-gen.*
     hut   build stay-SEQ house chop.down- chop.off-RLS[NON1SG]
     'Having builts a temporary shelter to stay in, he chopped down (trees for) a house.'

(73) *Mbegi-re mbutüp mbo ti-gen.*
     stay-SEQ house TOP build-RLS[NON1SG]
     'He staid and built the house.'

(74) *Kiambot po, wemin ge-gen   doro, murüp mbo ge-gen,*
     crocodile TOP night be-RLS[NON1SG] CNJ rain DUR be-RLS[NON1SG]
     kiambot po ro me-re   kimo ŋgane   törö-gen.
     crocodile TOP CNJ come-SEQ land short.distance go.up-RLS.[NON1SG]
     'The crocodile, during the night when it was raining, the crocodile came ashore a short distance (from there) and went up.'

(75) *Ogage   torogo ran   mbo ene Ketambö   mbo ege*
     Secretly go.up woman TOP her menstruation.blood TOP him
     terendi-r-an   doreto a[62] gokmo ran   mbo kurop[63]
     stick-RLS[NON1SG]-PAST CNJ   gut be.hot woman TOP theft

---

recognizable for the audience as such scenes play out almost daily in their own lives, in very similar ways. Missionaries tried to stop the endless claims and counterclaims related to deaths, insults, accidents, and many other things that formed (and forms) a key element in Greater Awyu communities to solve conflicts, to create conflicts and to establish, maintain and manipulate social relations. These cultural practices are still a key element in these communities.

61 The noun *mbutüp* means place, a place to live, clan territory. Making a place to live implies making a clearing in the rainforest by cutting downs trees and shrubs followed by the construction of a tree house. It is the custom to build a temporary hut, not in the trees, as a shelter to stay in during the clearing of the jungle and the construction of a tree house.

62 In all Greater Awyu languages the belly or intestines or gall are the seat of emotion and cerebration. Uncontrolled emotions are expressed in experiential constructions where the human experiencer is not the subject of the clause but topics. Nouns denoting belly, intestines and so on are the subject with which the verb agrees. Here the topic (crocodile) is implicit in the experiential clause with *a* 'belly' as subject.

63 Nouns denoting theft are also used in a broader sense of violating the rights of other people, especially in relation to sexuality and marriage in several Greater Awyu languages, e.g. Mandobo (Drabbe 1959: 56) and Kombai.

namo reŋendema-gen
  with sleep.upon-RLS[NON1SG]
  'secretly he went up and he had illicit sex with the woman whose menstruation blood stuck on him so he became angry'

(76) *Reŋendemo igia ok wüop korü-gen.*
  sleep.upon again river inside go.down-RLS[NON1SG]
  'He had sex with her and again descended into the river.'

(77) *Korü raŋ-gen do, wemin ge-r-an do,*
  go.down lie-RLS[NON1SG] CNJ night be-RLS[NON1SG]-PAST CNJ
  Koujap metere-gen.
  once.again come.up-RLS[NON1SG]
  'He went down and lay down and in the night, he came up again.

(78) *Koujap matera, ran koujap igia reŋendema-gen.*
  once.again come.up woman once.again again sleep.upon-RLS[NON1SG]
  'He once again came up, and again had sex with the woman.'

(79) *E-neti mbo, orat ke-r-an do, itigio-gen do,*
  her-father TOP light be-RLS[NON1.SG]-PAST CNJ see-RLS[NON1SG] CNJ
  e-metip no mbeman kogu mb' andondo-gen.
  his-daughter POSS breast wound TOP be-RLS[NON1SG]
  'Her father, when it became light, saw that his daughter's breast was wounded in several places.[64]'

(80) *Itigio tomamo-gen: ŋgo mbeman Kogu mbo kenema-gen*
  see ask-RLS[NON1SG] you breast Wound TOP what.do-RLS[NON1SG]
  de gej'o ne-gen.
  CNJ Q=CONN say-RLS[NON1SG]
  'He saw and asked, your breast is wounded, what did you do?'

(81) *Na-j-o no mbo wemin no raŋ-gen-ep to, küap koneni*
  father-LIG-VOC 1SG TOP night DUR lie-RLS-1SG CNJ man large
  eren mbo matere-ro no reŋendemo to, oro ok
  very DUR come.up-SEQ me sleep.upon CNJ SEQ river

---

64 The verb stem is a derived iterative stem from the experiential verb *kogu ando-* 'to wound' and this implies several wounds, according to Drabbe (1959: 57).

rürüoma-gen.
go.down.IT-RLS[NON1SG]
'Father, I was asleep at night and a very large man came up and had sex with me and went down to the river, several times'[65]

(82) *Ne-gen   doro, e-neti   ndot-ken.*
     say-RLS[NON1SG] CNJ,   her-father   hear-RLS[NON1SG]
     'She spoke, and her father listened.'

(83) *Matero   katoma-gen.*
     get.up   search-RLS[NON1SG]
     'He got up and looked (for a track)'

(84) *Katomo   itigio-gen   do,   ot   ra-gen   doro*
     Search   see-RLS[NON1SG]   CNJ   track lie-RLS[NON1SG]   CNJ
     kurüma-gen   do,   oro   ok   korü-gen.
     follow-RLS[NON1SG]   CNJ   SEQ   river go.down-RLS[NON1SG]
     'He went looking and saw there is a track and he follows it and it descends towards the river'

(85) *Itigio-gen   do, jendit wagot mba-gen.*
     see-RLS[NON1SG]   CNJ path   broad sit-RLS[NON1SG]
     'He saw that the path was broad.'

(86) *Mene   mbo kiambot   e-ana   no   metip   po   Kurow   namo mbe*
     this   TOP crocodile he-SBJ my   daughter TOP   Theft   with DUR
     reŋgendema   Gen
     sleep.upon   RLS[NON1SG]
     'This (broad track) here, the crocodile used to have illicit sex with my daughter

(87) *A   gokmo   matero   kotet   oru-gen,*
     belly   be.angry   come.up   brushwood cut-RLS[NON1SG].

---

[65] The verb stem *rü-rüo-ma* is a derived iterative stem, based on reduplication of the verb *rü-* 'to go down' and the verb *mo/ma* 'to do' that is often used in verb derivations (Drabbe 1959: 57). Drabbe (1959: 57) remarks that the iterative verb implies that the crocodile repeatedly entered the house under the cover of darkness (no visibility) and rain (tropical rains make a lot of noise so that he could approach unheard).

    tik   ŋgwamo-gen.
    rattan chop.down-RLS[NON1SG]
    'Upset he started cutting wood, he chopped down ratttan.'

(88) *Ro-me-ro*   *rurukma-gen*   *do, agop*
     Hold-come-SEQ   put.together.IT-RLS[NON1SG] CNJ many
     ke-gen   *doro, ndara koŋ-gen.*
     become-RLS[NON1SG] CNJ   fence put-RLS[NON1SG]
     'He collected (rattan and wood) until there was a lot, and then made a fence'

(89) *Ndara koŋ-gen*   *aro, ene jendit top*   *ŋgwamo-gen.*
     fence put-RLS[NON1SG] SEQ his path opening cut.out-RLS[NON1SG]
     'He put(them into) a fence and cut out an opening in his path.'

(90) *Top*   *ŋgwamo-gen*   *aro mbogombak ti*
     Opening   cut.out-RLS[NON1SG]   SEQ closing.gate make
     ketamo-gen.
     close.off-RLS[NON1SG]
     'After he cut out the opening, he made a closing gate and closed it off.'

(91) *Itigio-gen*   *kare e-gen*   *doro, igia tokmo*
     see-RLS[NON1SG]   fit   be-RLS[NON1SG]   CNJ again pull.open
     ro   *gen*
     put.down   RLS[NON1SG]
     'When he saw that it fitted, he again pulled it open and removed it.'

(92) *Terep*   *mbio-gen*   *aro, e-metip*   *n' itŋgombun*
     Gnemon.vine   twist-RLS[NON1SG]   SEQ his-daughter POSS forearm
     Kagoŋ Gen
     bind   RLS[NON1SG]
     'He twisted a Gnemon vine into a rope and tied it (around) his daughter's forearm.'

(93) *Kagoŋ-gen*   *aro kende*   *mbo tiri me-ro*   *e-neti*   *n'*
     bind-RLS[NON1SG]   SEQ other.end TOP take come-SEQ her-father POSS
     itŋgombun kago-gen.
     forearm   bind-RLS[NON1SG]
     'He tied and she tied the other end onto her father's forearm.'

(94) *Kagamo mba-gen do wemin ge-gen.*
bind   sit-RLS[NON1SG] CNJ night be-RLS[NON1SG].
Kinum riŋgio-gen
Sleep lie-RLS[NON1SG]
'They bound it and sat until it became night. They slept.'

(95) *Murup Koujap mbe ge-gen.*
rain   once.again DUR be-RLS[NON1SG]
'It was raining again.'

(96) *Kiambot koujap matero ko-gen.*
crocodile again come.up go-RLS[NON1SG]
'The crocodile again came up and went'.

(97) *ŋgane torogo-ro ndara top togo, ran koujap*
short.distance go.up-SEQ fence opening go.in woman again
mbe reŋgendema-gen
DUR sleep.on-RLS[NON1SG]
'He went up a short distance, went into the fence opening and again had sex with the woman.'

(98) *E-metip matero terep timo timo-mbima-gen.*
his-daughter rise rope take take-pull-RLS[NON1SG]
'His daughter got up, took the rope and pulled (it).

(99) *E-neti mbo ŋgiotke-ken.*
her-father TOP startle-RLS[NON1SG]
'Her father was startled.'

(100) *ŋgiotke matero terep koujap timo mbima-gen doro,*
Startle rise rope again take pull-RLS[NON1SG] CNJ
e-metip matero terep timo mbima-gen.
his-daughter rise rope take pull-RLS[NON1SG]
'He was startled, took the rope again and pulled it, then his daughter took the rope and pulled it.

(101) *E-neti matero terep po ogage o mbitöma-gen.*
her-father rise rope TOP secretly CONN pull.off-RLS[NON1SG]
'Her father got up and secretly pulled the rope off (his arm).'

(102) *Timo-koru-ro-gen.*
    take-go.down-put.down-RLS[NON1SG]
    'He took it and put it down.'

(103) *Ro-gen   aro   ogage   ngane   matero   ko   jombutop*
    put.down SEQ   secretly   short.distance   get.up   go   door
    top   keta-gen.
    opening   shut-RLS[NON1SG]
    'Put it down and then secretly went a short distance and shut the door.'

(104) *Ketamo   me-ro   in   ömböma-gen.*
    Shut   come-SEQ   fire   blow-RLS[NON1SG]
    'He shut it (in the fence), returned (to the house) and blew into the fire.'

(105) *Ömböma-gen   do   urut   ke-gen*
    blow-RLS[NON1SG]   CNJ   flame   come-RLS[NON1SG]
    doro   itigio-gen   do,   kaoro   go-gen.
    CNJ   see-RLS[NON1SG]   CNJ   flight   go-RLS[NON1SG]
    'He blew into the fire and the flame came, and he looked, but he (the crocodile) has fled (from the women's section of the house).'

(106) *Kaoro   go   top   mbo   itigio-gen   do   ümburüne-gen.*
    Flight   go   opening   TOP   see-RLS[NON1SG]   CNJ   be.closed-RLS[NON1SG]
    'He fled but saw that the opening was closed.'[66]

(107) *Eren   ge-gen   doro   raŋ-gen.*
    impossible   be-RLS[NON1SG]   CNJ   lie-RLS[NON1SG]
    'because it (fleeing) was impossible, he lay down.'

(108) *Ran   e-neti   ngou   matero   a   gokmo   mbendit   timo*
    Woman   her-father   Nggou   rise   belly   be.hot   bow   take
    kiambot   teembo   no[67] *wo-gen   doro,   kiambot   matere*
    crocodile   shoot   say   do-RLS[NON1SG]   CNJ   crocodile   rise

---

66 As in other Greater Awyu languages, clausal arguments of verbs of perception undergo argument distribution to the next clause in a biclausal conjoined sequence (see §5.5) (Lit. He saw and it was closed.)
67 See for quotative framing of intentions §5.3.

kujon tima-gen.
forbid take-RLS[NON1SG]
'The woman's father Nggou stood up, was angry, took his bow and wanted to shoot the crocodile, but the crocodile forbade it.'

(109) wo   mba-nog   eto orat ke-n   do orat ke-n
      wake sit-IMP   CNJ light be-[IRR]NON1SG CNJ light be-[IRR]NON1SG
      do, kenge-mo   to kotet   orü   giamo ro   me-ro,
      CNJ careful-do CNJ brushwood chop break hold come-SEQ
      tik   ŋgwamo-ro-me-ro   me-ro, keambuŋgujap
      rattan cut.off-hold-come-SEQ come   two.pieces.of.wood
      ü-[68]   to,   tik   ko-non
      put.in.ground CNJ rattan put.in-IMP
      'Do not shoot me, wait until the morning and then carefully collect brushwood and rattan, return and put two sticks in the ground and bind them together.'

(110) Keambuŋgujap   ü-nog   eto, mbegi-p   to,
      two.pieces.of.wood put.in.ground-IMP CNJ sit-[IRR]1SG CNJ
      aŋge   tik   komo-nok
      immediately rattan tie.loop-IMP
      'Put two pieces of wood in the ground, I'm there, you tie the rattan in a loop [around my body] and to a tree trunk and pull right away.'

(111) tig   gomo   to   tir-go   in-ondü   kagomo-mbimo-nok
      rattan tie.loop CNJ take-go tree-trunk tie-pull-IMP
      'you must tie the rattan in a loop [around my body] and to a tree trunk and pull.'

(112) mbimo rü-nog   eto, mbegi-p[69] to,   ŋgo mbo rigi-nog   eto,
      Pull   bind-IMP CNJ sit-[IRR]1SG CNJ you TOP stand-IMP CNJ

---

68 The idiomatic combination *keambuŋgujap ü-* denotes a series of actions: planting two sticks into the ground, one at each side of an object or person (here the crocodile) and then connecting the upper parts of the sticks in order to fixate the object, animal or person (Drabbe 1959: 59).

69 This is an example of the tendency in Greater Awyu verbal semantics to spell out sub actions (see §5.8). The O argument of the verb *rü* 'to bind' is expressed as the S argument of the next (chained) clause: you must bind and I will sit. Drabbe (1959: 59) correctly points out that such sequences must be translated as 'fasten me'.

9.2 Origin of the Ndumut river and the canoe

nen-arek tagamo to ŋgo ndare to karemo to, Kiambot
my-word Say CNJ you listen CNJ follow CNJ Crocodile
nöp ü-ro to, Joün tomü nü[70] ma-t[71] nene
me hit-hold CNJ Canoe make Say make-RLS[NON1SG] my
ŋgandöm mene karemo to tomü-nok.
lower.jaw this follow CNJ make-IMP

'Pull it tight, let me stay there, you must stand and listen to the words I say. You listen and obey and kill me the crocodile, and if you want to make a canoe, make it in the shape of my lower jaw.'

(113) Tagaŋ-gen doro, ndare mba-gen do, orat
say-RLS[NON1SG] CNJ listen sit-RLS[NON1SG] CNJ, light
ke-r-an do, in-ŋgembian
be-RLS[NON1SG]-PAST CNJ wood-type.of.wood
orü-giamo-ro-me-ro ndigio-gen do teleni-gen do,
chop-break-hold-come-SEQ give-RLS[NON1SG] CNJ bite-RLS[NON1SG] CNJ,
tik timo ŋgandöm mbo mbetekmo ruŋ-gun.
rattan take lower.jaw TOP do.tightly bind- RLS[NON1SG]

'When the crocodile said this, he (Nggou) listened and waited till it had become light and he chopped ŋgembian wood, broke, took and put it in the mouth of the crocodile (lit. he gave it and he (the crocodile) bit (the wood)), and he took the rattan and bound the lower jaw tightly.'

(114) Ruŋ-gun do mba-gen do, wegi timo
bind-RLS[NON1SG] CNJ stay-RLS[NON1SG] CNJ bamboo.knife take
wombut teengwamo ü-ro-gen.
tail cut.off hit-put.down-RLS[NON1SG]

'He bound (the crocodile's jaw) and he (Nggou) took a bamboo knife and cut off the crocodile's tail and killed him.'

---

70 The SS form of the verb of saying is used here to express intention as 'inner speech' (quotative framing, see §5.3).

71 Drabbe (1959: 32) describes the t-forms of Mandobo as conditional forms that are limited to clause chains with either an adhortative verb or an imperative verb in the final clause. But they also occur in Mandobo Past forms, with – t marking realis, as it does in the other Dumut languages. Drabbe (1959: 142) observes that realis forms are used in Yonggom Wambon in conditional topical clauses, of the type 'Given that X is the case, then Y'. Therefore, it could well be that in Mandobo – t is a realis marker in all contexts, including thematic/topical clauses that are contextually interpreted as conditional clauses.

(115) Ü   ro   kota   kotoma-gen.
      hit put.down skin   strip.off-RLS[NON1SG]
      'He killed (the crocodile) and stripped the skin off.

(116) Kotomo   mbokma-gen.
      strip.off cut.in.pieces-RLS[NON1SG]
      'He stripped it off and cut it (the crocodile) in pieces.'

(117) Mbokmo   ken   de   timop ro,   kende ŋ-gen.
      cut.in.pieces part roast hold   put.down part   eat-RLS[NON1SG]
      'He cut (the crocodile) in pieces and roasted a part and ate a part.'

(118) ŋ-gen   mba-gen   do, orat   ke-r-an   do,
      eat-RLS[NON1SG]   stay-RLS[NON1SG] CNJ light be-RLS[NON1SG]-PAST CNJ
      matero   ŋgweti   kende ŋgeremo, en'-etot   wandop
      get.up   crocodile part   take   his-longhouse previous
      koujap ko-gen.
      back   go-RLS[NON1SG]
      'He ate, stayed until it was light, got up and took part of the crocodile with him back to his previous.'

(119) Ko-ro   itio-gen   do   e-aŋen   omba   mbo, u   omba   to⁷²
      go-SEQ   see-RLS[NON1SG]   CNJ his-wife   other TOP   pig   other   feral feral
      ge mbe gee-r-an,   e-aŋen   mbo⁷³ ko u   mbo jo-ro
      be DUR go-RLS[NON1SG]-PAST   his-wife TOP   go pig TOP call-SEQ
      me-re   küap jendi-wüop   kiomo-gen.
      come-SEQ   man   road-middle   meet-RLS[NON1SG]
      'He went and saw that his (first) wife, who had been going after the other feral pig, had met a man while she was calling the pig.'

(120) küap mbo tagaŋ-gen   ŋgo-anomberi   koman   do
      man   TOP say-RLS[NON1SG]   your-husband   far.away   CNJ
      kee-r-an   doro ŋgo mbo   U   mbo   ro-man
      go-RLS[NON1SG]   CNJ   you TOP   pig TOP   hold-come. IMP.SG

---

72 *To* is an adjective used for domesticated pigs who wander off to the jungle and stay there.
73 Mandobo has, just like Kombai, a relative clause construction that is 'double-headed': the antecedent noun phrase is found at the beginning and the end of the relative NP. Mandobo marks both the relative NP as a whole and the initial antecedent with the deictic-based topic marker *bo* 'that'. See §4.2.5.4 for Mandobo and Kombai relative clause syntax.

nen 'etot   mene makwo   mbegi-w-on ne-gen
my longhouse TOP   together.be sit-IRR-1-PL say-RLS[NON1SG]
'The man had said, your husband has gone far away and so come with the pig to my longhouse and let us live together.'

(121) *Ne-gen   doro karema   ndot-ken.*
      say-RLS[NON1SG] CNJ follow listen-RLS[NON1SG]
      'He had said and she had followed and listened to him.'

(122) *Jok ne-gen.*
      yes say-RLS[NON1SG]
      'She agreed.'

(123) *Mbegi-ro e-gamben aŋen   ege   tima-gen.*
      sit-SEQ   his-mate wife   her   take-RLS[NON1SG]
      'He stayed and his mate's wife, he took her.'

(124) *Timo mba-gen   doro e-anomberi   ko-ro   tomamo-gen,*
      take sit-RLS[NON1SG] CNJ her-husband go-SEQ   ask-RLS[NON1SG]
      n- anggen o   Fiŋon   ku-r-an   gej'o ne-gen.
      my-wife   CONN Finggon go-RLS[NON1SG]-PAST Q   say-RLS[NON1SG]
      'He took and sat (= He took and after a while) her husband went asking where his wife Finggon had gone.'

(125) *Nda-j-o,[74]   ŋgo-aŋen   mbo ŋgo-gamben o   Kimitponop*
      No-LNK-CNJ,   your-wife TOP your-mate   CONN Kimitponop
      matero ŋgo-aŋen   mbo tima-gen.
      get.up your-wife TOP took-RLS[NON1SG]
      'Well, as for your wife, your mate Kimitponop has taken your wife.'

(126) *Ndare a   gokmo[75] togo   e-gamben ü   ro   matero e-gamben*
      hear   belly hot   enter his-mate hit hold get.up his-mate

---

[74] Drabbe (1959: 60) remarks that although the literal meaning is 'no, nothing', *ndajo* has become a general discourse marker for introducing answers. Digul Wambon *woyo* 'no' has the same function and can be used as the first word someone says to start a conversation.

[75] The SS non-finite verb *ndare* in (126) is followed by an experiential clause where the subject *a* 'belly' is non-topical and therefore does not trigger DS signals in the preceding clause. Notice that throughout (126) there is continuity of the topical participant 'he' (=Nggou). The switch

na   Taget   motu   tima-gen.⁷⁶
POSS kauri-shell little.bag take-RLS[NON1SG]
'He heard (them) and he became very upset, entered, killed his mate and
proceded to take the bag with his mate's money.'

(127) *Timo oro go en'-etot   ot-ken.*
Take SEQ go his-longhouse enter-RLS[NON1SG]
'Having taken it he returned to his.'

9.3 Yonggom Wambon text: The origin of the canoe

The following Yonggom Wambon text, transcribed by Ruth Wester, based on Drabbe (1959:148–150), is the Yonggom Wambon version of the origin story of the canoe, related to the Mandobo version of §9.2 but without the origin of the Mandobo river and with numerous details that are different. Drabbe (1959) does not say anything on the narrators or the circumstances under which he obtained the text.

(128) *Mbogokonon   jut   ri-t   te,   kotae kup, kom   kup,*
Mbogokonon   Jut   chop-RLS[NON1SG] CNJ, bark   with   chips with
mon-mon   kup,   tutupke   Ok   rira-t   te   ragae
small.pieces with   come.loose river go.down-RLS[NON1SG] CNJ fish
ke-r-an;   kotae e   wawot   ke-t,
become-RLS[NON1SG]-PAST bark CONN⁷⁷ wawot.fish become-RLS[NONS1SG]
Korom   ke-r-an;   Kom   e   ok
korom.fish   become-RLS[NON1SG]-PAST wood.chips CONN river   river
rira-t   te   ragae   kigip-kigip   ke-r-an;
go.down-RLS[NON1SG] CNJ fish   other-other become-RLS[NON1SG]-PAST

---

reference systems of Greater Awuy languages only track subjects which are discourse topics (see §4.5.2 and §5.7 and discussion there).
76 Notice that the same verb of taking is used: first Kimitponop took his wife and now Nggou takes Kimitponop's savings of shell-money. By killing Kimitponop and taking his money, the balance is restored.
77 Here and elsewhere in this text Ruth Wester glosses =e as a topic marker following the analysis Wester (2014: 151). I analyse it as a syntactic connective. See §4.4.3 for discussion.

mon-mon   e   ragae   mbe-mberon   ke-r-an.
small.pieces CONN fish small.small become-RLS[NON1SG]-PAST
'Mbogokonon chopped down a *jut* tree and bark, wood chips and small pieces came loose and fell into the river, they became fish. The bark became *wawot* and *korom* fish, the wood chips became other kinds (of fish) and the small pieces became really small fish.'

(129) *Jur   andui   e   tupke   rira-r=a^{78} te   woŋgopon   ke*
      jut.tree trunk CNJ fall   go.down-RLS[NON1SG]=SEQ CNJ long.time be
      te   uke   maturu   te   konoi   ke-t.
      CNJ from.water come.up CNJ canoe become-RLS[NON1SG]
      'The trunk of the *jut* tree fell down (into the river), after a long time passed, it came up from the water and had become a canoe.'

(130) *Maturu   te   nu   mene   ŋga^{79} ok   natin-in   nde-t   te*
      come.up CNJ 1SG here   CIRC   river row.IMP-PL say-RLS[NON1SG] CNJ
      'He came up and said 'row me here (across) the river!' and...'

(131) *Ok   ti-no   mboke-t   ran   Ja*
      River row-SIM stay-RLS[NON1SG] woman 3SG.POSS
      mimirop   Kup   undu-t.
      menstruation.blood With go.across-RLS[NON1SG]
      'while rowing across the river, a woman with menstrual bleeding went across.'

(132) *Mbanew   e   ŋgoropmo ok   rira-t.*
      crocodile CONN notice   river go.down-RLS[NON1SG]
      'The crocodile noticed and submerged.'

---

78 Wester (2014) and Drabbe (1959) analyse =*a* as a sequence marker. It could very well be that the grammatical meaning of =*a* is further 'bleached' and =*a* is developing into a more generic conjoining conjunction. For example, the last sentence of this text (165) is an example of the use of =*a* in non-sequential conditions.

79 Wester glosses this element -*ŋga* as an ergative marker. I reglossed it as a circumstantial case marker with peripheral phrases of time, location, instrument and so on, following Drabbe (1959: 144). The ergative function of – *ŋga* is restricted to its occurrence with core phrases in A function. See §4.3.1 and §4.4.2.

(133) *Mitik ke-t te, Ran e kinum ja-r-an.*
night be-RLS[NON1SG] CNJ Woman CONN sleep lie-RLS[NON1SG]-PAST
'It became night and the woman slept.'

(134) *Na ŋgin-o-kerop*[80] *warawae warimo-gen nde-t.*
1SG.POSS head- CONN-eye lightning do-RLS[NON1SG] say-RLS[NON1SG]
"My face is lightning' he [the crocodile] said.'[81]

(135) *Ema-t te matogo mende-r-an*
Thus.doing-RLS[NON1SG] CNJ come.in come-RLS[NON1SG]-PAST
'Thus he came inside.'

(136) *Me kinduma-t te Ran e kinum ja-r-an.*
come look-RLS[NON1SG] CNJ woman CONN sleep lie-RLS[NON1SG]-PAST
'He came inside and saw that the woman was sleeping.'

(137) *Janum ko mbarukrawa-r-an.*
Secretly go have.sex-RLS[NON1SG]-PAST
'He snuck in and had sex (with the woman).'

(138) *Ok ririopmo mbage-t.*
river go.down stay-RLS[NON1SG]
'He went down into the river.'

(139) *Ema-t te Ja nati matigo etaga-t te*
thus.doing-RLS[NON1SG] CNJ 3SG.POSS father get.up see-RLS[NON1SG] CNJ
ja matiw e mbemir e oksagat kun kup
3SG.POSS daughter CONN breast CONN mud trail with

---

80 This is an exocentric noun compound (see §3.2.4) with the main accent on the connective that links the two equal parts. It means 'face' (Drabbe 1959: 117).
81 'my face is lightning' is an experiential clause: the first person experiencer is not the subject and the verb agrees with the inanimate body-part noun that is the subject (see §4.3.2). The experiential clause is part of a quotative construction (see §5.3). This quotative framing is used to represent the emotions of rage and shame that engulf the crocodile who is the victim of the breach of a very strong pollution taboo: a man coming in contact with menstrual blood (see §9.2.1). An idiomatic translation would be: 'He felt very ashamed and angry.'

> ke-t;   mbemir   e   jugut   kup   ke-t.
> be-RLS[NON1SG]   breast   CONN rail   with   be-RLS[NON1SG]
> 'He did that and when her father got up he saw that his daughter's breast had a mud trail, that her breast had a trail.'

(140) *Randui   o   ŋg'   agaeopmo-gen   de   nde-t;*
      daugther   VOC you   what.do-RLS[NON1SG]   CNJ   say-RLS[NON1SG]
      mbanew   et   ke   Te   mbarukrap-ken   de   nde-ro   raga-t.
      crocodile SBJ be   CNJ have.sex-RLS[NON1SG]   CNJ   say-SS   speak-RLS[NON1SG]
      'O daughter, what have you done? he asked. 'The crocodile had sex with me' she said.'

(141) *Ema-t   te   kuk   ti-r-in-an.*
      thus.doing-RLS[NON1SG]   CNJ   fence   build-RLS-NON1PL-PAST
      'This happened and they built a fence.'

(142) *Kuk   ti-r-in=a   mbumo,   mitik   ke-r-an*
      fence   build-RLS-NON1PL=SEQ   finish   night   be-RLS[NON1SG]-PAST
      e   Tik   ra-me-ro   wir   atiga-t.
      SUB   rattan   hold-come-SEQ   arm   bind-RLS[NON1SG]
      'They finished building the fence, and when night came, he [the father] took a rattan rope and tied it to [his] arm.'

(143) *Ja   matiw   e   wir   atiga-t.*
      3SG.POSS   daughter   CONN   arm   bind-RLS[NON1SG]
      'His daughter tied [the other end] to [her] arm.'

(144) *Raga-t: randui   o   ŋguw=e   mitik   ke-t*
      say-RLS[NON1SG]   daughter   VOC   you=CONN   night   be-RLS[NON1SG]
      ki-n-in   ŋga,   mbanep   me   ŋgu   mbarukrawa-t
      be[IRR]-NON1PL-FUT SUB   crocodile come   you   have.sex-RLS[NON1SG]
      ke-t   ki-n-in   ŋga,   sapuk   nandap
      be-RLS[NON1SG]   be[IRR]-NON1PL-FUT SUB   pull   do.IMP
      te   ŋoropmo-p   nde-ro   raga-t.
      CNJ   know-[IRR]1SG   say-SS   speak-RLS[NON1SG]
      'He [the father] said: daughter, if it is night, if the crocodile comes and he has sex with you, pull [on the rope] and I will know."

(145) *Ndare-ro kinum ja-r-an.*
 hear-SS sleep lie-RLS[NON1SG]-PAST
 'She heard (him) and went to sleep.'

(146) *Mbanep mende-r=a mbarukrawa-t.*
 crocodile come-RLS[NON1SG]=SEQ have.sex-RLS[NON1SG]
 'The crocodile came and had sex [with her].'

(147) *Tik sapuk rawa-t te ja nati=e*
 rattan pull do-RLS[NON1SG] CNJ 3SG.POSS father=CONN
 ŋoropma-t.
 notice-RLS[NON1SG]
 'She pulled the rattan rope and her father noticed.'

(148) *Janem matigo-ro agatkande-r-an.*
 secretly get.up-SS go.long.way.around-RLS[NON1SG]-PAST
 'He secretly got up and took the round-about way.'

(149) *Agatkande-r=a ku-r=a*
 go.long.way.round-RLS[NON1SG]=SEQ go-RLS[NON1SG]=SEQ
 kuk riwirip ko ahap-piri=e koma-t.
 fence near go gate-?=CONN close-RLS[NON1SG]
 'He went a long way around, then went near the fence and closed the gate.'

(150) *Ema-t te kore matigo-ro enow*
 thus.doing-RLS[NON1SG] CNJ there get.up-SS fire
 uguma-r-in de mbanew=e ŋgirimo ku-t.
 light.by.blowing-RLS-NON1PL CNJ crocodile=CONN flight go-RLS[NON1SG]
 'He did that and they over there blew into the fireplace to increase the fire and the crocodile fled.'

(151) *Ku-r=a te ahap-piri oto-p te[82] te*
 flee-RLS[NON1SG]=SEQ CNJ gate-? go.outside-[IRR]1SG say CNJ

---

[82] This is an example of quotative framing of intention. Literally 'He fled saying I want to go out via the gate.'

```
jaju          ke-t.
impossible    be-RLS[NON1SG]
```
'He fled and wanted to go through the gate, it was impossible.'

(152) *Nde, ja   nati   ŋga raga-t: na   matip*
```
thus  3SG.POSS  father  AGT  speak-RLS[NON1SG]  1SG.POSS  daughter
mbarukrap-ken           ege  te,   komo-gen-ep  nde-ro  emo
have.sex-RLS[NON1SG]    TOP  CNJ,  close-RLS-1SG say-SS thus.do
nde-t
say-RLS[NON1SG]
```
'Yes, her father said, because you had sex with my daughter, I closed [the gate]'

(153) *Emo   nde-t   te   mbanep   raga-t:*
```
thus.do  say-RLS[NON1SG]   CNJ  crocodile  say-RLS[NON1SG]
ema-t                te   ŋgaŋguw=e  kowandut  menew=e    konoi
thus.do-RLS[NON1SG]  CNJ  2PL=CONN   now       now=CONN   canoe
ri-nan              tomŋgandi-n-in              o      nde-t
chop-[IRR]NON1PL    fall.down-[IRR]NON1PL-FUT   CONN   say-RLS[NON1SG]
```
'He said this and the crocodile answered: 'concerning canoes from now on you will have to fell (trees).' [Lit. you will have to chop and they fall]

(154) *Tumo-nan=a   mbumo   ŋgirapmo-ra   ko-nan=a*
```
chop.shape-[IRR]NON1PL=SEQ  finish   drag-SS       go-[IRR]NON1PL=SEQ
ok      riro        oro-n-an-in;                ŋgaŋgu  ŋgoton  ndomo
river   go.down     put.down-[IRR]NON1PL-FUT    2PL     tired   row
waepmo   n     An           in.
travel   LNK   [IRR]NON1PL  FUT
```
'You will then build it, finish it and drag it down to the river, you will put it in and you will get tired rowing.'

(155) *Waepmo-no mboke-nan   rakonmo   ok   kimbarukmo-nan-in.*
```
travel-SIM  stay-[IRR]NON1PL  capsize   river    swim-[IRR]NON1PL-FUT
```
'You will be traveling, capsize and [have to] swim in the river.'

```
Ajuk-nog-onin,    ran=e        nu    sumo-p           ten       o
not.want-IMP-1PL  woman=CONN   1SG   marry-[IRR]1SG   because   CONN
```

nde-ro   emo   nde-t.
say-SS   thus.do   say-RLS[NON1SG]
'Don't be so difficult! I did it because I wanted to marry the woman, he [the crocodile] said.'

(156) *Ja-nati   ŋga raga-t: kowandut Mene naŋgo   konoi tok,*
3SG-father AGT say-RLS[NON1SG] now   Now   3SG.POSS   canoe CNJ
kuk   ratokmo-wan   o   nde-t.   Oro   ok
fence open-[IRR]1PL   CNJ say-RLS[NON1SG] move   river
riro-n-o   nde-t.
go.down-[IRR]NON1SG-CNJ say-RLS[NON1SG]
'Her father answered: now that we have a canoe, let us open the gate. Let us take it down to the river.'

(157) *Nde-t   te   mbanew   arapke-t.*
say-RLS[NON1SG] CNJ crocodile protest-RLS[NON1SG]
'He said that, but the crocodile protested.'

(158) *Nu   i   ro-nan-in   o   nde-t.*
1SG hit put.down-[IRR]NON1PL-FUT CONN say-RLS[NON1SG]
'"Kill me" he [the crocodile] says.'

(159) *Na   tenorow   e   na   teŋger o   raramun ande-now*
1SG.POSS   ass   CONN 1SG.POSS   penis   CNJ women   eat-NOM
amow o   nde-t.
NEG   CONN say-RLS[NON1SG]
'From my ass and my penis, the women may not eat, he said.'[83]

(160) *Sinam Ŋga   nataem-inin   o   nde-t.*
bow   INSTR shoot.IMP-NON1PL   CONN say-RLS[NON1SG]
'"Shoot me with a bow' he said.'

(161) *Nde-t   te   taemba-r-in.*
Say-RLS[NON1SG] CNJ shoot-RLS-NON1PL
'He said that and they shot him.'

---

[83] Greater Awyu groups have dozens of food taboos. This passage in the origin story functions as a foundation for one of these food taboos.

(162) *Taemba-r-in   de   nan ip   tamburum rogo-na-ti-r-o*
      shoot-RLS-NON1PL CNJ 1SG name   lightly   speak-[IRR]PL-NEG-LIG-CNJ
      nde-t;   mun   mberon o   ran   mbari o   kagup
      say-RLS[NON1SG]   child small   COORD woman grown COORD   man
      pari   o   mimir atik kaendi-j-iw-e   o   nde-t.
      grown   COORD back   bite break-LIG-[IRR]1SG-FUT   CONN say-RLS[NON1SG]
      'They shot him and he said: 'Do not speak my name lightly, or I will break with my teeth the backs of small children, grown women and grown men."

(163) *Nde-ro   te   kima-r-an.*
      say-SS   CNJ die-RLS[NON1SG]-PAST
      'After he said that, he died.'

(164) *Ema-t   te   ra   ko   mbukma-r-in=a*
      thus.do-RLS[NON1SG]   CNJ hold go   cut.in.pieces-RLS-NON1PL=SEQ
      andi r   in   an
      eat   RLS NON1PL   PAST
      'Thus it happened, and they took and divided [the crocodile] into pieces and ate [it]'

(165) *Nde, konoi=e   ri-ri-mo-gon-in;   tuma-r-in=a*
      thus canoe=CONN   cut-cut-RLS-NON1PL   chop.shape-RLS-NON1PL=SEQ
      woŋopon   kegemo-gon-in.
      long.time   be-RLS-NON1PL
      'That is how they came to cut canoes; they make canoes and it takes them a long time.'

Index

Adverbial 86, 89, 102, 115, 116, 133
Aghu 14, 16, 21, 22, 24, 26–28, 30, 35,
    50–52, 66, 70, 72, 77, 81, 82, 91–93, 96,
    97, 104, 109, 125, 138, 150–152, 178,
    183, 186–187, 189, 194
Agreement 94, 110, 134, 135, 140, 201
Alignment 94
Argument distribution 120, 130, 139, 202,
    217, 239
Asmat 3, 5, 18, 46, 97, 153, 154, 173, 178,
    181, 182, 185, 200
Auxiliary verbs 26, 27, 41, 53, 68
Awyu subgroup 3, 5, 7–9, 14, 16, 27, 35, 44,
    52, 66, 71, 76, 143, 153, 159, 175, 176,
    186–189, 196, 198, 204, 205

Becking-Dawi 3, 10, 11, 16, 18, 21, 27, 33, 40,
    51, 53, 62, 65, 68, 69, 83, 91, 99, 108,
    143, 161, 169, 177, 199, 204
Biclausal 131, 132, 239
Bilingualism 112, 193, 194
Borrowing 7, 150, 174, 176, 187–189, 193,
    195, 197

Chaining 110
Clan 174, 184, 185, 190, 193, 195, 205, 206,
    217–219, 234
Clan names 25, 143, 146, 148, 149, 155,
    158, 159
Clause chaining 45, 47, 48, 55, 109, 111, 112,
    198, 206
Code switching 174
Comparative 120, 131, 132, 202
Conditional 133, 221, 241
Conflation 52, 62, 201
Coordinate 29, 46, 54–55, 77, 90, 92, 99
Copula 60, 93, 98–100, 109, 222, 232
Counting 71, 73, 75, 153, 195, 196, 198

Dani 44, 125
Deictic 36–39, 90, 107, 108, 117, 118,
    124, 126, 170, 172, 181, 202, 217, 221,
    225, 242
Denasalization 8, 187

Derivation 26, 37, 45, 236
Derivational 20, 21, 40–43, 77, 188,
    201
Dialect chains 5, 103, 150, 151, 174, 206
Digul Wambon 3, 5–7, 10–12, 16, 19, 25, 34,
    37, 39, 42, 45, 49, 51, 55, 57, 70–72, 74,
    75, 78–80, 82, 85, 86, 91, 92, 94, 99,
    103–105, 107, 116, 124, 133, 134, 147,
    179, 187, 188, 194, 196, 217
Discourse 19, 37, 50, 62, 111, 112, 115, 116,
    120–121
Dumut 3, 5, 7, 10, 16, 24, 27, 31, 33, 39, 44,
    47, 48, 52, 56, 57, 60, 72, 90, 99, 102,
    107, 108, 143, 175–177

Elevational 40, 170–172
Emotion 33, 125–129, 202, 222, 232, 234
Emotional 129, 218
Epenthesis 11, 12, 15, 17
Ergative 39, 94, 245
Event line 109, 110, 113–116, 118, 124, 136,
    139, 140
Exocentric 20, 28, 29, 93, 159, 246
Experiential 50, 87, 95, 114, 120,
    133–134, 200, 202, 217, 234, 235,
    243, 246
Extra-clausal 38, 39, 86, 87, 95,
    108, 109, 115, 116, 133, 134, 140,
    202, 203

False 50
'False' SS 114, 200
Final C deletion 8, 9, 14, 188
Final verb 45, 46, 51, 53, 61, 111, 122, 123,
    200
Focal 108
Focus 33, 35, 70, 90, 99–101, 107–109, 157,
    177, 232

Grammaticalization 49, 62, 91, 100, 101,
    103–105, 107, 202

Hesternal 52, 205
Hodiernal 52, 205

Inanwatan 131, 197
Intention 117, 122, 125–128, 202, 241, 248
Intonation 43, 70, 115, 121, 130, 137
Intonational 132
Intonationally 79, 87, 95, 115, 118, 132, 133, 203

Kinship 21, 23–26, 29, 89, 93, 154, 155, 158–160, 162, 163, 178, 179, 201
Kombai 14, 21, 30, 52, 53, 70, 71, 87, 88, 90, 93, 104, 124, 126, 127, 130, 134, 143, 147–149, 151, 152, 156, 157, 159–163, 169, 173
Korowai 1, 3, 7, 11, 14–17, 20–24, 26, 27, 30, 33, 36, 40, 41, 43, 50, 52, 53, 62, 65–70, 72, 80, 81, 83, 85, 91, 99, 102, 104, 110, 123, 128, 129, 132, 139, 143, 146, 147, 150, 156, 173, 177–178, 182, 187, 189

Language names 6, 143, 145, 151, 174, 205
Lexical similarity 3, 5, 178, 193
Lexical substitution 143, 145, 153, 154, 173
Linguistic avoidance 155, 173
Linguistic ideology 143, 185
Locative existential 60, 96, 97, 101

Malay 42, 65, 75, 143, 145, 148, 150, 152, 165, 167–169, 173, 190, 195
Manambu 45, 131, 148
Mandobo 7, 21, 22, 27, 28, 33, 37, 39, 43, 44, 48, 66, 72, 82, 87, 117, 118, 123, 125, 126, 128, 135, 136, 138, 139, 146, 147, 149, 151, 159, 176, 182, 183, 187–189, 191, 191–194, 203
Marindic 3, 5, 16, 18, 71, 112, 152, 181–182, 186, 188–189, 195, 196, 197, 198, 204, 205
Medial clause 111, 113, 140
Medial verb 20, 45–48, 51, 55, 110, 115, 221
Mian 131, 187
Motion verbs 40, 43, 62, 127, 172, 217
Multilingualism 18, 26, 75, 143, 167, 174, 183, 185, 190, 195, 205
Muyu 75, 187, 189, 190–193, 195

Names 4, 5
Ndeiram 3, 12, 52, 99, 143, 169, 175, 204
Negation 20, 27, 41, 60, 68, 69, 101, 176, 177, 206
Numo 125

Ok 5, 18, 21, 25, 27, 75, 131
Omaha 148, 160–162

Papuan 198–202, 205
Perception 131, 202, 239
Perception verbs 131
Periphrastic constructions 20, 26, 35, 53, 68
Personhood 145, 149, 150, 156–158, 169, 183
Phasal aspects 27, 53, 68
Pisa 3–5, 7, 47, 61, 82, 187–189
Posture verbs 27, 53, 61, 95–97, 101, 201
Prenasalization 10, 16, 198
Proto Awyu-Dumut 7–10, 13, 16, 18, 21, 24, 25, 33, 36, 40, 66, 68, 91, 175, 176, 179, 180, 187

Quotative 117, 120, 125–129, 202

Reduplication 24, 31, 35, 83, 236
Relative clause 78, 85, 87, 102, 203

Sequence 41, 46–49, 54, 55, 58, 111, 124, 136, 221
Serial verb 41, 43, 44, 131, 137, 138
Shiagha 3, 4, 7, 151, 187–189
SIL 2
Simultaneity 20, 41, 46–48, 54, 58, 61, 96, 110, 111, 200, 221
Sociocentric 149, 150, 169, 174
Sound changes 7, 33
Spatial orientation 40, 151, 169, 182, 217
Subordinate 47, 89, 109, 113, 115, 116, 118, 221
Subordinate thematic clauses 117
Suppletive stems 45
Switch reference 18, 19, 33, 41, 44–48, 50, 51, 58, 63, 65, 94, 111, 113, 114, 121, 130, 140, 200, 217, 227
Syllables 9–11, 15, 104, 198

Syncretism 52, 59
Syntactic connective 107, 244

Tail-head linkage 19, 116, 118, 121, 123, 125, 135, 139, 202
Temporality 41, 48, 55, 111, 112, 124, 200
Thematic clauses 89, 115
Thematization 87, 120, 132–134, 139, 202, 205
Topic 38, 39, 86, 95, 102, 107, 116, 117, 119, 133, 134, 140, 203, 206, 234, 242, 244
Topical 45, 46, 58, 87, 90, 112, 118, 121, 134, 136
Topicality 38, 50, 114
Tracking 113, 120, 121
Trans New Guinea 8, 16, 17, 20, 29, 38, 43, 46, 95, 110, 114, 115, 125, 132, 178, 180, 181, 185, 193, 198–199, 205
Tree house 43, 63, 121, 146, 170, 172, 185, 189, 218, 229, 233, 234

Verbal noun 27, 53, 60, 68, 110, 178, 201
Vowel harmony 9, 14, 17, 21, 22, 33, 221

Wambon 5
Witchcraft 148, 162, 165, 169, 174, 183

[(XP) V] 130, 131, 201

Yali 94
Yenimu 3–5, 7, 187–189
Yonggom 3
Yonggom Wambon 5–7, 19, 27, 30, 31, 35, 37, 39, 40, 42, 48, 49, 53, 54, 56–61, 66, 75, 84, 104, 105, 107, 113, 124, 128, 131, 134, 137, 187–189, 195, 196, 217, 221

www.ingramcontent.com/pod-product-compliance
Lightning Source LLC
Chambersburg PA
CBHW070758230426
43665CB00017B/2409